WITHDRAWN
UTSA Libraries

NEW DIRECTIONS IN ECONOMIC JUSTICE

New Directions in Economic Justice

EDITED BY
Roger Skurski

UNIVERSITY OF NOTRE DAME PRESS
Notre Dame & London

Copyright © 1983 by
University of Notre Dame Press
Notre Dame, Indiana 46556

Manufactured in the United States of America

LIBRARY
The University of Texas
At San Antonio

Library of Congress Cataloging in Publication Data

Main entry under title:

New directions in economic justice.

     1. Distributive justice—Addresses, essays, lectures.
2. Social justice—Addresses, essays, lectures.
I. Skurski, Roger. II. Title: Economic justice.
HB72.N48 1983   330.15'5   83-1254
ISBN 0-268-01460-4
ISBN 0-268-01461-2 (pbk.)

Contents

Contributors

STEPHEN T. WORLAND is professor of economics at the University of Notre Dame and has taught at the University of Dayton and Michigan State University. He is a specialist in the history and analysis of economic thought and author of the book *Scholasticism and Welfare Economics*. He has published a number of articles concerned with economic justice, political economy, and social economics. He has been active for many years in the Association for Social Economics and served as the president of the association in 1977.

DAVID L. NORTON is professor of philosophy at the University of Delaware and author of *Personal Destinies: A Philosophy of Ethical Individualism*. He became a professional philosopher only after accumulating experience as a smokejumper for the U.S. Forest Service, a uranium prospector for the U.S. Geological Survey, 2nd Lieutenant in the air force, a civil engineer for the California Highway Department, and finally as an architectural engineer for Norton Co., St. Louis. Philosophy, however, has been his principal field for the past two decades, and he has published many articles in that area. He is currently completing a book entitled *The Politics of Self-Governing Individuality*.

JAMES M. BUCHANAN is University Distinguished Professor and General Director of the Center for Study of Public Choice, Virginia Polytechnic Institute and State University. He has been a Fulbright Visiting Professor at Cambridge University, a visiting professor at the London School of Economics, and a member of the faculties of the University of Tennessee, Florida State University, and UCLA. He is a past president of the

Southern Economic Association and has also served as vice president of the American Economic Association. He has published a great number of articles and many books including: *The Calculus of Consent: Logical Foundation of Constitutional Democracy, The Limits of Liberty: Between Anarchy and Leviathan,* and most recently, *Freedom in Constitutional Contract: Perspectives of a Political Economist.*

HERBERT GINTIS, professor of economics at the University of Massachusetts, Amherst, is one of America's best-known scholars of the new left. He earned his Ph.D. at Harvard where he also taught for several years, and he has been a Fellow at the Institute for Advanced Study at Princeton. His early work in the political economy of education was published widely in education journals such as the *Harvard Education Review* and in economics journals from the *American Economic Review* to the *Review of Radical Political Economics.* More recently he has turned his attention to questions of democracy and justice and their compatibility with alternative economic systems.

DENIS GOULET is professor and holder of the William and Dorothy O'Neill Chair in Education for Justice at the University of Notre Dame. He sees himself as a philosopher of development working in the interstices between the various disciplinary approaches to the field and addressing questions of values, ethics, and justice. The wide variety of experiences he has had in Brazil, France, Algeria, Sri Lanka, and Washington can be viewed as successive apprenticeships in various economic, political, and social settings. He has published several books including *The Cruel Choice, A New Concept in the Theory of Development, A New Moral Order: Development Ethics and Liberation Theology,* and most recently *The Uncertain Promise: Value Conflicts in Technology Transfer.* He has also published more than fifty articles in a wide range of journals and continues to travel and lecture internationally.

GAR ALPEROVITZ is co-director of the National Center for Economic Alternatives, a Washington-based research organization. He has a Ph.D. in political economy from Cambridge University, an M.A. from Berkeley, as well as a B.S. from the University of Wisconsin. A Marshall Scholar, he has been a Fellow of King's College at the University of Cambridge, a

Guest Scholar at the Brookings Institution, and a Fellow at the John F. Kennedy Institute of Politics at Harvard University. He has testified before House and Senate committees, including the Joint Economic Committee, the Senate Subcommittee on Economic Stabilization, and the House Committee on the Budget. He has authored several books and a variety of professional and other articles which have appeared in such periodicals as the *New York Times,* the *Washington Star, Social Policy Magazine,* and *Wharton Magazine.* Currently, Dr. Alperovitz is completing a book entitled *Rebuilding America* with center co-director Geoffrey Faux to be published by Simon and Schuster.

ROBERT D. COOTER is assistant professor at the Law School, University of California, Berkeley. He earned his B.A. at Swarthmore, was a Fulbright Scholar at Oxford University, and received a Ph.D. in economics from Harvard University. He is one of those few people working on issues of common interest to the legal as well as the economics profession. He has published articles in such journals as *Quarterly Review of Economics, American Economic Review, Bell Journal of Economics,* and *Review of Legal Studies.* His forthcoming book is tentatively titled: *Price, Pleasure, and Principles: Ethical Foundations of Economic Theory.*

ROGER SKURSKI is associate professor and director of graduate studies in the Department of Economics at the University of Notre Dame. He earned his Ph.D. at the University of Wisconsin where his area of specialization was Soviet/Comparative Economic Systems. He has published a series of articles on the Soviet economy in journals such as *Slavic Review* and *Soviet Studies* and has recently finished a book titled *Soviet Marketing and Economic Development.* He was a Fulbright-Hayes Fellow at the University of Birmingham, and is currently the executive secretary of the Association for Comparative Economic Studies and consultant to the National Institute for Trial Advocacy.

Preface

Economists make their contribution to the good life by bringing the human community to a deeper understanding of the way the social system depends upon and is modified by its material base. Over the past decade, following the pioneer work of John Rawls, the efforts of economists to facilitate such communal self-understanding have frequently taken the form of efforts to formulate and justify theories of economic justice. This Volume IV of the Notre Dame Studies in Political Economy presents the contributions of seven scholars, operating from varying perspectives and from divergent points of the ideological compass, in an effort to articulate rules of justice that the community of mankind could adopt as the basis for economic and social cooperation. The papers are original essays specifically written and edited for this volume and are based on lectures delivered at the University of Notre Dame during the 1979-80 academic year.

In his essay, David L. Norton, finding that the demands of justice flow from each individual's responsibility to fulfill the unique demands of his personal *daimon,* takes good government to be but an "intermediate staging ground ... set to the ... nurturing of self discovery...." In this context, he finds contemporary efforts at workplace reform encouraging, though "insufficiently radical" to bring about the full matching of worker and job required for establishing a thoroughly just society. Warning that "an open society cannot survive if its government is viewed as an instrument for arbitrary transfers," James M. Buchanan in the next paper proceeds to a consideration of injustice in hiring practices. Finding that the competitive market may fail to achieve compliance with the basic justice precept of "equal treatment for equals," he expresses profound reservations about the "meanderings of the Supreme Court" in the judicial efforts to achieve better results in the Bakke and Weber court cases.

A deeper problem in the attainment of economic justice emerges in the following chapter. There Herbert Gintis finds that the liberal conception of rights provides a "tool of communicative discourse" common to both the private productive and political sectors of contemporary life, a conception that inevitably encounters a basic internal contradiction because of the capitalist tendency to treat labor as a marketable commodity.

The perspective shifts to the international scene as Denis Goulet, insisting that "justice ranks highest in the constellation of ethical goals," takes up the pressing moral dilemma raised by the immense disparity between standards of living in the Third World and in the industrialized nations. Next, in his paper, Gar Alperovitz argues that "if we are interested in social justice and wish to deal with reality," we will have to push beyond the received wisdom of contemporary conceptions of monetary and fiscal policy and develop "direct sectoral strategies to deal with an inflation which is neither demand-pull nor cost-push."

The analysis moves to a higher level of theoretical abstraction in the concluding paper where Robert D. Cooter proposes to clarify two disparate traditions in political theory—contractarianism and utilitarianism—by showing that the antagonism between them has a deep, deep source in a different mathematical conception of *consistency*. He concludes that the laws of justice as proffered by Robert Nozick cannot be relied upon as adequate.

Every generation of economists, as Professor Warren Samuels has observed,[1] has to reinterpret for itself one of the great classics of political economy—Adam Smith's *Inquiry into the Nature and Causes of the Wealth of Nations.* The way a community performs such a task of interpretation, so Samuel finds, becomes a "facet of the social control system" whereby a given society establishes guidelines for the constraint of economic activity. How a generation reads Smith helps determine a given community's conception of economic justice. This being the case, a review of recent developments in the interpretation of Adam Smith, as offered in the introductory essay by Stephen T. Worland, can provide a helpful initial insight into the work of the other authors presented in the following pages. Smith's heroic effort to demonstrate that capitalist institutions embody acceptable principles of justice fails at crucial points. Worland's reflections on his failure set the stage for considering whether today's economists succeed where Smith faltered and can thus contribute to a deeper understanding of the difficulties involved in the everlasting efforts of the human community to achieve economic justice.

Roger Skurski
Notre Dame, Indiana

NOTE

1. Warren Samuels, "The Political Economy of Adam Smith," *Nebraska Journal of Economics and Business,* Summer 1976, p. 3.

Acknowledgments

It is with great pleasure that I express my appreciation for the enthusiastic participation of the contributors to this volume: Stephen T. Worland, David L. Norton, James M. Buchanan, Herbert Gintis, Denis Goulet, Gar Alperovitz, and Robert D. Cooter. In addition to the scholarly papers that appear here, the visitors to Notre Dame spent many, many hours with our students and faculty and in the process provided fresh insights into the many problems and their potential solutions in the area of economic justice.

A special word of thanks is due to Charles K. Wilber, the chairman of the Department of Economics. The original idea for this annual visitors' program and the series of books built on it is his, and he has continued to supply inspiration and encouragement to these endeavors. Finally, without the cooperation of the University of Notre Dame Press and especially of its director, James Langford, this book would not have been possible.

Adam Smith: Economic Justice and the Founding Father

STEPHEN T. WORLAND

Taking the subject of economics to be a branch of moral philosophy, sharing the Enlightenment's faith in the ability of human reason to articulate the moral principles that ought to govern both individual conduct and the operation of social institutions, Adam Smith in *The Wealth of Nations* combines the search for a scientific explanation of how the market system functions with a systematic effort to discern the moral imperatives that rational men will admit as appropriate ethical guidelines for the governance of economic activity. "What are the rules," Adam Smith asks when introducing his analysis of the supply and demand mechanism, "which men naturally follow in exchanging ... goods ... for one another ...?"[1] Though the fact may not be apparent to a generation of economists misled by a prolonged flirtation with logical positivism, the "rules" referred to by Adam Smith in posing his fundamental question are in fact moral rules. And in asking what those rules are, Adam Smith raises the fundamental ethical question that provides the central theme for the following six essays offered in this volume.

An attempt to understand clearly Adam Smith's conception of economic justice might very well begin with a pervasive, popular but grossly inaccurate misunderstanding. According to a commonly held misconception, Smith was, the "rationalizer of greed," a victim of capitalist false consciousness who set out to write a scientific analysis of capitalism, but succeeded only in surreptitiously converting bourgeois class interests into unassailable moral imperatives. The result, so the editor of a widely used edition of *The Wealth of Nations* asserted some years ago, was that "the practical maxim of business enterprise achieved the status of theology."[2] No doubt, there is a large element of truth in Laski's finding that the

1

principles first enunciated by Smith have been twisted by subsequent generations into a psychological defense of capitalist class interest and bourgeois business practice.[3] However, if the general public and economists of today take him to be an admirer of businessmen and a naive spokesman for capitalism, then history has indeed played a nasty trick on Adam Smith. For the record in fact demonstrates almost the exact opposite.

Adam Smith conceived of human society as naturally divided into "three great original and constituent orders." The first were the landlord class, a largely ineffectual lot who, because of their particular position in the social system, would not find it advantageous to mislead their fellow citizens nor try to distort public policy in their favor.[4] Next, were the laborers, the working class whose combined productive efforts actually produced "all the necessaries and conveniences of life" which the community consumed,[5] and whose interests like those of the landlords, normally coincided with those of society at large. Lastly, there was the capitalist, employer class. And these in fact played the role of villain in Smith's version of the capitalist drama. For unlike the other two orders, they had a very, very clear understanding of just where their class interest lay. They knew very well how to make gain for themselves out of society's loss. They were adept at misleading both public and parliament into sacrificing the commonweal for the sake of their parochial class interests. They were identified by Smith as an order of men "who have generally an interest to deceive and ... oppress the public and who accordingly have, on many occasions, both deceived and oppressed it."[6] It was capitalist dominance of the political process that, in Smith's view, had produced that unholy alliance of business and government which he called "the Mercantile System," a system that he roundly denounced as exploiting consumers for the benefit of producers and protecting the "rich and powerful" while "oppressing the poor and indigent."[7] A careful survey of Smith's expressed attitudes toward each social class will show, as an insightful study of the problem once concluded, that Smith in fact "looked askance at the knavery and meanness of business men." "His wrath," like that of an Old Testament prophet or a medieval novelist, "was enkindled against the merchants and manufacturers, for he hated their invidious practices."[8]

To appreciate Smith's attitude toward businessmen and capitalism, it is essential to understand carefully his conception of the profit motive. Profit-seeking by entrepreneurs and resource owners is essential for the continued and efficient functioning of the market mechanism. But in analyzing the operation of the social system,

Smith regularly employs a philosopher's distinction between two kinds of causes—efficient and final causes.[9] His conception of the profit motive must be understood in such terms. Thus he proceeds on the assumption that the proper moral appraisal of economic institutions and practices must be grounded on a firm grasp of the intention of nature—that is, on a clear perception of what the proper "end" or "purpose" of economic activity ought to be. And as a humanist whose sympathy with the "humble and lowly ... was made plain for all to see," [10] Smith finds that the basic purpose, or final cause, to be achieved by the operation of economic institutions is not to provide maximum profits for the capitalist class, or to contribute to the military prowess of the national state but rather to provide a "plentiful revenue of subsistence for the people."[11] Capitalist manipulation of the powers of the state distorts the economic process and is denounced as moral outrage precisely because, in Smith's view, such distortion gives unjustified priority to producer over consumer interests and thus violates the "self evident maxim" that "consumption is the sole end and purpose of all production." [12] The final cause of economic activity, perception of which generates moral guidelines for appraising policy and institutions, is to provide the community with a plentiful supply of consumer goods, whereas profit maximization is but a secondary, or "efficient" cause. Thus, the profit motive gives rise to conduct which is desirable, not for its own sake, but only because and to the extent that such conduct contributes to attainment of the ultimate purpose of all economic activity—i.e., to providing "plentiful subsistence for the people."

In a well-known passage from *The Theory of Moral Sentiments,* Adam Smith uses his conception of the interaction between final and efficient causes in a rather crude, a priori manner, and reaches a conclusion that seems to have rather ominous ideological implications. The efficient cause in this case is a special kind of self-interest—i.e., the effort of the landlord class to achieve "gratification of their own vain and insatiable desires" for luxury goods. However, such "natural selfishness and rapacity" has, because of the natural interconnection between the two kinds of cause, an end result unforeseen and unintended by the agents who produce it. For such luxury consumption generates employment for the poor, thus providing them with the chance to acquire necessities, and in so doing contributes to the fulfillment of nature's purpose, here identified as "multiplication of the species."[13] It is in this passage from his moral philosophy that Smith first uses the famous "Invisible Hand" metaphor, and he does so here in what reads like an unedifying effort to justify social inequality.

However, to appreciate Adam Smith's conception of economic justice, one must take note of a difference in level of discourse between his two major works, a difference obscured by similarities in the rhetoric employed. The Invisible Hand metaphor may involve identical logic in the two works,[14] but when the metaphor recurs in *The Wealth of Nations,* it is used in the context of a purportedly scientific, and at the time newly discerned, understanding of the market mechanism. Instead of providing a metaphysical justification for the status quo, this scientific understanding in fact provides the rational basis for Smith's ringing condemnation of the corrupt business practices he found at work in his own society.

In *The Wealth of Nations,* the teleological assertion that "consumption is the purpose of production," is given operational content, translated from the domain of metaphysics into that of empirical science. For, in the latter work, Smith connects the basic moral purpose of economic activity with an observable variable—that is, with the level of net national product or, in his quaint terminology, with the "real value of the annual produce of society's land and labor." As the level of net product rises, so Smith's scientific model indicates, the ultimate purpose of economic activity is more fully achieved. The contribution of an efficient cause—the profit motive —to a morally desirable final cause—providing plentiful consumption—operates through the impact of the former on the level of net product.

Thus, according to a famous passage from *The Wealth of Nations,* "the annual revenue of society" (consisting mainly of a flow of consumer goods) is identified as "equal to the annual produce of its industry." The profit motive naturally induces investors and resource owners to transfer resources ("stock" and, with the capital goods, the labor to utilize it) from low-profit to high-profit sectors of the economy. But, as Smith's close reasoning indicates, profits are a function of value added by labor to raw materials in the production process, and net national product for the community at large consists of the aggregate of such values added. This being the case, when a private agent makes such a profit-increasing resource transfer, he is "led by an invisible hand to promote an end which is no part of his intention"—the unintended end being expanded net product and expanded consumption possibilities for the community at large.[15]

Another passage from *The Wealth of Nations,* not as well known as the one just cited, gives a clearer indication of Smith's understanding of the market mechanism. In the latter passage,

Smith invokes a distinction he usually makes between the "distant" and "nearer" employments of stock, that is, between two different branches of trade. He observes that if profits in the distant employment happen to rise above their equilibrium level, resources ("stock" and labor) will tend to be withdrawn from the nearer and reinvested in the distant employment. He then goes on to argue that the abnormally high rate of profit is "proof" that "those distant employments are somewhat understocked in proportion to other employments, and that the stock of the society is not distributed in the properest manner among all the different employments carried on in it. ..." After a confused effort to square the fact that distant employments can be "understocked" with his preconceived notion that such investment is normally less advantageous than the "nearer employment" of capital, Smith continues: "But if the profits of those who deal in such goods are above their proper level, those goods will be sold dearer than they ought to be, or somewhat above their natural price...." This being the case, the public interest "requires that some stock should be withdrawn from the nearer employments and turned towards that distant one, in order to reduce its profits to their proper level and the price of goods which it deals in to their natural price." Bringing the argument to its logical terminus, Smith concludes: "It is thus that the private interests and passions of individuals naturally dispose them to turn their stocks towards the employments which in ordinary cases are most advantageous to the society. ...Without any intervention of law, ... the private interests and passions of men naturally lead them to divide and distribute the stock of every society among all the different employments carried on in it as nearly as possible in the proportion which is most agreeable to the interest of the whole society." [16]

According to Smith's explanation of the market, as revealed in this passage, the play of supply and demand evens out the differential between prices and costs and in doing so brings the rate of profit in each sector down to the normal equilibrium level. In such a process, entrepreneurial profit maximization acts as the "efficient cause" that shifts resources from low-profit to high-profit sectors. But final cause is also achieved, and moral purpose thereby fulfilled, as resource allocation eventually settles into its "proper" pattern—that is, into that pattern which maximizes the level of net product and the level of per capita real income.

A deeper understanding of Smith's model requires only that the key "self evident maxim"—"consumption is the only end and purpose of production"—be analyzed carefully. As several commenta-

tors have emphasized, Smith is uniformly critical, almost contemp-
tuous, of the consumption behavior of the rich, especially the landlord class. They are accused of "selfishness and rapacity," and the
luxury goods they acquire are not, when all is said and done, really
contributory to authentic human happiness. Great wealth is included among those "trinkets of frivolous utility" which men may seek
but which, when acquired, do not provide "ease of body or tranquility of mind." Men may devote a lifetime to the acquisition of
power and riches, but such goods are in fact "operose machines ...
immense fabrics which threaten at every moment to overwhelm"
their processors.[17] And in order to fit such a conception of luxury
consumption into his overall scheme, Adam Smith is forced to press
the efficient-final cause distinction to an absurd limit. Conduct
that provides the efficient cause is not only self-motivated, but also
downright base. And such conduct can produce agent-unintended
but desirable end-results only because the Deity is willing to resort
to deception. The belief that wealth and luxury are truly desirable is
an "illusion" imposed on men in order to fulfill the hidden designs
of nature; nevertheless, such an illusion is ultimately beneficial. "It
is this deception which arouses and keeps in continual motion the
industry of mankind ..." leading them to "cultivate the ground,
build houses, ... found cities ... improve the sciences and arts ..."[18]
The Deity plays on human vanity, allows mankind to be misled by
the illusory belief that riches can bring true happiness, but with an
Invisible Hand directs the conduct that follows toward transcen-
dent, beneficial results.[19]

However, in interpreting Smith's views on consumption and
consumer behavior, it is well to pay careful heed to the characteristic
difference between his a priori moral doctrine expressed in *The
Theory of Moral Sentiments* and the economic analysis offered in
The Wealth of Nations. In the latter work, the key decision-makers
are not the landlord class motivated by a vain desire for power and
riches. Rather, it is the capitalist entrepreneur who, responding to
perceived price-cost differentials, shifts capital from one sector to
another, thereby providing labor with an inducement to migrate,
and in the process, contributing indirectly to an expansion of net
product. It is, indeed, the profit motive—"the constant and perpetual effort of every man to better his own condition"[20]—that guides
both these critical entrepreneurial decisions and the complementary
employment choices that ultimately give such decisions their socially beneficial result. But such decisions, as is explained more fully
below, are assumed by Adam Smith to be constrained both by the

legal system and by a sense of justice operating through the consciences of individual decision-makers. The rapacious, greedy landlords who play an important social role in *The Theory of Moral Sentiments* may deserve moral reprobation. But it is simplistic to extend such reprobation without qualification to the workers and investors who, as explained in *The Wealth of Nations,* make the critical moves in the market process. Moreover, consumption inspired by the vanity of the rich may be the motivating force or efficient cause of economic decisions in *The Moral Sentiments.* Consumption becomes a *final* cause—the factor that gives moral purpose to the whole economic enterprise—in *The Wealth of Nations.* The "plentiful revenue of subsistence" that provides the basic objective for economic policy and institutions in the latter work is expected both to fill true human need and, through the mechanism of an expanding market, to "diffuse itself through all the ranks of the society." [21]

To see the connection between the pioneer work of Adam Smith and contemporary works on economic justice, it is essential to realize that in his view capitalist institutions can make their appropriate contribution to political progress and the higher purposes of life, *only* when and if the operation of economic institutions is regulated, constrained, and controlled by strict rules of justice. A poet such as John Ruskin may denounce him as the "half-witted Scotchman who taught the deliberate blasphemy: 'Thou shalt hate the Lord, thy God, damn his law, and covet thy neighbor's goods,'" [22] but a more accurate understanding of Smith's system brings home the point that in his view both definite rules of justice and the moral commitment to comply with them are essential for the proper operation of the economy. In fact, in Smith's conception, political economy is defined as a branch of ethics concerned especially with an "articulation of rules of justice ... specifically those practices which concern the provision of ... a plentiful supply of material necessities ... to the citizenry...." [23]

In Smith's model of capitalism, government has a restricted, but definite and essential role to play. True enough, as a first step in the direction of rational and just public policy, a great body of existing legislation "which the clamour of our merchants and manufacturers has extorted from the legislature" and which is intended to "support their own absurd and oppressive monopolies" [24] must first be swept away. Laws which permit the importation of yarn but forbid the importation of lace; regulations which prescribe the minutiae of the packaging and transport of wool; prohibitions on the

export of sheep—violations of which were to be punished by impri-
sonment, mutilation and execution—must all be abolished in order
to bring about the demise of the Mercantile System.[25] Further con-
traction of the public sector is called for in recommending repeal of
the settlement laws—that is, of legislation which required a working
man to get official permission before shifting from one locale to
another. Repeal of such laws would allow for the free exercise of
what Smith takes to be the most "sacred" of all property rights—
the right of a poor man to employ the "strength and dexterity of his
hands" when and where he sees fit.[26] Repeal would also have a decided impact on the performance of the economy. Such a shift in the
political infrastructure would permit that occupational and geo-
graphical labor mobility essential for achieving an efficient, net-
product-maximizing, allocation of resources. But, though his critics
persist in misunderstanding him on this point, denouncing ineffi-
cient and unjust political interference with the market did not lead
Adam Smith to a simplistic recommendation of laissez faire.

For one thing, anticipating by a century a key discovery of students of public finance, Smith clearly realized that the market is not
an effective device for providing the community with those "public
goods" which are beneficial to the community at large but not profitable for private firms to produce. He also clearly perceived that
the exercise of free choice by some individuals can impose "external
diseconomies" on third parties. Thus he finds that the state must
provide for defense, education, and a transportation infrastructure.[27]
Public authority must also intervene with building codes and financial regulations in cases where, as in the issue of small-denomina-
tion bank notes, the "exertions of the natural liberty of a few... might
endanger the ... whole society."[28] And in what is really a basic inter-
jection of public authority into the capitalist system, Adam Smith
does not rely on the market to establish an optimum rate of interest.
He approves of usury laws establishing a maximum rate of interest
on the grounds that, without such regulations, capital will flow out
of productive, socially beneficial investment into the hands of
"prodigals and projectors" who will waste it.[29]

To take note of a more basic feature of his model of capitalism,
believing that "commerce and manufactures can seldom flourish"
unless property rights are secure and contracts enforced,[30] realizing
that a competitive economy cannot function without a "framework
of man-made law,"[31] Smith conceives of a vital, third, and distinct
function for government. The sovereign must not only provide public goods, establish a base transportation system, and intervene

when the market imposes external costs on third parties. The sovereign has the fundamental duty of "establishing an exact administration of justice." [32]

Smith's conception of this third and basic function of government can best be understood by noting the parallel between his model of capitalism and contemporary, twentieth-century versions of social-contract theory, such as that of John Rawls. In the latter, social decision-making takes place through a multi-stage sequence, with basic moral principles being chosen in an original, prepolitical state of nature or "original position," constitutional procedures being established at a later stage, and legislation being enacted at a still later stage. [33] In such a schema, economic institutions such as property and markets are envisioned as operating within a set of ground rules established at a prior, more basic level of social decision-making. Smith's model involves a similar conception of the relationship between economic and political decision-making. At an earlier stage of the social process, the community acting through its sovereign first establishes the procedures Smith refers to as an "exact administration of justice." That is, property rights are defined and enforceable rules of contract law are established. At a later and subsequent stage, and within the legal framework already established, the market comes into play as individuals begin to pursue their private interests—producing, exchanging, consuming, contracting—within the legal framework established at the initial stage.

On such an interpretation, Smith's rhetorical reference to an Invisible Hand (by which the Deity produces socially beneficial results from the pursuit of self-interest) actually obscures the real nature of his model. With his analysis of the market, Smith offers a rational, testable, explanation of how profit-maximizing self-interest can produce a desirable end-result, especially a product-maximizing pattern of resource allocation. If such desirable end-effects do flow from the market, as Smith's reference to the primordial significance of justice would indicate, this beneficial result is not in fact attributable to the mystic efficacy of the Deity manipulating men so that they "promote an end which is no part of their intention." On the contrary, the market produces desirable consequences for a perfectly rational reason. As rational decision-makers, men have deliberately and intentionally constructed an extramarket legal framework ("an exact administration of justice" that allows competition but forbids monopoly, for instance) that will cause such consequences to emerge from private profit maximization. The *final cause* or purpose of economic activity is perceived to be that of maximizing net product so as to provide a "plentiful revenue of subsistence for the people." On the basis of this moral perception, men establish a pattern of economic institutions that will bring the *efficient cause* (self-interested profit maximization) into line with achievement of such a final and moral purpose. [34]

Restrictions operating through the legal system are not, however, the only form of constraint on self-interest which Adam Smith takes as necessary for the proper functioning of free-market capitalism. Smith builds his model on the assumption that, in addition to restrictions imposed by the positive law, the social system also generates moral principles which, internalized so as to work directly on the individual conscience, also serve to modify and direct the pursuit of self-interest. Factors referred to by Warren Samuels as "nonlegal forces of social control"[35] play a crucial role in Smith's attempt to demonstrate that the market mechanism warrants moral approval. How these nonlegal control factors originate and how they are supposed to modify self-interest and the market process can best be understood by considering in some detail the connection between *The Wealth of Nations* and Adam Smith's other classic work, *The Theory of Moral Sentiments.* [36]

In the latter work, Adam Smith outlines an elaborate sociopsychological process whereby a community of men come to establish a set of moral standards that can be accepted as the basis of their common life. The foundation of the theory is an analysis of the process of moral judgment. When trying to ascertain the moral quality of human behavior, so Smith's explanation goes, a person must engage in a rather complicated thought-experiment. He must by the exercise of imagination transcend his personal interests and desires and bring himself to a point where disinterested observation and judgment are possible. That is, he must assume the role of an "impartial spectator," bearing witness to the conduct of others and, when testing his own conscience, of himself as well. Having done so, he must ascertain whether or not he can truly "sympathize" with the action of the agent in question. If the process of sympathetic identification indicates that the action is fitting and duly proportioned to the circumstances giving rise to it, the action is said to have the "propriety" appropriate for virtuous conduct. If the exercise of imagination by the spectator reveals that the gratitude felt by a third party affected by the agent's conduct is appropriate, such "indirect sympathy" with the patient's reaction indicates that the action is meritorious and deserving of reward. Cumulative experience with such moral decision-making leads eventually by inductive generalization to the formation of general rules of conduct. The latter provide an antidote to subjectivity. When "fixed in our mind by habitual reflection, such rules are of great use in correcting the misrepresentations of self-love."[37]

Over the years a great deal of ink has been spilt by commentators trying to specify clearly what Smith's crucial concept of "sympathy"—the capacity for "fellow-feeling" with the "passions" of others[38]—actually involves. One view, placing major emphasis on Smith's conclusion that moral perception must be the product of "immediate sense and feeling," rather than reason,[39] takes sympathy to be mainly a matter of emotive response by one person to the perceived emotions of another.[40] An alternative interpretation, noting that moral evaluation in Smith's model requires a judgment of what is "suitable" or "proportioned" in human conduct[41] insists that "judgments of what is appropriate cannot be made by mere emotion. They are bound to be rational ... sympathy is always united with reason."[42] However, whether sympathy be taken as emotional or rational, there seems to be general agreement on one crucial point. The process of sympathetic fellow-feeling which underlies moral judgment does generate the agreement on common standards necessary to allow social life to continue. Guiding his conduct by standards enunciated by an impartial spectator who represents his fellow men, realizing that happiness requires that we be "beloved, and ... know that we deserve to be beloved"[43] each member of society is led to pursue that perfection of character which renders him worthy of the love of others.[44] In Smith's model, the conscience of the individual is guided, not by a priori principle or by divine revelation, but by the "social experience" of the human community.[45] Thus the impartial spectator is said to "personify a process of interaction" which provides the social consensus necessary for ... the stability of society."[46] With his conception of sympathetic interaction, so another commentator concludes, "Smith charts the incremental development of standards ... which internalized ... in socialized behavior patterns of all men, evolve and emerge as general rules of conduct."[47]

The conclusion that sympathetic fellow-feeling is the source of social consensus and social stability, however, can obscure a basic difficulty in understanding the real nature of Smith's social theory. When sociologists first encountered *The Theory of Moral Sentiments,* they were quick to recognize that Smith's explanation of the origin of social norms coincided with their own views as to how a society sustains itself.[48] Interaction within the social community, rather than reference to philosophic principle, generates the norms which, internalized as imperatives by succeeding generations, provide social coordination and stability. Such a parallel between Smith's explanation of the genesis of moral norms and twentieth-century sociological theory has given rise to the view that the kind of ethical doctrine frequently associated with the latter can also be taken as characteristic of the former. Thus, in a careful study of Smith's moral philosophy, Campbell notes that the objectivity attributable to the decisions of the impartial spectator is only apparent and illusory, because such decisions do not in fact derive from "impersonal reason" or from "an external standard known through the exercise of some rational faculty." Emphasizing Smith's sensitivity to the opposition between custom and nature, and to cultural differences between one society and another, he concludes that Smith's theory implies acceptance of a position he designates as "moral relativity."[49]

According to such an interpretation, the moral norms which Smith takes as emerging from social interaction are "relative" not only in the sense that they are flexible, mutable, and adapted to the particular needs of a specific society. They are also "relative" in a much deeper, philosophic sense. According to such a more basic conception of "moral relativity," a decision as to what is good and morally binding for humankind cannot be definitely established by rational demonstration, as attempted for instance in Aristotle's classic offer to characterize the authentic "good life." Rather, a decision as to the good is man-made, created by human volition and agreement, the result—forever the result and never the original cause —of social agreement.

The conclusion that such *moral relativity* can be attributed to Adam Smith can be reached by a second route, one that emphasizes the similarity already noted between his model of society and latter-day versions of social-contract theory. For example, as the latter is formulated by James Buchanan, decisions as to the good must be carefully distinguished from scientific truths that are discovered and established by rational, scientific enquiry.[50] Such decisions, however, need not be reached by the kind of subrational, evolutionary adjustment process envisioned by Small and like-minded sociologists. Rather, what is to be accepted as society's good is determined by explicit, rational decision operating through the social-contract process.[51] Applying the tools of economic analysis to the political process will show, as Buchanan's version of contract theory indicates, that men who maintain their private, irreconcilably diverse, noncomplementary conceptions of the good will nevertheless find it rational and mutually agreeable to establish a political order with a framework of enforceable laws.[52] On such a view, the social mechanism is conceived as having only an instrumental value, and the ends that such a mechanism is to serve are determined not by attempts to specify the nature of human excellence, as in Greek political philosophy, but by the free choice of those who set up the mechanism through the device of social contract. Smith's observation that "society may exist among different men ... from a sense of utility, without any mutual love or affection"[53] has led to the suggestion that his social philosophy can be understood as an anticipation of such a version of contract theory. [54] Thus the decision to set up that "exact administration of justice" which, for Smith, provides the legal framework essential for the proper operation of the market mechanism can be considered as part of the social-contract procedure. Rational, self-interested individuals find it mutually advantageous and efficient to establish first a set of property rights and contract law, and having done so, to begin then the process of pursuing private self-interest through the system of division of labor plus exchange.

The social norms that provide the coordination necessary for community life may be conceived of, with the sociologists, as the product of an instinctive adaptation or, with the latter-day social-contract theorists, as the result of explicit rational agreement. In either case, according to the point of view designated by Campbell as "moral relativism," the basic value judgments legitimizing conduct and institutions are ultimately conventional, not demonstrated by philosophical enquiry but established by human volition. A classic study of his social philosophy makes a strong case for attributing such a conception of the human good to Adam Smith.

According to Joseph Cropsey,[55] Smith takes vital motion, the "infinite protraction of the life of nutrition and generation," to be the "highest good ... desired for its own sake." "The purpose of nature is endless existence or vital motion as a thing good in itself."[56] Thus Smith is said to have rejected the Aristotelian notion that the "state exists for the sake of a good life, and not for the sake of life only,"[57] in favor of the view that "society is for the sake of ... preservation ... rather than the perfection of life."[58] On such a view, economic activity is embedded in a biological life cycle, and the "self-evident maxim" that "consumption is the sole end and purpose of production" is taken to mean that consumption itself is desirable only for its contribution to the continued vital operation of the human species. In Cropsey's reading of Smith, mere biological preservation is the *natural* end of social life and economic activity. If such

biological process is to be elevated to a higher humane or moral purpose, ground for the elevation is found in free human choice. "Nature
seeks life, but man creates a criterion of the good life." The natural
end of biological sustenance "becomes the means to a non-natural,
supranatural end constructed by man."[59] To say that the "end" to
which natural biological process is subordinate is "superimposed"
and "constructed by man" indicates that, as in Buchanan's contract
theory and as in the ethical theory attributed to such sociologists as
Westermarck and Small, Smith's model of society presupposes that
decisions as to the good have no rational basis. "The very words right
and wrong," as Cropsey understands Smith, "can have no other
meaning than what by our emotions we sympathize with and approve...."[60] On such an interpretation, Adam Smith's elaborate
attempt to specify the economic functions of government and to
discern the moral rules that men naturally follow in exchanging with
one another, finally rests on the assumption that the ultimate ends
to be achieved through economic activity are arbitrary, determined
and selected by unrestrained human volition.[61] If Cropsey's interpretation were accepted as final and definitive, it would indeed be
difficult to avoid Campbell's conclusion that the doctrine of "moral
relativity" is fundamental and characteristic of Adam Smith's social philosophy. Such a conclusion would, of course, qualify decisively one's understanding of whatever rules of economic justice
can be derived from Smith's model of society and the economy. If it
is indeed true that economic activity is naturally oriented merely to
endless existence and vital motion for the human species, if whatever higher ends such activity might subserve are conventional and
arbitrary, then the rules of justice formulated to restrain and channel such activity are ultimately arbitrary and conventional also.
Several recent developments in the scholarship related to Adam
Smith, however, indicate that such an understanding of his moral
theory and of his conception of economic justice involves serious
misunderstanding.

   The suggestion that Smith takes continued existence or mere
biological preservation as the definitive and controlling end of social life has been challenged by no less an authority than the University of Glasgow's Adam Smith Professor of Political Economy. In a
careful review of Cropsey's work, A.L. MacFie points out that such
an interpretation attributes to Smith a mechanical psychological
theory whereby animal activity is reduced to "motion." Such a view,
however, is said to run counter to Smith's concerns not only for
prolongation of life, but also for "prosperity" and "betterment."

"No merely mechanical theory can explain improvement," MacFie finds. "Yet Smith certainly believed in improvement." [62]

The Theory of Moral Sentiments does indeed provide an explanation of how social interaction generates a common set of moral norms which, internalized in the conscience of the individual, constrain private conduct into patterns that stabilize the social system. However, the fact that such moral norms are discovered by social interaction rather than by philosophic enquiry does not necessarily imply that they are subjective or arbitrary. Smith's recognition of the process of socialization should not obscure the fact that the rules themselves are taken by Smith to be "objective, or at least intersubjective." [63]

Careful textual analysis of *The Theory of Moral Sentiments* will reveal, so some students of Smith indicate, that there is a twofold standard operating in Smith's explanation of the source and validity of moral principles. First and fundamentally, there is the criterion referred to by Smith as "the idea of exact propriety and perfection;" secondly and derivatively, there is "that degree of approximation to this idea which is commonly attained in the world." [64] It is the second standard—referred to by Lindgren as the "norm of performance" [65]—which reflects the moral rules established by social consensus and actually operative in a particular society. Compliance with such a standard is important to the moral maturity of an individual since adherence to prevailing norms of performance acts as a practical corrective for egoism—for what Smith called the "misrepresentations of self-love." [66] But it is the first criterion—the "ideal of performance"—which in fact comes into play when one appeals to the hypothetical judgment of the supposed impartial spectator in an effort to evaluate human conduct. [67] And rules derived from such an impartial standard are not mere derivatives of current social practice. In fact, Smith is said to have proposed a theory to show "how moral ideals can detach themselves from social morality." An agent begins by testing his behavior against the prevailing "norm of performance," asking whether other members of the community find his conduct "proper." But this initial question leads naturally to a second. Is the behavior "in fact proper"—that is, consistent with that Lindgren referred to as the "ideal of performance"? A search for objective moral truth thus gets underway. "Instead of the propriety of social morality ... we are thus led to ... judge ourselves in terms of an 'absolute' propriety...." [68] According to such a reading, Smith's moral norms may first be perceived through a process of social interaction, but such perception tends naturally to become critical and reflexive. Those who take the impartial spectator to be merely the "personification of customary norms,"[69] or who conclude that "conscience for Smith is purely a reflection of social attitudes"[70] overlook the crucial distinction between (i) the ideal, and (ii) the norm of performance. And sociologists who like Westermarck "believed that ... Smith ... was convinced ... that moral judgments lack objectivity, that there is no basis upon which men might assess the correctness of normative claims,"[71] have oversimplified and not recognized that his moral theory involves a search after "absolute" and "objective" principles.[72]

According to Smith's understanding of moral knowledge, general rules of conduct emerge as adaptive consequences of social interaction. Such rules stabilize the social system and provide guidelines for the individual conscience; "once in existence, they are quite capable of directing our moral evaluations."[73] Such a process, at least as understood by some of Smith's commentators, is progressive, involving a development from the prevailing "norms of performance" to a clearer perception and conformity with an objective, "absolute," "ideal of performance." Thus social life is based not, as moral relativism seems to require, upon values arbitrarily selected, but upon a communal search for an ever more adequate formulation of moral norms which, conceived as ultimately objective, can provide the ethical basis for a good society. Though Smith's rhetoric obscures the fact, the "System of Natural Liberty" sketched as a moral and economic ideal in *The Wealth of Nations,* is based on a crucial moral principle—the statement of an "ideal of performance" —which was apparently discerned and articulated through reflection on capitalist social experience.

In Smith's model of capitalism, the competitive market is commended not only as an efficient mechanism for "providing a plentiful revenue of subsistence for the people"; the "universal opulence" generated by such a mechanism is also expected, through a trickle-down distributional procedure, to "extend itself to the lowest ranks of the people."[74] The root moral principle on which he makes his case—"consumption is the sole end and purpose of all production"—is described by Smith as "so perfectly self-evident that it would be absurd to attempt to prove it."[75] With such a peremptory justification for his own most basic premise, Smith oversimplifies intellectual history and does not acknowledge a crucial instance of his own theory of moral knowledge at work. For the principle he asserts to be self-evident was not in fact, and for very good reasons, clearly perceived by those who preceded Smith in trying to come to an accurate understanding of capitalism. In his analysis of the market system, Smith had to disentangle such a critical moral premise from a welter of ethical ambiguity. After his perceptive genius had done its work, the proposition would then appear as obvious, or, as he put it, as a "self-evident maxim."

Advocates of mercantilism are criticized by Smith for their perverse tendency to reverse the proper teleological connection between production and consumption, such perversity being attributed to the base selfishness of those producer interest groups who have been "the contrivers of this whole mercantile system."[76] Laying the blame for the exploitative misguided principles of mercantilism on a capitalist conspiracy gives Smith yet another opportunity to express his contempt and loathing for the businessman social class. But in this case, as in most others, resort to the conspiracy explanation involves oversimplification.

"Consumption is the purpose of production" may be an obvious truism so long as economic activity is confined to the household or intertwined with political and social relations in an institution such as a feudal manor. However, once the market mechanism emerges and the economy comes to be "disembodied" from the rest of the social system, personal responsibility for economic behavior is obscured—e.g., prices are determined by supply and demand, not by personal decision—and the community's perception of economic activity tends to blur.[77] According to one common line of interpretation, the Mercantile System was not deliberately created by capitalist conspiracy, but arose because such a system served as a halfway point on the human community's progress from a stage of ambiguity and confusion to an advanced stage of greater moral insight. If economic activity is guided and directed by an impersonal market mechanism, wherein the predominant motive force appears to be only the profit motive, the question arises: is it possible for such activity to be subordinated to the rule of moral principle, and if so, what are the nature and ground of such a principle? Mercantilism can be understood as offering an answer to such a question, an answer the inadequacy of which was eventually discerned through accumulated social experience and formally rejected as Adam Smith laid the basis for his System of Natural Liberty.

Thus, as the story is told by anthropologists and historians, the historical emergence of modern market capitalism shattered the prevailing pattern of social relationships and the institutions, such as guild and manor, previously designed to regulate economic activity. Social relations based upon considerations of *status,* so Sir

Henry Maine's classic thesis holds, gave way to relationships governed only by *contract.* The inner nature of human society was transformed, from a *Gemeinschaft* wherein communal relations predominate, to a *Gesellschaft* held together by free contractual choice.[78] The concomitant restructuring of society, according to a well-known interpretation, degenerated into "complete moral chaos," and the Mercantile System is found to have emerged as the antidote to such disorder. For "there was one factor ... strong enough to reduce anarchy to order," as the British historian William Cunningham found: "men were forced in their dealings to have a due regard for the power of the state."[79] On such a view, the Mercantile System, casting about in moral confusion for a defensible point of reference, found the moral imperative appropriate for regulating economic activity and institutions in a consideration for the power and might of the newly emerging national states.[80] "National power," rather than consumption or providing plentiful revenue for the people, was thus taken to be the objective of economic activity and the purpose of economic activity. The particular rules and regulations of the Mercantile System—tariffs on imports; protection for agriculture; subsidies for shipping—were established, not as Adam Smith held because they were profitable to the capitalist class, but because such measures were necessary to fulfill what was taken to be high moral purpose—i.e., enhancing the power of the state.

Understood against the background of such an interpretation of the Mercantile System, "consumption is the end of production" is neither a common-sense platitude, nor the "self-evident maxim" Smith asserted it to be. Economic activity directed by the market appears to superficial observation to be governed by no moral principle except a selfish profit motive. Mercantilism tried to bring ethical principle to bear on such activity by subordinating it to the end of national power. Adam Smith also appeals to end, or final cause, in trying to specify moral guidelines for economic behavior and policy. But his intuition led him to locate the appropriate end or purpose of economic activity in consumption. For this reason, he lays down as the "first object of political economy considered as a branch of the science of the legislator," a definite and specific policy goal. The goal is that of "providing a plentiful revenue of subsistence for the people."

Though Smith himself does not make the point, the discernment and articulation of such an utterly basic moral imperative is a prime example of how Smith's own theory of moral knowledge functions. Coming to the realization that the immense and complicated congeries of market-related institutions has a definite and special purpose, and eventually identifying that purpose as consumption rather than national power or private profit, are themselves the result of the kind of social process whereby moral knowledge emerges to clear formulation out of sustained reflection on accumulated communal experience.

Smith's moral theory thus offers an explanation of how the critical role of consumption as final cause could be discerned. His broader social theory also suggests how such a critical proposition, once articulated, should be understood in the evaluation of economic activity and institutions. If Smith's model of society is taken, as Cropsey suggests, as implying that economic activity and social life are but an extension of a biological life cycle, then consumption might be the end of production, but such consumption would serve only as the nutritional means of maintaining life for the individual and the species. On the other hand, if Cropsey's critics are correct, social life is progressive rather than cyclical, moral rather than merely biological. If the latter is the case, consumption is not only the purpose of production; consumptive activity in its turn is directed to an end beyond mere sustenance. Embedded in a more comprehensive teleological pattern, economic activity is contributory not only to continued biological existence, but also to higher human and moral values.

In this connection, it is important to note that Smith finds economic efficiency and political stability to be complementary goods which, taken together, contribute not merely to biological maintenance but also to the attainment of leisure and tranquility. These latter, in turn, are necessary prerequisites for mankind to undertake the study of science and philosophy, enterprises which may generate useful side effects but which ultimately are sought for their own sake as fulfilling the basic human desire for pure speculative knowledge. Consumption achieved through expanded net national product may be the "end and purpose of production," but the further end to be achieved through consumption and leisure, as one commentator puts the point, "is greater refinement ... an increase in the variety, the beauty and the purposeful activity of human life." [81]

The notion that economic activity contributes to higher moral purpose is reflected in Smith's conception of the complementarity between economic and political progress. For instance, in his analysis of the transition from feudal anarchy to capitalism, he develops an elaborate, though not particularly convincing, argument to demonstrate how the spread of commerce and industry "gradually introduced order and good government, and with them, the liberty and security of individuals."[82] Contact with the East led to a shift in consumer tastes among the nobility. The increased desire for luxury goods, the attempt to gratify "the meanest ... sordid vanities," led to increased emphasis on rational, maximizing behavior. The result was a basic transformation of the political process. The maintenance of retainers gave way to market, contractual relationships between landlord and tenant. The nobility were led to barter away the arbitrary political authority that had been theirs.[83] The system of market relationships that emerged, so recent scholarship finds, was understood by Smith as providing a bulwark for individuals' natural rights, freeing them from subordination to arbitrary authority.[84] Thus, when the market mechanism analyzed in *The Wealth of Nations* is fitted into Smith's wider notions of cultural and political development, it becomes evident that economic activity (in his view) is oriented first to biological sustenance, but ultimately also to moral progress, cultural development, and the attainment of political freedom.

The rules of justice appropriate for regulating economic activity will emerge and achieve articulation through social interaction within the human community, at first being crude and imperfect but eventually evolving into objective form as what Lindgren calls "ideals of performance." As to the content of such a potential ideal of economic justice, the basic motivational assumption of Smith's model of market capitalism is, of course, the principle of self-interest, or "the desire of bettering our own condition," a quality of character that leads the individual to the steady, unrelenting pursuit of his private economic advantage. Such a drive is utterly basic, natural, and crucial to the system. It "comes with us from the womb"; it is "the principle from which ... opulence is originally derived," a principle strong enough to surmount "a hundred impertinent obstructions" and to carry society to wealth and prosperity.[85] It is this principle that leads capitalist investors to respond to market signals, to shift resources from low profit sectors to high profit sectors and, in the process, to bring about the pattern of resource allocation which maximizes net product.

However, as MacFie points out, the trait identified as self interest in *The Wealth of Nations* is but a special economic form of the personal quality referred to in *The Moral Sentiments* as *prudence*.[86] In the latter work, Smith takes prudence—"steadiness of ... industry and frugality" in the care of one's health, fortune, and rank—to be a virtue, that is, a quality of character that warrants the moral approval of the impartial spectator."[87] Objecting to the belief that only altruistic, benevolent conduct is morally commendable, Smith points out that "habits of economy, industry ... are generally supposed to be cultivated from self-interested motives, and at the same time are apprehended to be very praiseworthy qualities."[88] Prudence in *The Moral Sentiments*, economic self-interest in *The Wealth of Nations,* are understood as morally desirable character traits, not only for the utilitarian reason that such traits conduce to prosperity but also on the ground that they pass Smith's ultimate test of moral intuition. They would be approved by the impartial spectator.

A crucial qualification in Smith's argument must, however, be carefully noted. Appeal to the hypothetical judgment of the disinterested, impartial spectator is the device he uses to introduce rationality into moral judgment.[89] Acknowledging that behavior is basically self-interested, Smith allows the individual to follow the prompting of each human "affection" or psychological propensity, but to do so only within due limits or proper measure. What those limits and measures are is determined by the judgment of the impartial spectator, the latter being taken as "the natural and original measure of the proper degree of all the affections."[90] And judgment of the spectator poses a distinct restraint on the individual's pursuit of economic self-interest. "In the race for wealth," so reads an oft-quoted passage from *The Moral Sentiments,* an individual "may run as hard as he can, to out-strip his competitors. But if he should jostle, or throw down any of them, the indulgence of the spectators is entirely at an end. It is a violation of fair play which they cannot admit of."[91]

A similar moral restraint on self-interest is also explicitly imposed at a crucial point in *The Wealth of Nations.* Bringing his long and detailed criticism of alternative "systems" to a close, Smith provides a summary statement of the requirements necessary for his own "System of Natural Liberty"—the system that, in his view, would allow for economic efficiency and progress—to operate effectively. The government must provide defense, education, and a legal framework for the market—i.e., "an exact administration of justice." Within such a framework, the individual is left "perfectly free to pursue his own interests in his own way, and to bring both his industry and capital into competition with any other man." However, the argument involves a moral proviso comparable to that noted in *The Moral Sentiments.* "Every man" is left free to pursue his self-interest "as long as he does not violate the laws of justice."[92] According to Smith's model, economic activity is motivated by the laudable virtue of self-interest—by the individual's prudential desire to "better his own condition." But such behavior must also conform to a further "ideal of performance." The profit seeking, self-interested economic agent must not "violate the laws of justice."

A summary view of Smith's analysis of market behavior indicates that the "laws of justice" he refers to here are moral rules which, according to a philosophic tradition leading all the way back to Aristotle's distinction between *commutative* and *distributive* justice in *Ethics* V, have been identified as having to do with interaction between one private individual and another, particularly in acts of exchange.[93]

"What are the rules which men naturally observe in exchanging?"[94] asks Smith as he opens his analysis of the market mechanism. And the final inference to be drawn from his condemnation of monopoly, his denunciation of the Mercantile System, his defense of his own System of Natural Liberty is that the rules he finds applicable reduce ultimately to the requirements of commutative justice. This is not to say that Smith's heroic effort to understand market capitalism finally produces only a restatement of the ancient principle of the just price, embellished with rhetoric and enlivened by moral fervor. For it is the genius of Smith to have demonstrated that compliance with commutative justice in private acts of exchange has an immensely important social consequence, a side effect unintended by the individuals themselves and a result not immediately apparent to casual observation. For it is justice in exchange, allowing market prices to equate supply and demand and to bring prices into line with costs which, so Smith's explanation of the resource allocation mechanism demonstrates, is essential for maximizing net product and thus permitting society to "provide a plentiful revenue of subsistence for the people." Neither Aristotle nor his many followers in the medieval tradition had been able to establish the critical linkage between justice in exchange and society's communal welfare. Smith forges such linkage in his System of Natural Liberty.

One must admire Adam Smith's sustained effort to combine insight into market relations with a grasp of the moral purpose of economic activity so as to demonstrate how compliance with the rules of commutative justice would contribute to building the material base for a humane and just society. And yet, the immense endeavor fails at crucial points. Inconsistencies in Smith's analysis, and much social experience over the past two centuries, combine to suggest that, whatever its advantages in providing a "plentiful revenue of subsistence," the System of Natural Liberty also produces its own special form of social degeneracy.

As with many an individualistic social theory that tries to build the good society on the single ground of commutative justice, Smith's theory encounters special difficulties. It requires scrupulous regard for individual rights—e.g., of the worker to use the strength and dexterity of his own two hands when and where he chooses, or of the capitalist investor to bring his resources "into competition with any other man." For this reason, the theory denounces as immoral any interference with freedom of contract or any failure to carry out contractual agreements once entered into by private parties. But Adam Smith's individualistic social theory provides no procedure whereby the community could come to a reasoned consensus as to the relative merits of its members and distribute goods accordingly. That is, there is no way for the community to discern or to carry out the moral obligations of what the Western philosophic tradition recognizes as a second form of social imperatives, the demands of *distributive justice*.[95] Like the similar theories of Hume,[95] Smith's model provides no normative principles for evaluating the pattern of asset distribution prevailing prior to the inception of market interaction, no moral justification either for accepting or modifying the initial configuration of resource ownership. Thus those who start out in undeserved penury because they are denied their fair share of society's productive property will end up, even though all subsequent transactions comply scrupulously with commutative justice, in comparable undeserved end-state penury.

Nor is this inability to perceive and articulate the special kind of obligation involved in distributive justice accidental for Smith's model. According to his conception of moral knowledge, ethical insight emerges through social interaction and progresses toward objectivity as men learn to evaluate conduct according to decisions of a hypothetical impartial spectator. As Peter Danner has shown, appeal to the impartial spectator does indeed suffice to rectify human behavior—forestall a violation of an individual's right—in the process of commodity exchange where there is a definite quid pro quo on both sides of the transaction.[96] But reference to an impartial spectator, apparently, cannot be relied upon to discover the special kind of knowledge needed to implement distributive justice.

"People of the same trade seldom meet together, even for merriment or diversion," goes a famous passage from *The Wealth of Nations*, "but the conversation ends in a conspiracy against the public or in some contrivance to raise prices."[97] Following up this initial insight with magnificent consistency, Adam Smith provides a chilling illustration of individualistic social theory at work. Government cannot effectively prevent people of the same trade from gathering together, but government can at least not "facilitate" or "render necessary" such assemblies. And as an example of wrong-headed facilitating legislation, Adam Smith refers to "a regulation which enables those of the same trade to tax themselves in order to provide for their sick, their widows and orphans."[98] Such regulations create a focal point of common interest among the members of a trade. And such a pursuit of common interest is, according to Smith's reading, bound to be sinister. If people of the same trade meet not merely for merriment or diversion, but also to care for their poor, their sick, their widows and orphans, the result is likely to be a conspiracy against the public.

Smith's comprehensive social theory envisages a process whereby social interaction leads to a progressively clearer formulation of normative rules. His warning of the likelihood of conspiracy indicates that men can come to objective moral judgments—to conclusions consistent with the decision of the supposed impartial spectator—when engaged in impersonal exchange relations, but are likely to be seduced into conspiracy if the social situation is less atomistic. The fact that objectivity is attainable in one situation but not in the other suggests that the impartial spectator mechanism for testing the validity of moral judgments works only if men keep a social distance between one another, a distance so great that only root natural properties, the same for all men, are taken into account. Taking note of nonnatural properties, such as would be the case when men "of the same trade" interact, would obscure moral vision, so Smith's example indicates, and lead to evil conduct. But it is precisely the nonnatural properties which differentiate one man and his social position from that of another which have to be taken into account if *distributive* justice is to be made operative in social life. To abstract from such differences, to treat all men as equal, obliterates the classical distinction between the two kinds of justice. Smith's moral theory seems to involve precisely such obliteration. It would thus deprive the community of any rational grounds for either changing the existing distribution of property or approving the initial distribution as legitimate.

Deprived by his own theory of moral knowledge of grounds for formulating critical principles of distributive justice, Adam Smith accepts the class divisions of capitalist society as natural. Given compliance with his brand of justice, commodities sell at just prices, and the revenue derived from such sale divides into three functional shares—wages, rent, and profits. And these functional shares devolve upon three distinct social classes, the "three great, original and constituent orders of every civilized society."[99] The capitalist class structure being taken as given, Smith's humanitarian concern for the poor takes on a special and characteristic form. The "universal opulence" generated by capitalism is expected to "diffuse itself through the lower ranks of society." And the mechanism that is to make such a trickle-down process work is not redistribution, but economic growth—capital accumulation and expansion of net product at rates faster than population growth. The demand for labor, pulling up wage rates and raising working-class living standards, "necessarily increases with the revenue and stock of the country and cannot possibly increase without it."[100] Should the growth process falter—if society were to relapse from continuous expansion into a stationary or declining state—increase in their numbers would soon reduce the working class to utter poverty. They can rise to a position of decent comfort only if the process of capital accumulation is allowed to flourish.[101] Since such accumulation is done by the rich, rising living standards for the worker will not eliminate social inequality. In fact, one of the basic functions of civil government is to protect the property of the rich from the "envy" and "indignation" of the poor.[102]

The moral ambiguity of Smith's model becomes apparent when the process of capital accumulation is analyzed further. According to the crude theory of production employed in *The Wealth of Nations,* capital accumulation leads to growth of output, but it does so only because greater capital per worker enhances the division of labor. National opulence is the by-product of greater and greater specialization raising output per worker, and such productive subdivision of tasks can take place "only in proportion as stock is previously more and more accumulated."[103] In the last analysis, it is division of labor that raises output per capita and consumer living standards. But according to a well-known argument from *The Wealth of Nations,* this same process that contributes to national opulence also has a devastating impact on the personality and character of the working class. Workplace experience is the source of intellectual challenge for most of the population. And an individual confined to simple and repetitive operations within a system of division of labor "has no occasion to exert his understanding." As a consequence, he "generally becomes as stupid and ignorant as it is possible for a human creature to become," incapable alike of rational conversation, noble sentiment, and participation in civic life.[104]

Capital expansion is essential to forestall poverty. Yet such expansion is indeed a mixed blessing. Economic growth raises consumer living standards—but does so by spawning a working class too stupid and ignorant to participate in civilized life. Capitalist development as envisioned by Smith may lead, first, to greater consumption and ultimately, as Grampp and Thompson find, to greater leisure, culture, refinement, and political progress. But, on Smith's own showing, capitalism also systematically deprives the working class of the ability to share in any of these benefits except the animal, biological good of greater consumption. Given capitalist growth, "the poor we have always with us" proverb will be disconfirmed. Instead of the poor, we will have a rabble of well-fed, but ignorant and alienated worker-consumers.[105]

NOTES

1. Adam Smith, *The Wealth of Nations,* (New York: Random House, Modern Library Edition, 1937), p. 28. Cited hereafter as *WN.*

2. Max Lerner, quoting Harold Laski, in *WN,* p. ix.

3. For an explanation of how the process referred to by Laski came about, see W.S. Gramm, "The Selective Interpretation of Adam Smith," *Journal of Economic Issues,* March 1980. According to Gramm's "epistemological thesis," Smith's originally critical model of capitalism has been converted by the present generation into an apologia for the status quo because of a "rebalancing of ... positive and normative elements," an interpretive "transformation" whereby "ingredients most compatible with the existing power structure come to be regarded as the essence of the system." Ibid., p. 133.

4. *WN,* pp. 248 ff.

5. *WN,* p. lvii.

6. *WN,* p. 250.

7. *WN,* pp. 608 ff., 625.

8. Eli Ginzberg, *The House of Adam Smith* (New York: Columbia University Press, 1934), pp. 11 ff.

9. See Adam Smith, *The Theory of Moral Sentiments,* with an Introduction by E.G. West (Indianapolis, Ind.: Liberty Fund, 1976), p. 168. Cited hereafter as *TofMS.*

10. Jacob Viner, "Adam Smith and Laissez Faire," in *Adam Smith, 1776-1926* (Chicago: University of Chicago Press, 1928), p. 154.

11. *WN,* p. 397. In his formal statement, Smith asserts that economic activity has "two distinct objects"—to provide (i) subsistence for the people; and (ii) revenue to finance public services. In his total schema, however, the second objective is subordinate and contributory to the first.

12. *WN,* p. 625. Herbert Thompson found that the reference to consumption constitutes the "fundamental value judgment," and the "revolutionary normative judgment," for the *WN.* See "Adam Smith's Philosophy of Science," *Quarterly Journal of Economics,* Winter 1965, pp. 212-33, esp. p. 230. According to T. D. Campbell, Smith's "advocacy of the system of natural liberty is ultimately based on an assessment of its utility in increasing *per capita* consumption." *Adam Smith: The Science of Morals* (Totowa, N.J.: Rowman and Littlefield, 1971), p. 213.

13. *TofMS,* p. 304.

14. A.L. MacFie, *The Individual in Society* (London: George Allen & Unwin, 1967), p. 77.

15. *WN,* p. 423.

16. *WN,* pp. 594 ff.

17. *TofMS,* pp. 301 ff.

18. *TofMS,* p. 303.

19. Smith is sometimes said to have anticipated Veblen's belief that the motive for acquiring wealth is based upon a desire for "pecuniary emulation" of the rich. Cf. J. Ralph Lindgren, *The Social Philosophy of Adam Smith* (The Hague: Martinus Nijhoff, 1973), pp. 102 ff.

20. *WN,* p. 324.

21. *WN,* p. 11.

22. Glenn R. Morrow, "Adam Smith: Moralist and Philosopher," in *Adam Smith, 1776-1926* (Chicago: University of Chicago Press, 1928), p. 165.

23. Lindgren, p. 85.

24. *WN,* p. 612.

25. *WN,* p. 607-13.

26. *WN,* pp. 121 ff.

27. *WN,* pp. 651, 653 ff., 681 ff.

28. *WN,* p. 308.

29. *WN,* p. 339.

30. *WN,* p. 862.

31. Scott Gordon, *Welfare, Justice, and Freedom* (New York: Columbia University Press, 1980), pp. 4 ff.

32. *WN,* pp. 651, 669.

33. John Rawls, *A Theory of Justice* (Cambridge, Mass.: Harvard University Press, 1971), pp. 195-97.

34. As a classic study of Smith and his successors once put the point, "the invisible hand which guides men to promote ends which were no part of their intention, is not the hand of some god ... it is the hand of the lawgiver." Lionel Robbins, *The Theory of Economic Policy* (London: Macmillan, 1953), p.56. For a similar interpretation of the Invisible Hand metaphor, see MacFie, p. 129. For a different interpretation of Smith on the relationship between government and market, see Warren Samuels, "Adam Smith and the Economy as a System of Power," *Review of Social Economics,* October 1973. According to Samuels, "Smith analyzed the ... role

of the invisible hand ... in the market allocation of resources ... but he also analyzed the economy as a broader system of power ... and in this broader analysis ... he considered the use of government as an economic variable." Ibid., p. 134.

35. *The Classical Theory of Economic Policy* (New York: World, 1966), p. 17.

36. The apparent inconsistency between his two major works has been a perennial problem for Smith scholarship for nearly a century. See Garry Wills, "Benevolent Adam Smith," *New York Review of Books,* January 1978, pp. 40 ff. For an expanded treatment of how the virtue of *justice* provides the basic "organizing concept" of *The Wealth of Nations* and the "critical link between Smith's social philosophy and his political economy," see Leonard Billet, "The Just Economy: The Moral Basis of *The Wealth of Nations,*" *Review of Social Economy,* December 1976, pp. 295-315.

37. *TofMS,* p. 266. As a classic work in moral theory, *The Theory of Moral Sentiments* has always provided ample grist for the mills of philosophic commentary. According to one recent exposition of how the impartial spectator procedure works:

> By means of sympathy we try to create a spectator position towards ourselves; we try to take up that view-at-a-distance which we perceive others take of us...Next we try to imagine whether...such a spectator would be able to enter into our real position ... We then try to estimate the outcome of this second sympathetic move to see whether there will be agreement between our original motives and sentiments and those ... of the imagined spectator—that is, whether the imagined spectator approves or disapproves of our original sentiments and motives. Finally, we try to make this spectator approval or disapproval our own ... In this way we come to judge of our own behavior by the same standard with which we judge of the behavior of others ...

Cf. Knud Haakenssen, *The Science of a Legislator* (London: Cambridge University Press, 1981), p. 53. For other explanations, see Lindgren, p. 12; Joseph Cropsey, *Polity and Economy* (Westport, Conn.: Greenwood Press, 1977), p. 12. The impartial spectator procedure is sometimes described as a device for avoiding the two extremes of "Mandeville's pernicious sophistries, that self interest in any respect is beneficial," on the one hand, and Hutcheson's unrealistic belief that "a totally disinterested benevolence is possible," on the other. See also Peter Danner, "Sympathy and Exchangeable Value: Keys to Smith's Social Philosophy," *Review of Social Economy,* December 1976, pp. 317-33, esp. pp. 321 ff.

38. *TofMS,* p. 49.

39. *TofMS,* p. 506.

40. According to Joseph Cropsey's interpretation of Smith, "the

principle of approbation is not reason, but sentiment and feeling, via sympathy," cf. A.S. Skinner and T. Wilson, eds., *Essays on Adam Smith* (Oxford: Clarendon Press, 1975), p. 141. See also Cropsey's metaphor of the soul as a tuning fork in *Polity and Economy,* pp. 15 ff.

41. *TofMS,* p. 61.

42. MacFie, pp. 64, 67.

43. *TofMS,* p. 207.

44. Lindgren, p. 20.

45. MacFie, p. 67.

46. Campbell, pp. 137 ff.

47. Samuels, p. 26. Smith's explanation of the genesis of moral principles is said to involve an interaction between efficient and final causes similar to that operative in *The Wealth of Nations.* Sympathetic interaction is an efficient cause which, acting as a "selection mechanism" to weed out antisocial behavior, leads to fulfillment of an overarching final cause, the stability of society. Cf. Haakenssen, pp. 55, 59.

48. See the references to Small and Westermarck in Campbell, pp. 137, 152, and in Lindgren, pp. 36, 57.

49. Campbell, pp. 139-45. Campbell draws the logical conclusion that, having adopted "moral relativism," Smith could not consistently condemn as immoral any practice comfortable with existing social mores. But see Lindgren, pp. 36 ff.

50. See his criticism of the "Platonic faith that there is 'truth' in politics remaining only to be discovered" and of the "truth judgment approach" to political theory in *The Limits of Liberty* (Chicago: University of Chicago Press, 1975), pp. 1, 15. See also his careful formulation, based on a comparison of the thought of Frank Knight and Michael Polanyi, of the difference between politics and science in *Freedom in Constitutional Contract* (College Station: Texas A & M University Press, 1977), chap. 5. Buchanan's distinction between the rational truths of science and perceptions of the good coincides closely with Smith's belief that, though reason has an inductive function in formulating moral principles, the belief that reason "pointed out the difference between right and wrong in the same manner in which it did that between truth and falsehood" should be rejected because "it is altogether absurd ... to suppose that the first perceptions of right and wrong can be derived from reason...." Cf. *TofMS,* pp. 504, 506.

51. See Buchanan's definition of the "'good'" as "that which emerges from agreement among free men..." *Limits of Liberty,* p. 167.

52. Cf. *Freedom in Constitutional Contract,* pp. 86 ff.

53. *TofMS,* p. 166.

54. Smith is said to have made a "departure from Greek traditions" and to have adopted a "functional" view of politics which shows how a "constitution can be expected to emerge ... whose function is simply to allow the coexistence of heterogeneous people." E.G. West, "Introduction," *TofMS,* pp. 24 ff.

55. *Polity and Economy.*

56. Ibid., pp. 3, 4.

57. *Politics,* III, 9.

58. Cropsey, p. 33.

59. Ibid., p. 96.

60. Ibid., p. 13, "general approbation of conduct is not to be regarded as the sign but as the origin of moral good and virtue...." Ibid., p. 17.

61. Smith's ultimate intention, Cropsey finds, was to demonstrate how a society relying upon competitive self-interest—rather than on benevolence or virtue—could achieve social progress and, ultimately, freedom from both ecclesiastical and civil authority. Cf. ibid., pp. 93-95.

62. MacFie, pp. 126-30, esp. p. 127. In what MacFie characterizes as a "very subtle final footnote" to his main argument, Cropsey points out that mere life or bare existence might after all be subordinate to excellence, to living well or nobly, so that there is ambiguity in taking Liberty—freedom from ecclesiastical and civil authority—as the ultimate end of civil life.

63. Emily Gill, "Justice in Smith: The Right and the Good," *Review of Social Economy,* December 1976, pp. 275-95, esp. p. 276. See also Jacques Maritain's observation that Smith's conception of "sympathy" as the source of moral knowledge involves recognition of the profound truth that such knowledge is originally "pre-philosophical," not acquired through "conceptual discourse," but nevertheless possessed of its own certitude. *Moral Philosophy* (New York: Scribner's, 1964), p. 95.

64. D.D. Raphael, "The Impartial Spectator," in Skinner and Wilson, pp. 83-100, esp. p. 95.

65. Lindgren, p. 65.

66. *TofMS,* p. 266.

67. Lindgren, p. 30.

68. See Haakenssen, p. 56 "... the seeking of social approval ... has a strong tendency to become a search for another and higher judgment ... for a standpoint of absolute impartiality...." Ibid., p. 58.

69. Lindgren, p. 26.

70. Raphael, p. 90.

71. Lindgren, p. 36.

72. Raphael (p. 98) finds a significant development in Smith. Replying to the objection that his theory deprives the individual of rational grounds for following his conscience in opposition to community standards, Smith was led in successive editions of the *Moral Sentiments* to place increasing emphasis on the capacity of the individual to form objective moral judgments that can stand against those of society, eventually coming to the position that "moral rules are equivalent to divine laws and that conscience has an authority superior to social approval and disapproval."

73. Cf. Haakenssen, p. 61 "... by our gradual evolution of moral rules ... from innumerable cases ... we develop those human institutions which are at once the safeguards and growing points of human societies," MacFie, p. 57.

74. *WN,* p. 11.

75. *WN,* p. 625.

76. *WN,* p. 626.

77. Cf. Karl Polanyi, "Aristotle Discovers the Economy," in K. Polanyi, C.M. Arensberg, and H.W. Pearson, eds., *Trade and Market in the Early Empires* (Glencoe, Ill.: Free Press, 1957), pp. 64-93.

78. Polanyi, pp. 69 ff.

79. William Cunningham, *The Growth of English Industry and Commerce* (Cambridge: Cambridge University Press, 1910), p. 467.

80. "... mercantilist statesmen and writers saw in the subjects of the state means to an end, and the end was the power of the state itself." Eli Heckscher, "Heckscher on Mercantilism" in H. Spiegel, ed., *The Development of Economic Thought* (New York: Wiley, 1952), p. 35.

81. Cf. Thompson, pp. 216 ff., 227. Cf. William Grammp's conclusion that Smith "approved of a market economy because on balance it promoted the good life—the life of learning, beauty, personal virtue and good works." *Economic Liberalism,* vol. II (New York: Random House, 1965), p. 7.

82. *WN,* p. 385.

83. *WN,* p. 389.

84. For development of this interpretation, cf. T.J. Lewis, "Adam Smith: The Labor Market as the Basis for Natural Right," *Journal of Economic Issues,* March 1977, pp. 21-49. Lewis finds that there are two conceptions of natural price implied in Smith's model, an "efficiency" price and a "normative natural price." Opening of the market allows market price to converge toward the latter, and thus the market serves to exempt both parties to exchange from domination by arbitrary authority. According to a similar view of Smith, expanded political freedom was one of the most important consequences of the growth of capitalism. Cf. Gordon, p. 60.

85. *WN,* pp. 324, 326, 329, 508.

86. Cf. MacFie, pp. 74 ff.

87. *TofMS,* p. 351.

88. *TofMS,* p. 480.

89. MacFie, p. 65.

90. Ibid., p. 65.

91. *TofMS,* p. 162.

92. *WN,* p. 651.

93. "Of particular justice ... one kind is ... manifested in distributions of honour or money or other things ... among those who have a share in the constitution ... and one is that which plays a rectifying part in transactions between man and man ... the justice which distributes common possessions is always in accordance with proportion .... But justice in transactions is a sort of equality...." Aristotle, *Nicomachean Ethics,* V. 2.4.

94. *WN,* p. 28.

95. Haakenssen, p. 27.

96. Danner, p. 322.

97. *WN*, p. 128.

98. *WN*, pp. 128 ff.

99. *WN*, p. 248.

100. *WN*, p. 69.

101. To drive the moral home, Adam Smith tells a horror story. In the stationary state of China, where economic expansion has come to a halt, working class poverty has reached the uttermost extremity. The situation is so desperate that a gruesome specialized trade has grown up among the poor, the trade of drowning unwanted babies "like puppies in the water." *WN*, p. 72.

102. *WN*, p. 670.

103. *WN*, p. 260.

104. *WN*, pp. 734 ff.

105. Lindgren concludes that, though Smith was "indeed outraged by the oppression of the working poor," and despite his recommendation that government support of education be introduced to protect them, "Smith did not address himself squarely and directly to the question of how laborers could find dignity and self respect...." Lindgren, pp. 131 ff. Lewis, having explained how capitalist development for Smith contributes to political progress and freedom, points out that as a result of division of labor "the worker's right to 'self direction' is now vacuous; because the capacity to use it has been destroyed." Lewis, pp. 41 ff. In a comparison between Marx and Smith, E.G. West has challenged the view that the worker in Smith's model suffers because of workplace alienation on the ground that "participation in the division of labor enables them to...move away from animal-like existence...." "The Political Economy of Alienation: Karl Marx and Adam Smith," *Oxford Economic Papers,* March 1969, pp. 1-23, esp. p. 12.

Good Government, Justice, and Self-Fulfilling Individuality

DAVID L. NORTON

I. INTRODUCTION

I will begin by contending that when we speak of good government we properly speak not of one best form of government, but of several best forms of government. The premise behind this contention is that persons, as the subjects of government, are relevantly and distinctively different at different points in their lives. If the character of good government is determined by the character of the subjects who are governed, and if the subjects who are governed undergo important changes—if they grow or develop in relevant aspects—then what constitutes good government will be different at different stages in the development of subjects. To take the development of persons seriously is, I think, to recognize that it is not a pure continuum, a mere "getting bigger" of what is throughout the same thing. There are decisive qualitative changes which mark development stages, each with its own intrinsic ends. To be a child or adolescent is not to be a small adult, but to be a creature with responsibilities different from those of adulthood. Correspondingly what constitutes good government with respect to children, adolescents, and adults is distinctive in each case. I will try to briefly characterize each of these cases, to illuminate the political problem that arises.

Let us posit as the defining characteristic of childhood the characteristic of dependence; and let us agree to understand by this not that children are incapable of spontaneous behaviors, but that they cannot self-supply the regulatory principles which transform random changes in behavior into sustained development. By its nature as dependence, then, childhood requires regulation by external authority, and the question of good government with respect to children becomes the question of the criteria by which to distinguish trustworthy authority from spurious authority.

33

For contrast we will temporarily bypass adolescence and next consider adulthood. Many of us will be quite ready categorically to distinguish adulthood from childhood by employing for adulthood a term that is the contradictory of the dependence of childhood, namely, the term "autonomy." Granted, the word is treacherous and has been badly abused. I think in particular we must avoid the pitfalls of identifying autonomy with asociality, as in the "atomic" individualism of classic liberalism. The truly autonomous individual, I would argue, is no less an intrinsically social being than is the dependent child, but his sociality is different in kind from the sociality of dependence. And we must avoid the mistake of identifying autonomy with the complete self-sufficiency of the individual, as promulgated for example by Rousseau, by Marx, and by the romantic individualists.[1]

But the origin of this last mistake is fruitful to speculate upon, and I offer the following. In our everyday social situation, each of us counts upon others to do certain things for which we deem them responsible; and they often fail us. Against the disappointment and inconvenience of such failures, one resort is a self-ideal of perfect self-sufficiency. But this ideal is a dangerous mistake if true individuality is intrinsically social in some sense of interdependence; for in this case, ironically, the ideal of perfect self-sufficiency precludes individual fulfillment. The ideal itself is, I think, a reaction-formation, a compensatory ideal. If persons in situations of interdependence often fail one another, this fact should turn our minds to the problem of discovering the conditions under which persons—ourselves included—become reliable at doing what they are responsible for doing. A conception of interdependence which is consistent with autonomy is one in which each individual determines for himself what services he will provide for others, and what utilities he will derive from the self-determinations of others.

As distinguished from dependence, then, autonomy means self-regulation. Through the ages much social and political theory has felt obliged to take a stand on the disjunctive questions, "Are human beings essentially dependent creatures or are they autonomous individuals?" The contradictory character of *dependence* and *autonomy* has been thought to dictate that definitive predication of one of the terms renders the other inapplicable. But the contradiction between dependence and autonomy does not preclude the noncontradictory predication of both terms to an entity which undergoes development, for they can be predicated seriatim, as defining characteristics of successive stages of development.

Where do the principles of order of self-regulating adulthood come from? On the view I am presenting they are not arbitrary constructs, internalized in persons by conditioning. Principles of social and personal order are identical, and they are implicit in personhood from the beginning, to be explicated progressively by personal development. Because they are explicit and operative only as the outcome of development, there can be no question of doing away with positive law. But to justify the existence of a framework of positive law it is not enough to show that only by its means can social order be maintained. The question must be answered, "Social stability for what?" And the answer here proposed is, "Social stability for the purpose of achieving the self-fulfillment of individuals."

By the model of personhood here employed, to be a person is to be a unique potential excellence with responsibility for self-discovery and progressive self-actualization. To put it another way, human being is unfinished, with responsibility for taking up the work of its own self-completion. This conception originated in ancient Greece and found its first systematic formulation in the work of Socrates, Plato, and Aristotle. To acknowledge this origin I will term the conception *eudaimonistic.* Since everything to be said here about government and justice is rooted in the eudaimonistic conception of personhood, I will first try to set forth the conception as clearly as possible. I believe the interest of brevity will be served if I do this by countering four deep-rooted misconceptions about eudaimonism.

First, eudaimonism is not a form of egoism. It posits as the native motivation of persons the desire to live a life of worth. The worth which is aspired to is objective worth. This is to say it is of worth not to the individual himself exclusively or primarily, but in principle to all persons, and in fact to such persons as in themselves fulfill the conditions of appreciation[2] of worth of the distinctive kind manifested by the given individual. For example, as a work of objective worth, Beethoven's Ninth Symphony is of worth not exclusively or primarily to Beethoven himself, but in principle to all persons, and in fact to persons who fulfill the conditions of appreciation of worth of the kind which the Ninth Symphony represents. An obvious condition of such appreciation is acquaintance—one cannot appreciate the Ninth Symphony if one does not know of its existence. But some conditions are developmental: to appreciate the Ninth Symphony requires cultivated capacities in the hearer.

Second, eudaimonism is not a variant of hedonism. According to eudaimonism persons are not natively pleasure-seeking but worth-seeking. Nor are they inevitably pain-avoiding. With development, every person learns to distinguish between pains which interfere with his or her self-actualization, and pains which are indispensably attendant upon that self-actualization and may even be welcome as secondary indicators of it. What has been said is descriptive and is directed against psychological hedonism. Normatively, pleasure is not the *summum bonum,* or even a guide to the good or the right. We mean by pleasure the feeling that attends gratified desire, and "happiness" is pleasure in the long run, or a sum of pleasures. But eudaimonism goes beyond this to interrogate desire. Is the desire in question right or wrong with respect to the person whose desire it is? Because pleasure itself is noncriteriological, attending gratification of wrong and right desires indifferently, it affords no moral guidance whatever.

Third, eudaimonism is not a form of subjectivism. True, it exhibits great concern for the subject, i.e., the self of each person. But what the self is, is a task, a piece of work, namely the work of self-actualization; and self-actualization is progressive objectification. The eudaimonistic position is that the categories "subjective" and "objective" constitute a fallacy of abstractionism when wielded in mutually exclusive fashion. Every human impulse is subjective in its inception and objective in its intended outcome, and because its intended outcome is implicit within it at its inception, there is nothing in personhood which is "merely subjective" in the exclusive sense.

Finally, eudaimonism is not an elitism. It was elitist in its original Greek formulation, but the connection there is historical and contingent, not logical. And in modernity some eudaimonists have been elitists, but again the connection is contingent. Eudaimonistically conceived, to be a person is to possess innate potential excellence, with responsibility for self-discovery and self-actualization. But the contingent association of eudaimonism and elitism has been frequent enough to oblige an advocate of eudaimonism today to offer an account of it. I think this requirement is to be accounted for as a twofold failure on the part of eudaimonistic elitists.

First, it seems clear today as it did to the ancients, that the number of persons who live self-responsible, self-determined lives, manifesting unique irreplaceable worth, and experiencing the distinctive intrinsic rewards which, as Aristotle says,[3] they will trade for no other—in short, the number of true individuals—is small. Eudaimonism is obliged to account for this, and the handiest way is by concluding, perhaps with a sigh, perhaps gloatingly, that by the

natural lottery of birth only the few are endowed with potential excellences, while the majority are left empty-handed. But this handy
account is both lazy and self-serving. The challenge lies in an equally
viable alternative, namely, that all persons possess innate potential
worth, but that much potentiality goes unactualized, while at the
same time some kinds of actualized worth go unrecognized. In this
case the immediate questions are *why* much potentiality goes unactualized, and *why* some kinds of actual worth go unrecognized. Our
proposed answer to the first question is that self-actualization has
conditions, some of which cannot be self-supplied by persons, and
some of which cannot be expected to obtain by happenstance and
inadvertence. Our proposed answer to the second question is the
parochialism of eudaimonistic elitists which limits the range of
diverse kinds of human value that they can recognize. But parochialism is an endemic human condition, characterizing persons and
cultures alike, and fully deserving of the term "normal madness"
applied to it by Santayana.[4] Yet it is a tractable condition, suscep-
tible of amelioration by education. To renounce elitism, then, is to
take up the twin challenges of discovering and socially instituting
the conditions of self-actualization which cannot be self-supplied,
and designing educational programs which progressively expand
the capacities of persons to recognize and appreciate diverse kinds
of human value.

To return to the thesis of good government on a developmental
model, I will try to show that our eudaimonistic conception of personhood resolves the primary theoretical problem that the thesis
presents. The problem is this. We have identified three stages in the
development of persons, each of which calls for a distinctive kind of
government. The three forms of government must operate concur-
rently, because any society at all times comprises persons in each of
the three stages. Yet the three forms of government appear to be not
merely heterogeneous, but mutually repellent. The form of government appropriate to dependence is trustworthy external authority.
The form of government appropriate to the intermediate stage, of
which we have as yet said little, but which I will call the stage of pre-
individuated autonomy, is collective self-government, i.e., participation by or consent of each in the government of all. And the form
of government appropriate to autonomous individuality is each individual's exclusive self-government. A great deal of classical political theory has worked to demonstrate the incommensurability of
these three forms of government, but I think it can be shown that

they are commensurated by what we here propose as the fundamental aim of sociality and politics, namely, the support of self-responsible, self-determined individuality.

Consider the external authority that is entailed by the dependence of the first stage of life. It has classically been argued that external authority is incompatible with self-responsibility. But this argument ignores development. Self-responsibility is not an unvarying *fait accompli* but a developmental outcome which, as an outcome of prior dependence, entails authority as one of its own preconditions. There can be no contradiction between an outcome and one of its own preconditions. Rather, there is a criterion here for distinguishing trustworthy from illegitimate authority. For if self-responsibility is to be the developmental outcome of prior dependence, then the dependence is provisional dependence. And the authority that is entailed by provisional dependence is provisional authority. The test of such authority is clear. It is trustworthy when its exercise serves to diminish progressively the dependence of its subjects, and illegitimate (on eudaimonistic principles) when its exercise serves to perpetuate or increase the dependence of its subjects.

Consider next the collective self-determination of second-stage government. The familiar form of collective self-determination constitutes what Michael Oakeshott terms "collective enterprise association," organized around a common purpose or set of common purposes. And a major theme in Professor Oakeshott's recent book, *On Human Conduct,* is the demonstration that the collective enterprise association of governments is antithetical to the individual determination that Oakeshott takes to be the basic moral responsibility of persons.[5] This demonstration is scrupulous and telling, but it does not, I think, cover one exceptional case. The exceptional case is where the collective purpose of the enterprise association is precisely the nurture of that self-responsible, self-determined individuality that Oakeshott prizes. If the goal is self-responsible, self-determined individuality and the distinctive kind of association entailed by it, then it must be recognized that this outcome presupposes a prior stage in which the preconditions of such individuality are undertaken as a social, i.e., collective, problem. And the reason for this is that some important preconditions cannot be self-supplied by individuals. Without this prior stage of government, true individuals will be too few to matter, and the virtues of what Oakeshott means by civil association (the mode of association of true individuals) will go unrecognized.

II. THE EUDAIMONISTIC CONCEPTION OF JUSTICE

We have been speaking of conditions of self-responsible, self-determined individuality, and the eudaimonistic conception of justice centers in the idea of such conditions. The crux of it is that persons are entitled to the necessary conditions of their own self-discovery and progressive self-actualization. These entitlements constitute individual rights, but it is important to see how they arise. They do not appear in the irreducibly minimal conception of personhood. Instead, they derive from something that does appear in the irreducibly minimal conception, namely, responsibility. Eudaimonistically, to be a person is to be responsible for discovering and progressively actualizing one's innate potential worth. This is the fundamental moral "ought," and rights derive from it by the logic that "ought" implies "can." It cannot cogently be said that someone ought to do something which he cannot do; and if there are conditions to his ability to do it, then our ascription of the ought entails the presence of the conditions. Thus if each person is responsible for self-discovery and progressive self-actualization, each person is entitled to the necessary conditions of such self-discovery and self-actualization.

I will term eudaimonism "responsibilities-primitive" because responsibilities appear in its minimal conception of personhood, whereas rights do not. The interest here is that the Anglo-American tradition in political theory has been rights-primitive for 400 years, and continues to be so today. If we consider the recently revived interest in bedrock re-examination of the concept of justice, we can say that in my discipline—philosophy—it is epitomized in three studies, namely, John Rawls's *A Theory of Justice*, Robert Nozick's *Anarchy, State and Utopia,* and Ronald Dworkin's *Taking Rights Seriously*.[6] For the most part the attention of commentators has been directed to differences among the three. If we leave aside some admittedly fascinating differences in method, the deepest substantive difference can be said to center in the question, "Which human right is the most fundamental?" For Nozick quite clearly the answer is the right to liberty, which he finds implicit in an autonomy of the numerical individual as attested by the "fact of our separate existences."[7] Dworkin on the contrary contends for the right of equality, which he says is "axiomatic," and must be "assumed" if man is to be accorded the "moral personality" which distinguishes him from other animals.[8] At first sight Rawls seems to endorse the priority of the right to liberty by his first principle of justice, which is a staunch principle of liberty. But when we ask *why* liberty is the first principle, Rawls's answer is that it is so because it would be chosen as such by persons—not, however, by just any persons, but by those persons who ought to do the choosing. These are persons in an "original position" which has been achieved by a "veil of ignorance" which eradicates all differences among them. We learn here that in Rawls's exposition, the right to equality has been presupposed and is logically prior to the right to liberty.

Beneath differences, what is common to Rawls, Nozick, and Dworkin is rights-primitivism, i.e., a position that begins with a conception of man which includes rights. As Dworkin correctly indicates, this axiomatizes rights, it defines them into man. Four hundred years ago, when political theorists sought to enfranchise the newly emergent individual against the corporate powers of church and state, their chosen strategy of rights-primitivism had contextual warrant. They were in an extreme situation calling for militance, and by axiomatizing the rights of individuals they rendered them unarguable and inalienable.[9] But it is not excusable today to suppose that the only way to render rights inalienable is to axiomatize them. Rights that derive from inalienable responsibilities will be inalienable. In short, responsibilities-primitivism can, in Dworkin's phrase, "take rights seriously."

The great difference between rights-primitivism and responsibilities-primitivism is that rights-primitivism sets up what I will term a general *recipient* orientation by which persons learn to conceive of themselves in the first instance as beings to whom some things are due, whereas responsibilities-primitivism sets up a *productive* orientation by which persons learn to conceive of themselves in the first instance as beings who have something worthy to contribute.

If we follow eudaimonism in conceiving of rights as conditions of the exercise of responsibilities, then the next step is to acknowledge two important categorical distinctions among kinds of rights. The first has been alluded to heretofore: it is the distinction between conditions which can be self-supplied and conditions which cannot be self-supplied. The second is the distinction between entitlements obtaining to persons by virtue of pure, unactualized potentiality in those persons, and entitlements obtaining by virtue of persons' actualized potentialities. I will speak briefly about the four classes of rights set up by these distinctions, and then say something about concrete implications for current public policy.

If we picture to ourselves those individuals we know who are the very best examples of self-responsible self-determination, we will observe in them the self-acknowledged responsibility to supply for themselves many, and indeed most, of the conditions of their own further development. But we reflect here upon an advanced level of self-actualization, encompassing keen self-knowledge and resourcefulness. On the other hand, at the beginning of self-actualization, self-knowledge and resourcefulness are rudimentary, unconfident, and faltering, whereas certain of the conditions of further development are complex, profound, and very difficult to secure. They cannot be self-supplied by groping, neophyte individuals, and to suppose that they should be is to condemn such neophyte individuality to floundering and developmental arrest. Moreover, childhood precedes even this neophyte individuality, and to recognize it as dependence is to affirm that most of the conditions of its development cannot be self-supplied. From the central aim of nurturing self-responsible individuality it follows that persons are to self-provide those conditions of their own development which they can self-supply without serious deflection from their responsibility for that development. What cannot be thus self-provided is to be provided by government and constitutes the basic raison d'être of the state.

Turning to the classes of rights set up by the distinction between unactualized and actualized potentiality, those rights that obtain by virtue of unactualized potentiality are uniform, absolute, and inalienable. They include entitlement to material conditions of subsistence, but also to the educational and social conditions by which to transform subsistence into growth. A key social condition is the respect by others which is due to every person by virtue of merely potential worth.

Potentiality is actualized by degrees, and it adds entitlements to those that derive from unactualized potentiality. It also introduces a qualitative criterion that I will term the criterion of commensurability. Whereas entitlements from unactualized potentiality are uniform, absolute, and inalienable, entitlements deriving from actualized potentiality are differentiated, qualified by degree, and self-alienable. They are self-alienable, because actualized potentiality can lapse, either by moral "backsliding," or by the choice of the individual to exchange the course of life upon which he has been engaged for another and different course of life, requiring the cultivation of different abilities.

The qualitative criterion enters because actualization of potentiality is the process of qualitative individuation. Eudaimonism is *normative individualism,* as distinguished from normative uniformitarianism. Normative uniformitarianism regards all qualitative differences among persons on the model of the mole upon one's cheek, or the color of one's eye, i.e., as normatively irrelevant. But from the eudaimonistic standpoint it is potentialities that are normative, and the innate potentiality of every person is unique. Because self-actualization proceeds by degrees, in its early phases it produces only a differentiation of rough types, for example, intellectual, voluntarist, sensualist. But prolonged self-responsible living within one's type eventuates in manifest uniqueness, as the music of Beethoven is unique, or the administrative style of Disraeli was unique. In short, the basic moral responsibilities of individuals are qualitatively distinguished, and correspondingly the entitlements that derive from those responsibilities are differentiated entitlements. The principle is that persons are entitled to those distributable goods whose potential values they will actualize in the course of their own self-actualization. They are not entitled to distributable goods whose potential values will not be actualized in the course of their own self-actualization. For in this case, either the potential values of the goods will go unactualized, constituting waste, or else they will be actualized at the expense of the self-responsibility of the individual, constituting self-deception or self-betrayal. Mario Andretti is entitled to his Lotus race car, but I am not entitled to one. You are entitled to your edition of Adam Smith's *The Wealth of Nations,* but your pretentious neighbor is disentitled to all of the unread great works that fill his shelves to impress his guests.

If we again picture to ourselves those individuals we know who are the very best examples of self-responsible self-determination, I think we will recognize their living expression of the above conception of distributive justice. They do not lay claim to anything and everything under the supposition that equality means that they are at least as entitled to anything as is anyone else. They claim only what they require and can utilize in the production of value. They openly disavow any claim to incommensurate goods, recognizing that such goods represent seductive distractions. Indeed, they actively will such goods to those individuals for whom the goods are commensurate, first of all for the special pleasure they experience in the sight of proportionality or fitness; but equally because they know that they cannot fulfill themselves in solitude—that self-fulfilling individuality entails the sociality of other self-fulfilling individuals on the principle of the complementarity of diverse excellences.

If we turn now to programmatic implications of eudaimonism, we must notice, first of all, that within the eudaimonistic framework, collective self-government is not the supreme political achievement, but an intermediate step and staging ground for higher political achievement corresponding to further individual development. Here is a response to the well-known problem of the "tension" (or come would say, contradiction) between equality and excellence. For by eudaimonism, collective self-determination and the quality it implies are set to the purpose of nurturing individual self-discovery and self-actualizing excellence. And here is a response as well to those observers today who find our democracy purposeless by contrast to some collectivized societies and to militant nationalisms. There is a distinctive purposefulness implicit in our democracy, one that attacks neither individuality nor excellence, but serves both. The task is to make it explicit.

But this is very general, and it is important to show that the perspective of eudaimonism, while rich with implications, can achieve sharp focus upon priorities. In my judgment it identifies as the key social problem the problem of meaningful work, and it identifies the developmental locus of the problem at the place well prior to the locus of current initiatives in work reform (about which more will be said shortly)—namely, in adolescence. I will say something to support these two contentions.

III. MEANINGFUL WORK AND SELF-ACTUALIZATION

In the first place, by the eudaimonistic conception of personhood worthy living is work—the work of self-actualization. To use an expression that has some currency, it is the individual's "meaningful work." The supreme rewards of living are the intrinsic rewards of one's meaningful work, such that one who knows them will, as Aristotle said, exchange them for no other. Moreover, as I have sought to demonstrate elsewhere,[10] what are traditionally recognized as the personal virtues—honesty, courage, fidelity, generosity, justice, wholeheartedness—are natural products of the conjunction of persons with their meaningful work. The reason that, on the one hand, work has had a bad press through history, and on the other hand human beings have lent themselves to the characterization, as by Hobbes and the classical British economists, that they are by nature lazy and averse to work, is that historically, very little of the work to be done has been done by the persons whose meaningful work it is to do. The problem, quite simply, is that of *matching*. And it is a problem because of individuation, for what individuation means in this

context is that persons are highly selective, and also widely diversified, in the work that each finds intrinsically rewarding. Amid the
great variety of recognizably productive kinds of behavior, there are
many kinds which each of us as an individual is disinclined to do,
and only a small number which we find intrinsically rewarding. This
fact has not gone unrecognized, but it has typically been dismissed
as idiosyncrasy, "mere subjectivism." By eudaimonism's lights, this
disregard does humankind a crippling disservice.

If we take the fact seriously, it directs us to adolescence and
calls for a restructuring of that stage of development. The logic in
this contention is the following. Meaningful work is chosen work,
and criteriologically chosen work. The paramount criterion is the
innate potentiality of the individual, but it cannot be discovered by
introspection; it can only be discovered by experimental enactments
in the world followed by evaluation of the results. And such experimental enactment at the same time affords the knowledge of available alternatives which is the prerequisite of genuine choice. Devel-
opmentally, adolescence is the place for such exploration, for it
possesses the requisite autonomy, while it is as yet unburdened by
adult commitments and their requirement of fidelity. What is to be
discovered is the individual self, but the self is a task, a meaningful
work to be enacted in the world. The job of adolescence, then, is exploration in the interest of self-discovery, but it has formidable conditions which adolescents cannot provide for themselves. One such
condition is precisely the public understanding that this is what adolescence is, for by this understanding adolescence is released from
the imposed authority of childhood and safeguarded from prema-
ture imposition of the demands of adulthood. What adolescence
next requires is carefully designed and socially implemented programs to facilitate fruitful exploration among alternative vocations
and life-styles. And these it most certainly cannot provide for itself,
for to render exploration fruitful requires, in the first place, the very
best in the way of a logic of discovery that cumulative human knowledge and the ages of human thought can provide.

It is when adult commitments are true choices that the individual's engagement at them becomes wholehearted, for it is undis-
tracted by the seductiveness of untried options. And it is in wholehearted engagement that the productive resourcefulness of the individual becomes manifest. This wholeheartedness is a virtue long
associated with the eudaimonic individual, the self-responsible,
self-determined individual whose portrait I have twice asked you to
picture in your mind's eye. This portrait has fascinated moral and

political philosophers through the ages. But political modernity can be characterized by its decision to disregard this portrait in favor of a "realistic" depiction of persons as nasty and brutish, avaricious and indolent. Indeed, as a father of realpolitik Hobbes himself recognized the eudaimonic individual and declared him to be the securest foundation of justice.[11] Why, then, was this individual adjudged politically irrelevant by Hobbes and modernity? The answer is clearly given: it is because such individuals were too rare to build a system of social order upon. But this judgment was made 400 years ago, and its warrant has evaporated today. Unlike the fathers of political modernity, we today can recognize the eudaimonic individual as the conditional developmental outcome of potentialities that all persons possess. And we know enough about development to uncover its necessary conditions and make a working program of the ideal of generalized eudaimonic excellence.

There is an urgency in the need for such a working program that should be spelled out. So-called morphologists of culture are not wrong in discerning a life-cycle to cultures which is roughly analogous to the life-cycle of individuals. Cultures wear out their initial inspiration and undergo declining vitality, ending as composites of empty institutional forms that are enacted, not by full-blooded persons, but by hollow role-performers. Yet there is within every culture a source of perpetual regeneration consisting in the vitality of fresh generations of persons. But to capture this intrinsic regenerative source requires that precedence be given to persons in each newly ascendant generation, and not to the institutional forms which are the remnants of past generations. Each newly ascendant person bears within him or her the source of a personal inspiration which, if cultivated in persons generally, is a prime social asset and the wellspring of cultural vitality and renewal. To the extent to which antecedently determined social utilities take precedence over each newly ascendant generation of persons as persons, institutions and practices become empty forms, and persons experience alienation, anomie, and residual hopelessness. Yet for every person there is a meaningful work which affords to that person intrinsic rewards that will not be exchanged for work of any other sort, or for idleness or unproductive self-indulgence. This work is this individual's self-actualization, and it is likewise productive of social utilities. For recognition of this double aspect of productivity the *locus classicus* is Aristotle's observation that "Every virtue or excellence both brings into good condition the thing (person) of which it is the excellence and makes the work of that thing (person) be well done."[12] On this recognition, giving precedence to persons over social utilities secures superior social utilities and secures to the society in question the perpetual renewal of institutional vitality.

IV. EUDAIMONISM AND WORKPLACE REFORM

To its credit, our decade of the 1980s evinces mounting concern over the troubled condition of work and has initiated a multiplicity of striking experimental correctives under such titles as "job enrichment," "job restructuring," and "the humanization of work and the workplace." This concern is epitomized in the U.S. by *Work in America,* the report issued in December 1972 by the Department of Health, Education, and Welfare. In Europe its most ambitious expressions are the Scandinavian and Yugoslavian experiments in industrial democracy and job restructuring. Among many smaller experiments, both in the U.S. and abroad, widespread publicity and interest has attended the job enrichments undertaken at American Telephone and Telegraph between 1964 and 1968; the introduction of "flex-time" by Lufthansa Airlines in 1970; the Gaines Pet Food experiment with autonomous work groups at its plant (opening in 1971) in Topeka, Kansas; and the work restructuring by joint union-management collaboration at Harmon Industries in Bolivar, Tennessee, begun in 1972.[13]

Early reports on these and related experiments have in general been glowing, crediting them with, on the one hand, increasing the job satisfaction in workers, and on the other hand producing such key employer benefits as increased productivity, reduced absenteeism, and diminished worker turnover. But it has also in general been the case that as the experiments have matured, follow-up studies have introduced doubts of several kinds. This latter circumstance was unquestionably epitomized in the minds of most observers by the remark of one of six American automobile workers who had just returned from four weeks' experience in the team-assembly experiment at the SAAB auto works in Sweden. He said, "If I have to bust my ass to be meaningful, forget it; I'd rather be monotonous."[14]

The six auto workers went to SAAB as part of a Ford Foundation study in cooperation with the United Auto Workers, General Motors, and Chrysler. One of their findings was that the SAAB experiment with team assembly (dispensing with the assembly line) was restricted to only a small proportion of the assembly work, the rest being done on a conventional assembly line. Moreover, many of the regular Swedish and Finnish workers shunned team assembly on grounds very like those of the American worker quoted above, namely, that the work was harder. The work was also more diversified, with each worker doing five or six operations instead of just one; and it was flexible in that teams could apportion the work among themselves as they chose each day. For the most part these features failed to impress the Americans, however, some of them labeled it "just a different kind of boredom."[15] True, the extended and flexible work took longer to learn, but it was doubted that the work would be any less boring when it had been learned.[16] Some of the Americans surmised that in the end the motivation of SAAB workers was identical to their own—auto work is good money. In their four weeks the Americans had little exposure to the effects of Sweden's initiatives at industrial democracy (by Swedish law, employees of all firms with more than 200 on the payroll can elect two of their number to the company's board of trustees), but they were dubious. The board of trustees seemed too remote from the shop floor; and the union likewise seemed remote from the shop floor, perhaps because the adversary relationship between unions and management does not obtain in Sweden, leaving workers uncertain of support. As one American worker put it, Swedish workers cannot say, as in the U.S., "That's it ... get me the committeeman right now."[17]

As epitomized by the observation, "If I have to bust my ass to be meaningful, forget it ...," the report on our auto workers' reactions to their experience at SAAB has become something of a focal point for mounting skepticism concerning the basic presuppositions of current work reform endeavors. The author of the report on the auto workers' experience observes himself that "The relatively relaxed tone of the workers' discussion about job satisfaction contrasted sharply with the urgency in the literature of work reorganization. In effect, the Americans said that they had to make a living and auto work was good money. They did not expect the job to give them all or most of their satisfaction in life..." In a similar vein but more general and emphatic is the following observation by George Strauss of the Institute of Industrial Relations at the University of California. "[The] evidence suggests," he says, "that for workers at all levels—even managers and professionals—lack of challenge is much less oppressive than lack of income. People as a whole are willing to tolerate large doses of boredom if they are paid enough. In so doing they are perhaps selling their souls for a mess of pottage. By my elitist standards this may be a raw deal ... but why should my elitist standards govern?"[18]

What calls for attention is that the skepticism expressed here is entirely compatible with the eudaimonistic theses that for every person there is meaningful work, and that the well-lived life is a life of meaningful work. They are rendered compatible by the proposition that present work reform in all of its variety is insufficiently radical to touch the problem. The problem cannot be attacked by beginning with dull jobs and bored workers and "enriching," "enlarging," or "democratizing" the jobs. The reason for this is that what we have termed meaningfulness subsists, not in jobs, considered in independence of workers, or in workers, considered in independence of jobs, but in the relationship of job and worker. It is the relationship of a given kind of work to the person, qua individual, whose work it is to do. It would be useful to rescue the term "vocation" from indiscriminate usage and restrict it to the designation of this relationship. Where this relationship does not exist the given kind of work does not constitute the meaningful work of the given worker, and no amount of enriching, enlarging, or democratization can alter the relationship. In this case the work is not intrinsically rewarding. It will be done exclusively for the extrinsic rewards it offers, and intrinsic rewards will be sought elsewhere. As Robert Goldmann says of the American auto workers, "They did not expect the job to give them all or most of their satisfaction in life...."[19] But there is a deep-seated contaminant here. It is the supposition that *work per se* is an unpleasant necessity, and not a source of intrinsic rewards. Under its influence the "elsewhere" in which satisfactions are sought becomes not productive activity of another sort, but unproductive self-indulgence.

As Leo Strauss has written, "Political freedom, and especially that political freedom that justifies itself by the pursuit of human excellence, is not a gift of heaven; it becomes actual only through the efforts of many generations...."[20] In our political tradition our conception of freedom is associated with a "public sector/private sector" bifurcation. In the minds of our profounder political fathers—Jefferson, for example—it meant, in the private sector, freedom from externally obligatory and intrinsically unrewarding work for the chosen and meaningful work termed by Strauss "the pursuit of human excellence." But the pursuit of excellence is work, and it will not occur if work per se is thought to be intrinsically unpleasant. The conception of freedom as freedom from work has as a consequence that political freedom does not justify itself by the pursuit of human excellence and persons are deprived of intrinsically meaningful living. For Aristotle is profoundly correct when he identifies human happiness as productive activity in accordance with the *arete* (innate potential excellence) of each individual.[21]

Current work-reform initiatives are commendable for their shared presupposition that public-sector work can be intrinsically rewarding. This presupposition bridges the discontinuity between public and private sectors, a discontinuity that has worked to subjectivize the satisfactions sought in the private sector, draining them of meaning. Meaningful living is self-fulfilling living. Self-fulfilling living is progressive actualization of the individual's potential worth. This worth is objective and therefore public, hence self-actualization cannot be confined to a "private sector." This much can be seen, upon reflection, to be implicit in the shared presupposition of current work-reform initiatives. But the truth of the presupposition can be demonstrated only in the experience by individuals—including persons typified by that statement "If I have to bust my ass to be meaningful, forget it..."—of their meaningful work. And such experience is not produced by "enriching" or "enlarging" (etc.) the work of persons who are by their nature disinclined to do so.

A better place to begin would be by studying the leisure-time pursuits of the disaffected workers, for there it will be discovered that some of them, at least, will be genuinely investing themselves in a chosen activity—perhaps fly-fishing—which is highly productive in the self-actualization sense, generating knowledge, skills, resourcefulness, and concern for quality. Indeed, that preference for monotony, or tolerance for "large doses of boredom" in the workplace, often represents the conscious choice of the worker to conserve his energy and resourcefulness for his leisure-time pursuits. Two of the American auto workers, for example, were engaged in evening studies toward university degrees. They experienced great satisfaction in these studies and invested themselves unstintingly in them. And they both resisted "job enrichment" in order to conserve their energy and initiative for their studies.[22] But meaningful work is necessarily (though I will not develop the argument here) productive in the double sense which appears in our earlier citation from Aristotle. It actualizes the potential excellence of the individual, and it produces social utilities. The evening study of the two auto workers clearly implies productivity of both kinds. But the subjectivization of the private sector by its divorce from the public sector has produced a climate in which the two auto workers will be judged to be "busting their asses," and the consensus preference will go for boredom, or the disguised boredom of undemanding amusements.

Meaningful working is meaningful living, and it is not to be sequestered in a "private sector" without degenerative consequences. The primary social responsibility and the principal raison d'être of government, as argued previously, are to make the necessary preconditions of meaningful work available to all persons. The way to do this is to set aside the question of social utilities and give precedence to persons and their meaningful work, generating social utilities therefrom. The focal point is adolescence, and the central measure is an educational program that emphasizes and cultivates self-knowledge, i.e., knowledge of oneself as a task of self-realization, a meaningful work to be enacted into the world and productive there of social utilities. Because self-discovery only occurs a posteriori, by participatory enactments and evaluation of the results, classroom study must accept a secondary place as supportive of apprenticeship, while patterns of exploratory apprenticeship must be designed to afford experience of the spectrum of alternative kinds of productive employment. The requisite teaching emphasizes elicitation over inculcation, calling for the cultivation of distinctive skills. Teachers must, for example, be able to recognize the signs of eudaimonia and dysdaimonia, first identified in systematic form by Aristotle, but perceptively catalogued for use today by Abraham Maslow.[23]

This added investment in adolescence will be repaid with generous interest by the dividends from adulthood. Today, productivity in the workplace is dependent upon an extensive and growing support-industry engaged in the manufacture of largely ornamental work incentives together with externally imposed quality controls. The investment in adolescence will work to dismantle this support-industry through the recovery of work incentives native to every person, together with the intrinsic quality control that meaningful work secures in the form of pride. Doubtless our best efforts at extending the opportunity of meaningful work to all persons and all jobs will in the end leave some jobs and some persons unaffected. But these will no longer be the norm, nor will the "compensation" they continue to require be mistaken for the universal relation of man and work. To persons engaged at their meaningful work, "compensation" is gratuitous, and the paycheck becomes the subsidy that enables them to continue to do what they want to do, and do best.[24]

Finally, our focus upon jobs in the last few pages must not be allowed to obscure the eudaimonistic thesis that one's meaningful work is one's life, conceived as a whole and as a task of unification. Just as this recognition restores continuity between "public" and "private" with respect to work, so it establishes continuity between self-responsibility and social order. In the end, order does not impose a penalty upon the self-expression of persons which they are obligated to pay in the interest of self-preservation—it is the principle of that self-expression. To declare self-disciplined self-expression politically irrelevant, as Hobbes did, is to deprive social order of its natural foundation and its place in human fulfillment. The task is not to invent an artifactual and nonnatural or anti-natural order, but to construct intermediate systems that will foster in persons their self-disciplined self-expression as a developmental outcome.

NOTES

1. In Rousseau, human beings in the primitive condition are free because they are independent of one another, thanks to self-sufficiency. Each is self-sufficient because nature is bountiful, the needs of the individual are minimal, and his powers to gratify them are sufficient. "It is impossible to imagine why, in this primitive state, a man should need another man any more than a monkey or a wolf should need another of its kind." Jean-Jacques Rousseau, *Second Discourse,* in G.D.H. Cole, ed., *The Social Contract and Discourses by Jean Jacques Rousseau* (New York: E.P. Dutton, Everyman's Library, 1950), p. 220. The parallelism Rousseau seeks to establish in civil society includes a self-sufficiency resting in the proposal by Rousseau that each individual, in willing the good of all, is an instantiation of the General Will. Each individual is self-sufficient because, as an instantiation of the General Will, he is in himself universal humanity. Rousseau, *The Social Contract,* in Ernest Barker, ed., *Social Contract* (New York: Oxford University Press Galaxy Book, 1962), p. 196. Marx's vision of harmony in the final historical stage rests upon a self-sufficiency closely akin to Rousseau's General Will. The individual is the *totaler Mensche,* the whole man, of whom it is characteristic to "do one thing today and another tomorrow, to hunt in the morning, fish in the afternoon, rear cattle in the evening, criticize after dinner, just as I have a mind...." Karl Marx, *The German Ideology,* ed. C.J. Arthur (New York: International Publishers, 1974), p. 1. The individual here is self-sufficient because he is the undifferentiated instantiation of the "species-being," i.e., he is in himself universal humanity. On romantic individualism, its glorification of solitude is typified in the following by Schopenhauer. People are sociable, he says, in proportion to their "vacuity of soul," and their consequent inability to endure solitude. But "Great minds are like eagles, and build their nest in some lofty solitude." *Essays of Arthur Schopenhauer,* trans. T. Bailey Saunders (New York: A.L. Burt, n.d.), pp. 116, 143.

2. "Appreciation" here is meant to include utilization. Utilization of another and his works is nonexploitive when it does not obstruct, but follows upon, his self-determination. Indeed, it is a necessary condition of his self-fulfillment. For as objective, his worth is of worth to others, and is incomplete without this valuation.

3. Aristotle, *Nichomachean Ethics,* 1166a20-23.

4. George Santayana, "Normal Madness," in *Dialogues in Limbo* (New York: Scribner's, 1948).

5. Michael Oakeshott, *On Human Conduct* (London: Oxford University Press, 1975, Parts II and III.

6. John Rawls, *A Theory of Justice* (Cambridge, Mass.: Harvard University Press, 1971). Robert Nozick, *Anarchy, State and Utopia* (New York: Basic Books, 1974). Ronald Dworkin, *Taking Rights Seriously* (London: Duckworth, 1977).

7. Nozick, p. 33.

8. Dworkin, pp. vx, 181.

9. McTaggart on the claim to immediate intuitive certainty is equally applicable to axiomatization: "When a man asserts that he has an immediate certainty of a truth, he doubtless deprives other people of the right to argue with him. But he also—though this he sometimes forgets—deprives himself of the right to argue with other people." J.M.E. McTaggart, *Studies in Hegelian Cosmology* (Cambridge: Cambridge University Press, 1918), p. 72.

10. Tentatively entitled *Political Individualism, A Eudaimonistic Perspective.* To be published by Princeton University Press.

11. See Michael Oakeshott, "The Moral Life in the Writings of Thomas Hobbes," in Oakeshott, *Hobbes on Civil Association* (Oxford: Basil Blackwell, 1975), esp. p. 124.

12. Aristotle, *Nichomachean Ethics,* 1106a15-17.

13. For a useful résumé of the experiments mentioned, see e.g., Paul Dickson, *The Future of the Workplace* (New York: Weybright & Talley, 1975).

14. See the report by Robert Goldmann, "Six Automobile Workers Abroad," in Robert Schrank, ed., *American Workers Abroad* (Cambridge, Mass., & London: MIT Press, 1979), pp. 15-55. The citation appears on p. 42.

15. Ibid., p. 45.

16. Ibid., p. 54.

17. Ibid., p. 47.

18. Ibid., p. 35.

19. Ibid., p. 18.

20. Leo Strauss, *Natural Right and History* (Chicago: University of Chicago Press, 1953), p. 131.

21. *Nichomachean Ethics,* Bk. I, chaps. 8, 13.

22. *American Workers Abroad,* pp. 25-26, 35.

23. The characteristics are set forth in Maslow's *Motivation and Personality* and *Toward a Psychology of Being,* but for succinctness without loss of depth, see Abraham H. Maslow, "A Theory of Metamotivation: The Biological Rooting of the Value-Life," *Journal of Humanistic Psychology,* vol. 7, no. 2, Fall 1967.

24. For this idea I am indebted to Lawrence Haworth, *Decadence and Objectivity* (Toronto: University of Toronto Press, 1977), pp. 110-11.

Fairness, Hope, and Justice

JAMES M. BUCHANAN

I. RULES FOR A FAIR GAME

In my book, *The Limits of Liberty*,[1] I discussed the problem of distribution at some length, but I did not explicitly raise normative issues of "justice." Several critics have interpreted my efforts as supporting the "justice" of the distributional results that emerged from my analysis, but I did not, at least in any conscious sense, consider myself to be offering any such argument. My primary concern in that book was to show that contractarian agreement, at some initial and prelegal stage, might emerge that would involve the definition, the guarantee, and the enforcement of a distribution of rights and claims (endowments) among persons in a community. I was concerned to show that such a distribution of rights and claims is necessarily prior to the simple as well as the complex exchanges that a market economic process embodies, the process which, finally, determines a distribution of end-items or product values, final goods and services, upon which attention tends to be directed when we talk loosely about "distribution."

Though my analysis was essentially positive rather than normative, there are direct implications for the methodology of discussing matters of distributive justice. My whole argument suggested that the focus of attention should be on the distribution of rights and claims prior to or antecedent to the market process itself rather than on some final distribution of social product.

I shall return to this central point later, but let me now plunge directly into my main topic and ask the personalized question: Are the nominal claims to income and wealth that I now hold "just"? Am I "entitled" to these claims which allow me to translate values into measured quantities of goods, services, and real assets produced by others in the economy?

53

Let me first point to some considerations that must be reckoned with in my answer. Perhaps the most important of these to keep in mind is the relative or relational characteristic of "justice in holdings" or "entitlements." Are the nominal claims that I now hold "just"? Now, let me pose the question differently. Is there anyone else "more entitled" to these holdings than I am? And, even more specifically, are you more "entitled" to my nominal holdings, to the cash in my wallet or in my bank accounts, than I am? If you choose, you may include everyone in the "you" in thinking about this question. Would a revised distribution, with you holding the cash or claims rather than me be more "just"? Or is the "state" or the "government" somehow more entitled to them? If so, what is "the state"? Who is "the government"? Who is "entitled to act as 'governor'"?

As you can surmise, it becomes very easy to translate all such questions into the oldest and deepest issues in political, moral, and legal philosophy, issues with which we are all familiar. And of course the reason such issues are the oldest and the deepest is that they are the hardest to resolve satisfactorily.

A second consideration, already suggested by the first, involves the prospect of disagreement. Let us suppose, provisionally, that I believe that my entitlement to my holdings is at least as strong, in a moral sense, as that of anyone else. If you accept this judgment— that is, if you acknowledge my relative claim—then we really do not need to argue further about the larger issues of the "moral-ethical" supports for such claims. It is critically important here to recognize that most of our ordinary economic dealing proceeds on the basis of just such a mutual acknowledgment of the justice of the holdings that exist in the status quo. I can go to the university bookstore and buy a book with relatively minor transactions costs because I fully acknowledge the bookstore's claim to ownership of the book before I buy it, while at the same time the bookstore accepts my claim to the cash in my wallet. Neither of us need be concerned at all about "justice" in the large.[2] Serious issues arise only when disagreement emerges. Let us suppose that I believe I am more entitled to my holdings than you are, but that you do not agree with me. You think that you are really more "entitled" to the cash in my wallet than I am.

If you act out your beliefs, you will simply take my wallet if you have the power to do so, and I will, at the same time, exert every effort to prevent you from so doing. We fight unless one of us is protected in our claims by the force of law, of the state. In my example, if you attempt to take my wallet, I can call the local policeman and he will arrest you. In the foreknowledge of this probable scenario, you may refrain from attempting to take the wallet by force; that is, you may be observed to acquiesce in my holdings while at the same time you may continue to think that you remain more "entitled" to these holdings than I: In this case, you may then seek to modify the existing set of claims by political action that would involve the government levying a tax on me while at the same time making cash transfers to you. If you succeed, I may acquiesce in the tax-and-transfer program, but I shall do so only because I am unable to violate the tax law without probable penalty. The basic conflict remains. We continue to fight by political rather than by more direct means.

In any such fight or conflict, questions of "justice" necessarily get mixed up and intermingled with pure self-interest. You may want to take my wallet simply because you want the money, quite independently from any consideration of entitlement or justice in holdings. If you cannot take the holdings directly you may be quite willing to let the agency of government do it for you. I may want to keep my holdings because I want to keep them, and I may be quite happy to allow government to prevent you from taking these by force. "Justice" need not enter at all, on either side of the potential conflict. Your utility function may dictate that you would like my money under any conceivable distribution; but you may be constrained from taking these holdings by law. If, however, the law is not effective, either directly or indirectly, you will take the money unless additional constraints are present. And among these additional constraints are your attitudes toward the "justice" of my holdings. [3]

We come back, therefore, to agreement. What are the conditions or characteristics that determine whether or not you agree that my holdings are "just," that my entitlements to these holdings are superior to anyone else's? There are, of course, many ways of getting at this question, but I want to concentrate on what we call the contractarian response.

II. GAMES WITH FAIR RULES

The response may be summarized in the subsidiary question: Can my claims to holdings be interpreted and understood as one component in the outcome of what we might agree is a *fair game*? This question, in this turn, raises several subsidiary ones. What is a fair game? What is fairness? Is the game analogy appropriate for interpreting the economic interaction process?

I shall deal with the last question very briefly here. The contractarian position is distinguished from its alternatives by its dependence on criteria that are internal to the individuals who are participants in the interaction. It becomes illegitimate to invoke external criteria for evaluating either processes or end-states. Once this is recognized, the game analogy emerges almost necessarily, with the qualifications as noted in the discussion to follow. For those who do not accept the basic contractarian logic, and who would want to invoke external norms of evaluation, there is little to be said.

Let me, therefore, return to the other questions concerning what is a fair game, and what is the meaning of fairness. The contractarian response, not surprisingly, comes back again to agreement. A "fair rule" is one that is agreed to by the players in advance of play itself, before the particularized positions of the players come to be identified. Note carefully what this definition says: A rule is fair if players agree to it. It does not say that players agree because a rule is fair. That is to say, fairness is defined by agreement; agreement does not converge to some objectively determined fairness.

One way of proceeding from this point would be to discuss the derivation of what we might call "ideally fair rules" or even "plausibly fair rules." That is essentially the approach taken by John Rawls in *A Theory of Justice.*[4] While I have considerable affinity with Rawls, this method of proceeding would take me too far afield for my purposes. I find it useful to commence with an existing or even an abstracted status quo and to try to use the fairness criteria to determine the possible correspondence between the results, actually or potentially observed, and personal attitudes toward the "justice" of these results. To return to my personal example, could my claims, my current holdings, have emerged as one outcome of a game that we might agree has been carried out under tolerably fair rules?

It is first necessary to look at the factors that might determine distributional results, under real or imagined institutional structures. Anyone who would argue that a person's holdings are "unjust," or indeed that they are "just," by fairness criteria, must presume genuinely monumental knowledge of both economic analysis and statistical interpretation. Too often our academic colleagues, in economics and other disciplines, as well as commentators outside the academy, are unwilling to undertake the chore of understanding how distributional patterns actually might emerge under differing sets of rules. They tend, instead, to stand ready and willing to "jump" directly into evaluative-normative judgments about existing distributions of holdings, and hence about particular personal holdings within these distributions, before they really know what they are talking about. This point is made emphatically by my former colleague at the University of Virginia, Professor Rutledge Vining. He has for a long time argued that students of distributions (of any kind) should be forced to understand stochastic patterns, should be thoroughly grounded in the elementary principles of probability theory, before they are allowed to advance evaluative diagnoses.

It is evident that if we take Vining's admonition strictly, none of us could say much of anything about income and wealth distribution. I think that we can, however, take the Vining admonition as a warning to temper all of our efforts at discussing distribution. Here, as elsewhere in economic policy analysis, we must be careful to remain with relevant comparisons. And we can start to lay out the factors that determine the distribution of claims to economic value in differing institutional settings, in different games, under differing rules.

In the United States economy of today, the institutional setting is one that combines markets and politics in an extremely complex web of intersecting and often conflicting relationships. To attempt to model this structure, this game, in any plausibly acceptable manner, even when allowing for highly abstracted models, is beyond my competence or purpose here. I propose, instead, to abstract from the politics, from the manifold governmental influences on distributional patterns in the economy that we observe, and to look directly at the market process, and at the distributional patterns it might generate in the absence of governmental intervention. That is to say, I want to look at a relatively pure market structure, a relatively pure market game, a game operating within a legal-political framework that is limited to the protection of life and property and to the enforcement of contract. For labels here, we can say I shall be discussing distribution in the market economy in a minimal or protective state.

As noted above, this model is not at all realistic, but by examining the distributional patterns that might be predicted to emerge from it, we may begin to get some feel for what we mean by the terms "justice" or "injustice" applied to distributive results, again both terms as interpreted within the fairness conceptions.

One way of avoiding the pitfalls that Vining warns against is to forego discussion of "distributions," as such, and to stick with the simple personal example introduced earlier. Take a single person, take me. What are the elements or factors that have determined my relative share in the status quo claims to economic value or, rather, would have determined my share in these claims in the relatively pure market economy, as defined?

At this point, let me call on my own professor, Frank Knight of the University of Chicago, who said that, in a market economy, claims are determined by "birth, luck, and effort" and "the least of these is effort." Knight's three determinants offer us a good starting point for discussion, but let me add only one additional determinant, "choice." As you can already envisage, there are interdependencies among these elements. Let me take these four determinants in the following order: choice, luck, effort, and birth.

Choice. Surely my own choices have in part influenced the value of my current claims on economic product, or more generally, my current holdings. It must, I think, be readily acknowledged that any person's claims have been influenced by his own choices, of course with varying degrees of importance. With the proviso noted above, take my own personal history. I chose, deliberately, to undertake an academic career at a time shortly prior to the academic boom of the late 1950s, 1960s and early 1970s. That is to say, I chose to enter an industry that was shortly to experience extremely rapid growth, with the predictable consequences for the income levels of its participants. Even before I made this occupational choice, however, I had chosen to continue with my education, even at the cost of forgone earnings (which admittedly were pretty dismal in the late 1930s). I do not, of course, suggest that my various choices along the way were fully informed. In a very real sense, I was personally lucky in these choices, and as I noted above, we cannot really separate some of the determinants I have separately listed. Persons necessarily choose under conditions of great uncertainty, and I could have chosen a declining industry rather than an expanding one, in which case the consequences for my relative income-wealth position would have been quite different.

My purpose is not, however, to discuss in detail the influence of choice on individual or family shares in the claims to total economic value. I want only to suggest here that, insofar as personal differentials in the relative sizes of such claims can be attributed to choices freely made, there is no legitimate argument for assessing such differentials as being "unfair" or "unjust." The wino in Chicago who "might have been" a success had he chosen differently may, it seems to me, appeal to the compassion of his fellows; but he cannot, and should not, be allowed to appeal to their innate sense of "fairness," which has in no way been violated in his own situation.

Luck. Choice merges with and intersects with luck, fortune, or chance as an element that influences the distribution of claims. Though a person may not have deliberately and explicitly chosen to do this or that, his share in the claims to value may have been shifted unexpectedly and dramatically, upward or downward. The farmer who tills the family farm in the standard manner did not choose to have oil discovered under his land. He was simply lucky. Others may be unlucky, and see their holdings vanish into nothing by flood, fire, or pestilence. Again, I do not propose to discuss the relative significance of luck in the total imputation of claims to value, in the United States economy of 1980, or anywhere else. My point, once again, is to suggest that, to the extent that luck is the acknowledged causal influence, and provided all persons "could have been" in the game, so to speak, there would seem to be no violation of basic fairness precepts in observed relative differences in the sizes of claims.

Effort. There need be little discussion of effort. To the extent that a person's share in claims are traceable to his own efforts, there must be near-universal agreement, on fairness or any other set of criteria, that his claims are "just." Indeed, we could argue that, in the absence of such effort, there would have been no value existent to claim. In a very real sense, therefore, this value attributable to effort involves no opportunity cost to anyone in the community, even in the narrow context of potential value available for redistribution.

Birth. We are left with birth as the remaining influence or element in determining the distribution of claims, and it is not at all surprising that most of the charges of "injustice" and/or "unfairness" concerning income and wealth distribution arise or are alleged to arise from this source. Few persons could say that the economic game is intrinsically unfair just because some persons are lucky, or because some persons make better choices, or that some persons exert more effort than others. Unfairness in the economic game described by the operation of market institutions within a legal framework of private property and contract tends to be attributed to the distribution of endowments with which persons *enter* the game in the first place, *before* choices *are* made, *before* luck rolls the economic dice, *before* effort is exerted.

III. THE EASTER-EGG HUNT—A MARKET ANALOGY

I can introduce some of the issues raised indirectly by resort to an analogy, that of the Easter-egg hunt, an analogy that I borrow from my former colleague, Professor Richard Wagner of Auburn University. The distributive patterns in a market process are not too different in kind from those of the Easter-egg hunt. In large part, "finders are keepers," and the final division of product depends on the historical accidents of person, time, and place—on luck, talent, capacity, and effort, which were discussed to some extent earlier. But as I noted in connection with effort, there is no fixed sum to be "found"; there is no fixed quantity of total economic value to be somehow shared among all participants. The fact is that unless the hunt is properly organized, many of the eggs will not be found at all. Product of potential value will remain "undiscovered," "unproduced." The person who, by luck, talent, or effort, finds a cache of eggs is not necessarily "entitled" to keep them in some basically moral sense, but surely no one else, individually or collectively, is similarly "entitled" since, by supposition, the cache might not have been located at all by anyone else.

All of this is, of course, merely a way of emphasizing the positive-sum nature of the competitive economic process. But the attribution of "justice" or "fairness" to the rules of the finders-keepers game depends critically on the presence of one of two conditions. Either there must be many "games in town" *or* the starting positions must be approximately equivalent. There need be little or no concern about relative starting positions if there are "many games in town" so that any player who joins a particular game does so voluntarily and at the same time retains the option of exit from the game. If, however, there is "only one game in town," and if everyone, willy nilly, must participate, attention is immediately drawn to relative starting positions. Before we can even begin to evaluate results in terms of justice or fairness criteria, the starting positions must be reckoned with. If there are some players endowed initially with superior capacities, which they possess through no choices on their own part, these players will be relatively advantaged in any playing of the game. Our ordinary sense of "fairness" seems to be violated when such players are put on equal terms with those who are relatively less advantaged but who must, nonetheless, participate in the same game.

Must an acceptable fair game, therefore, embody handicaps? Many of us will recall Easter-egg hunts when older and larger children were deliberately handicapped by being placed behind the young and smaller children, in distance or in time. Presumably, all children must have been entrants in the same hunt; the smaller children were presumed unable to have their own game, at least advantageously. In a sense, this setting offers a reasonably appropriate analogy to social process, at least for my purposes of discussion here.

If there are demonstrable and acknowledged differences in endowments, talents, and capacities, differences that are discernible at or before the effective starting point, there would seem to be persuasive arguments for discriminatory handicapping, even at a reckoned cost in lost social value. But if we postulate an idealized veil-of-ignorance, in which no person knows what position in the predicted array of initial endowments, talents, and capacities he or she might occupy, expected value is maximized only in the absence of handicaps. Social product is largest by allowing the market process to operate without redistributional encumbrances, and if each person has the same opportunity to secure each share in product value, rational precepts, defined on expected values, seem to reject any discriminatory handicapping at all.

Expected value will not, however, be the only criterion. If the predicted distribution of starting points—defined by endowments, talents, and capacities to produce value—extends over a wide range, then variance matters. Empirical estimates concerning actual as well as perceived differences among persons become important in determining possible departures from expected value maximization. If we agree with Adam Smith about the absence of natural differences between philosophers and porters, the starting-position problem becomes immensely more tractable than it is if we agree with Plato about inherent natural differences. In addition, the relative importance of differentials in starting positions in influencing final shares in consumption value will, of course, affect the attitudes toward possible adjustments in starting positions. That is to say, if choice, luck, and effort dominate birth in the determination of any person's actual command over economic value, the fairness issue in the possible distribution of starting points may be of relatively little import.

This point is, I think, important enough to warrant some elaboration here. The sources of the observed and the imagined differences in command over final product values, at the potential consumption stage, are relevant for any attribution of "justice" or "injustice" to the economic game. Consider a simple two-person example. Suppose, first, that the incomes of A and B are exclusively determined by the initial endowment of each, which, for A is double that for B. Hence, A's income is two times that of B. Contrast this setting with one in which initial endowments remain as before, with A's being double B's. Assume now, however, that income shares also depend on choice, luck, and effort. Before these additional determinants enter, the expected value of A's income share will exceed that of B. In observed results, however, B's income share may well exceed that of A. In this setting, there will tend to be less concern about the disparity in initial endowments than in the first.

Two further points need to be made. In the political-economic "game," the inequalities in starting positions that become relevant for considerations of "justice" are inequalities among the opportunities to produce whatever is deemed to be "valuable" for social order and stability. These values need not, and normally would not and should not, include all observed differences among persons in preferences, talents, and endowments. This recognition of the multiplicity of values is closely related to a second point. In the extremely complex "game" that modern social order must represent, capabilities to produce value take on many different forms. In effect, there are many subgames going on simultaneously within the larger "game," each one of which might require a somewhat different mix of endowments and talents for success. "Equality of starting position," even as an ideal, surely does not imply that each person be qualified to enter each and every subgame on all fours with everyone else. Properly interpreted, "equality of opportunity," even as an ideal, must be defined as some rough, and possibly immeasurable, absence of major differences in the ability to produce values in whatever "game" is most appropriate for the particular situation for the person who participates.

With all the qualifications and provisos, however, rules of fairness would seem to suggest some imposition of what we may call handicaps so as to allow an approach to, if not an attainment of, something that might be called equality in starting positions, or, more familiarly, equality of opportunity. Before this implication of "justice as fairness" is accepted too readily, however, we must ask and try to answer the awesome question: Who is to do the handicapping? There is no external agent or overlord, no benevolent despot, who can spot the differences among the players in advance and adjust starting positions. And, indeed, the individual who conceives himself to be in some original position behind the Rawlsian veil of ignorance would be foolhardy to turn the handicapping task over to that subset of persons who might be temporarily or permanently assigned powers of political governance over their fellow citizens. Genuinely fair rules might include some equalization of starting positions, but if some of the players are also allowed to serve as umpires, it may well be best to leave off consideration of such rules altogether.

The implementation of handicapping rules, even those upon which conceptual agreement might be reached most easily, presents any community with a formidable institutional dilemma. If those persons who are to be assigned powers of governance are not to be, and cannot be, trusted to use their own discretion in carrying out the rules that are given to them because of some fear that they will exploit these rules for their own self-interest, how can "equality of opportunity" be promoted, even in a limited and proximate sense?

Some resolution of this dilemma may be secured by resort to *constitutional* order, to the selection of institutional rules that are chosen independently of political strife and conflict, and which are designed to be quasi-permanent constraints on the behavior of governments as well as private parties. Constitutional rules may be laid down that establish institutional structures within which some equalization of starting positions may be encouraged. If this constitutional, as opposed to the political, route toward implementation is taken, however, the inability to accomplish any "fine tuning" among possibly widely disparate opportunities must be acknowledged. At best, constitutional design might allow for institutions that take some of the more apparent rough edges off gross inequalities in starting positions. I shall discuss two such institutions in the next two sections.

IV. CONSTITUTIONAL DESIGN AND INEQUALITIES

Could a polity that allows intergenerational transfers of assets to proceed unencumbered pass any test of fairness? Such intergenerational transfers are perhaps the most blatant and most overt devices that are seen to create *inequalities* in starting positions, and hence to run directly counter to any objective of equalization. Even when the above-mentioned difficulties of implementation are recognized, some system of taxation of asset transfers would almost surely emerge from any agreement on a set of fair rules. Some such tax structure would seem to be almost a necessary part of any set of starting-position adjustments.

This conclusion is not affected by the various arguments that may be, and have often been, advanced against transfer taxation. It may be fully acknowledged that such taxes are Pareto-inefficient, that saving, capital formation, and economic growth are adversely affected, and that such taxes necessarily interfere with the liberties of those persons who are potential accumulators of wealth and potential donors to their heirs. These arguments do suggest the relevance of some trade-offs between the requirements for fairness in the rules and the objectives for economic efficiency and growth. But they do not imply that the latter objectives somehow dominate or modify those for fairness. They imply only that the fairness objective be tempered by a recognition of the costs of achieving it. Nor does a second, and possibly much more important, set of arguments modify the basic role of transfer taxation in a "fair" society. These arguments are based first on the substitutability between wealth in potentially taxable and nontaxable forms, and, second, on the inherent nontaxability of endowments in human capital, endowments that may be transferred genetically. Such nontaxable endowments may well be more significant in determining ultimate command over product value than potentially taxable endowments. If this should be the case, what is the moral-ethical basis for taxing the transfer of nonhuman assets?

As I have noted above, one such reason lies in the blatancy or overtness of such transfers; there is a fundamental ethical difference between nonhuman and human capital, even if modern economists can treat these two elements of endowments equally for their analytical purposes at hand. A second reason lies in the potential taxability itself. To an extent, such taxation, no matter how limited it might be in ultimate effect, represents a movement toward the objective of equality in starting points. The fact that the nontaxable elements in the transfer of endowments exist so as to make this objective ultimately unattainable should lend support rather than opposition to faltering efforts to go on as far as is possible.

A second institution that seems justified on basic fairness criteria, and still within the objective of equalizing starting positions, is publicly—or governmentally—financed education. It might be predicted that this institution would emerge from conceptualized contractual agreement even in recognition of the difficulties of implementation already noted.

The second set of arguments against transfer taxation noted in the preceding section is also applicable here. Natural differentials, in part genetically determined, in human capacities cannot, of course, be offset in their effects by education, even if instruction should somehow be organized with idealized "efficiency," whatever this might mean. But the availability of education serves to reduce rather than to increase the effects of such differences in starting positions in determining relative commands over economic value. In this sense, education acts similarly to transfer taxation.

Economists, and public-finance economists in particular, may have shifted attention away from the central issues when they classify education as a "public" or "collective consumption" service in the formal Samuelsonian sense. In such a schemata, public or governmental financing tends to be justified only to the extent that the benefits spill over or are external to the child that is educated and its immediate family. The whole public-goods approach, however, presumes that persons are "already in the game." A conceptually different justification for publicly financed education emerges when we look at potential adjustments in starting positions, at handicaps aimed at making the game "fair." Note that, in this context, the argument over governmental financing is not at all affected by the extent of spillovers or external economies, at least in the ordinary usage of these terms.[5]

As I have emphasized, the taxation of transfers and publicly financed education are not capable of equalizing starting positions even in some proximate manner. Inequalities will remain; opportunities will remain different for different persons. Nonetheless, these two basic institutions can reduce the impact of differences, and they can be seen to accomplish this result. To such an extent, the "game" will be seen to embody criteria of "fairness" in its rules.

What else might be done from fairness criteria at the starting position level? In subsequent discussion, I want to concentrate attention on additional aspects of the problem, specifically institutions aimed at insuring reasonably "fair chances to play." Even if persons may recognize that starting positions can never be equalized, steps can be taken that allow all persons to have the same opportunities to participate. In terms of an example, the child of a sharecropper can never possess an equal opportunity to become president with that of the child of a billionaire. But institutions can be organized so that the child of the sharecropper is not overtly *excluded* from the game, as such. And if he is so much as allowed to play, and by the same rules, there remains at least some chance that he can win. Later I shall discuss these aspects of "economic justice" in considerable detail. "Hope" is an extremely important component of any social order that makes claims of "justice."

V. DIVISION OF THE PRODUCT

At this juncture, I want to shift from the starting-position problem and to examine more carefully possible redistributive adjustments in results or end-states, in income shares after the economic game is played. Using the same basic precepts of fairness, what scope for redistributive income transfers exists?

In order to concentrate on end-states, let us provisionally assume that starting positions, inequalities in opportunities, have been satisfactorily mitigated. Nonetheless, the interdependence between the two stages of potential application of fairness criteria should be kept in mind. To the extent that starting positions are satisfactorily adjusted, that the game is appropriately handicapped, there is surely less persuasive argument for any operation of redistributive transfer among results, and vice versa.

I have previously noted that if differences in results, in relative income shares, can be attributed to choice, luck, or effort, elementary precepts for ex ante fairness are not violated. So long as all players enter the game on proximately equal terms, and have the chance to play the same rules, the rules are "fair" in a very fundamental and basic sense. The predicted, and observed, results may, however, exhibit wide differentials in the shares assigned to separate persons. The efficiency of the "finders-keepers" rules in maximizing total product value may be acknowledged. But fairness precepts, more extensively interpreted, may suggest some postproduction *redistribution*. That is to say, even if the expected values of all income shares should be equal ex ante, the actual distribution of shares, ex post, may exhibit such variance as to command rejection on contractarian grounds.

The issues here are, in part, empirical. As noted earlier, the contractarian logic labels that rule as fair upon which general agreement is reached. And prospects for agreement depend critically on the expected or predicted pattern of results. With genuine equality of opportunity, what form would the actual distribution of income shares in a market economy take? I do not think any of us here can really answer this hypothetical question, and we are reminded again of the Vining admonition discussed above.

The prospects for agreement on any set of rules also depend upon the potential acceptability of alternatives. The generalized finders-keepers rules that are embodied in the market may not meet first-best criteria for "justice," at least in the attitudes of most persons, but unless alternative rules exist upon which more agreement may be secured, these rules may remain superior in some consensual context. That is to say, the distributive rules of the market may represent some sort of Schelling-point outcome of the conceptualized contractual process; there may be no alternative set of rules upon which agreement can be attained. This "defense" of the distributional results of market order has been advanced by Frank Knight, and, more recently, by Dan Usher.[6]

There would seem, however, to be no convincing logical argument to demonstrate that distributive rules of the competitive market would *necessarily* emerge from generalized contractarian agreement among potential participants, even under the presumption that starting positions are equalized. The market rules *might* emerge from this postulated setting; but these are only one set of rules from among a larger number of sets. Plausible arguments could be made to the effect that some posttrading, postproduction adjustments in income shares would be embodied in any contractual agreement, at least if the difficulties of implementation should be neglected. The rough edges of market-share distribution might be tempered, so to speak, with some guarantees from those persons whose luck turns sour, even at the expense of those persons who are more fortunate. There is no logical basis for rejecting the Rawlsian "difference principle" as one possible outcome of the contractual agreement. Rawls's error was in suggesting that this principle for redistribution was somehow the unique rule that would, in fact, emerge under his postulated conditions.

For my own part, both in a positive predictive sense and a normatively preferred sense, I should remain relatively undisturbed about the distributional results of competitive market process if rough fairness in the distribution of initial endowments and capacities could be guaranteed. Much of the socialist-inspired criticism of the market economic order has been misdirected. The institutions of the market have been criticized for their failure to produce distributive results that meet stated normative objectives when, in fact, these results are more closely related to disparities in premarket endowments and capacities.

Consider a very simple oranges-and-apples example. Suppose that, as a posttrading result, we observe that Tizio has 16 oranges and 14 apples, whereas Caio has only 3 oranges and 2 apples. This postmarket imputation, taken alone, however, tells us nothing at all about the premarket imputation of endowments. If, before trade, Tizio should have had 19 oranges and 13 apples, while Caio had no oranges and 3 apples, the trade of one apple for 3 oranges by Caio has surely improved his position, as well as that of Tizio. The distributional impact of this trade is dwarfed in significance by the premarket disparity in endowments.

The market rules are rarely put to the test in situations where differences among premarket endowments and capacities can be neutralized or isolated. If the distinction between the distribution of value potential in premarket positions and the distributional effects of trade, as such, is recognized, several principles command acceptance, whether on fairness or other criteria. Attempts to mitigate distributional inequities or injustice that may be due largely to premarket inequalities should not take the form of interferences with the market process, as such. Minimum-wage laws are perhaps the best example. Such restrictions harm those whom they are designed to benefit. In this, as in many other cases, the distributive justice of Adam Smith's system of natural liberty should be acknowledged and emphasized. Attempts to modify distributional results should be directed at the sources of the undesired consequences, which is the distribution of premarket power to create economic values.

VI. FAIRNESS IN POLITICAL RULES

It is necessary to return to the question posed earlier. Who is to do the adjusting? Who is to impose the handicaps? Precisely because the redistributional arrangements must be chosen and implemented by persons internal to the community involved, the contractarian-constitutional ethic seems to offer the only available standard for evaluation. The "laws and institutions" of society provide a continuing and predictable framework within which individuals interact. It is important that these laws and institutions be seen to be fair, and to do so they must contain features that to some extent rectify differences in opportunities, as previously noted. In this respect, I have already suggested the importance of the taxation of transfers and the governmental financing of education. But, perhaps even more important, the institutions of political decision-making must also be seen to be fair and just. This critical element in any structure embodying "economic justice" tends to be overlooked almost entirely by socialist critics of the market. If political adjustments are to be made, the political game itself must embody precepts of fairness even more stringent than those sometimes attributable to market dealings.

Political adjustments in claims to values can only be made to appear fair on contractarian grounds. That is to say, the arms and agencies of the state, the government, cannot be used directly to transfer incomes and assets from the politically weak to the politically strong under the disguise of achieving "distributive justice" or anything else. The citizenry cannot be fooled by such empty rhetoric. Distributional adjustments that are implemented politically must, first of all, be strictly "constitutional" in the sense that they must be embodied in permanent or quasi-permanent institutions of social order. No short-term legislative or parliamentary manipulation of distributive shares could possibly qualify by genuine fairness criteria. In terms of practical programs, the argument here suggests that a progressive income tax might possibly emerge as one feature of an acceptable fiscal constitution, but the overtly political jiggling with the rate structure to reward political friends and to punish political enemies would, of course, violate all contractarian precepts. Similar conclusions apply to the pandering to politically dominant coalitions by jiggling expenditure programs.

Libertarian critics of efforts to transfer incomes and wealth should concentrate their attacks on the unwarranted use of democratic decision structures. An open society cannot survive if its government is viewed as an instrument for arbitrary transfers among its citizens. On the other hand, libertarians go too far, and reduce the force of their own argument, when they reject genuinely constitutional or framework arrangements that act to promote some rough equality in premarket positions and act so as to knock off the edges of post-market extremes. The libertarian may defend the distributive rule of the competitive process on standard efficiency grounds, and he may, if he chooses, also develop an ethical argument in support of this rule. But this is not the same thing as defending the distributive results that might be observed in a market economy in which there is no attempt to adjust starting positions. The libertarian who fails to make the distinction between the two separate determinants of observed distributive results makes the same mistake as his socialist counterpart who attacks the market under essentially false pretenses.

Having indicated that (i) institutions of transfer taxation along with (ii) institutions that involve governmental financing of education are likely to emerge in any agreed-on fair rules, I want now to look at additional institutions that may be required to mitigate particular forms of starting-position inequalities, always as evaluated with basic criteria of fairness.

VII. JUSTICE AND FAIR CHANCES

More specifically, I want to elaborate the notion of "fair chances" that I have already touched on only briefly. In a fundamental, but limited, respect, "fair chances" amount to "equal opportunity." Each person is insured that the claims to economic value assigned to him are determined by elements *within himself* and by chance factors that affect all persons *equally.* This criterion does not require equalization of expected values among all persons, evaluated at the starting positions. As suggested, the more restrictive definition of equal opportunity implied in the latter criterion could never be achieved, or even closely approached. But the "fair chances" criterion does require the absence of effects on expected values that are exerted by elements external to the persons themselves and discriminatorily distributed among persons.

It is not easy to articulate the precise meaning of this criterion apart from examples to be introduced below, in which I think the notion becomes evident as well as familiar. Let me say at the outset, however, that I think the criterion of "fair chances," or, in perhaps a more descriptive appellation "equal treatment" is vitally important in the generation of personal attitudes toward the "justice" of any social order. So long as each person considers himself to have a "fair chance" to play the game, he can hope for a favorable outcome despite his own recognition that the expected value of the outcome for him may remain below that for other players.

Consider my earlier argument to the effect that elementary precepts for ex ante fairness are not violated if income shares can be somehow attributed to choice, luck, or effort. To the extent that the rules allow everyone to play on equal terms, the pattern of outcomes, including the distribution of shares in command over final goods and services, cannot be adjudged to be "unfair." But, as I have also noted, to "play on equal terms" could be strictly interpreted to require that all players possess equal capacities-endowments at the starting point. In this narrow interpretation, and even with the imposition of institutionally appropriate handicapping, the game can never really be labeled to be "fair." But life in civil community means that all persons must, willy nilly, participate, so what is to be done?

To the extent that a person accepts his own lot in the genetic-cultural distribution of basic or natural capacities and talents, he can also think of this lot as his own "luck," considered in the more inclusive pregame sense of the term. None of us can change his or her genetic-cultural heritage (we cannot choose our own parents). And we may, therefore, look on that heritage that we do have as our own particular "luck in the draw of history," while at the same time we may acknowledge that this heritage may itself be of major importance in determining just where we will stand in the allocation of shares to value in the community. For better or for worse, we may accept the necessity to live with our lot, and especially as the political-economic rules of the game do not seem to operate so as to add to, or to exacerbate, the differences in value shares emergent from the distribution of natural talents.

In order to discuss this distribution of "natural talents" more systematically, let me postulate, for purposes of argument, that all persons in the community make roughly the same quality of choices, have roughly the same luck within the game itself, and exert roughly the same basic effort. In this abstract setting, if the distribution of natural talents or capacities-endowments is known, and if each person can be readily identified in terms of where he or she stands in the distributional array, a distribution of expected values of claims to final values can be mapped as a direct correspondence with the initial distribution of talents-capacities-endowments. As noted earlier, to the extent that choices, luck, and effort vary among persons, this precise mapping between the distribution of starting positions and the distribution of final claims to product value breaks down. Considerable ranges for intersections and overlapping may emerge in the latter distribution as the game is actually played out. And as I suggested previously, there will be a direct relationship between the importance of these "nonnatural" or "nonstarting point" influences and the perceived "fairness" of the game itself.

We know, however, that persons cannot be readily identified in terms of their "natural talents," their basic capacities to generate economic values, independently of demonstrated or proven performance in the economic game itself. In part at least, and perhaps in large part, the differences in the capacities of persons to create economic value, to produce what we may call "social income," can only be seen in retrospect, after individuals act. To an extent, persons necessarily *enter* the game unidentified and unclassified. Unobserved differences in capacities may exist, and they may be important in determining the distribution of final claims to value, but there may be no way of judging these initial differences until the course has been commenced. The simplistic Easter-egg hunt analogy used above breaks down; the "faster runners" cannot be identified in advance.

If the distribution of assigned claims to final product value could somehow be put off or delayed until full information about comparative productivities is available, there is no particular problem created by the absence of such information during those initial periods when economic activity takes place. But in the economic-political game described by a market economy operating within a legal setting of property and contract, we must think in terms of extended calendar time. Persons could hardly be expected to wait for the length of a working life, or even a relatively small part thereof, before some shares of product value are passed out. Some payments scheme must be worked out and implemented that will assign per-period claims in the absence of full information about relative productivities. During some initial sequence of time periods, which we call a "demonstration period," while individualized productivities are being determined, the market will tend to generate pay assignments, "wages," that are valued at some average for the whole group of entrants from the relevant subgroup. The calendar length of such a demonstration period will, of course, vary significantly among different occupational groupings. For common labor the period may be so short as to be almost insignificant; for professors it may be quite long.

VIII. A FORMAL MODEL

At this point, I find it necessary to introduce somewhat more formal analysis through a set of simplified and highly abstract models. Let me first assume that there are N entrants into the working-producing force for a defined set of occupational categories. (I do not want to get into detailed discussion here about wholly "noncompeting" groups, with the distinctions among these being determined by the range of genuinely natural talents and abilities, e.g., artists and athletes.) For purposes of my argument, we may either assume that all potential entrants may enter all occupations, in which case we need not refer to groupings, or, alternatively, we may restrict our analysis to the single set of occupational categories which all of the N entrants considered can enter and in which they can produce meaningful economic results.

The N entrants are cohorts in terms of time profiles; they enter the working-producing force at the same time, say, 1980. Let me postulate that the entrants differ in starting positions, in their basic capacities to produce economic values. If each person in the group of N entrants should make the average quality of personal career choices, if each should have roughly the same luck, and if each should exert roughly the same effort, the array of market-value productivities would follow the array of natural talents, as noted above. Let me plot such a distribution in Figure 1, where, on the abscissa we measure expected values of economic productivity for the N persons and where numbers of persons are measured on the ordinate.

Let me postulate that the economy is fully competitive. Once information about individual productivities is known, individuals

Figure 1

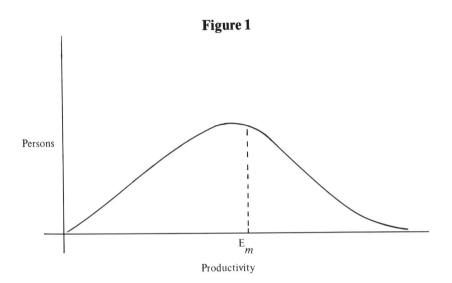

Persons

E_m

Productivity

will be able to receive income shares commensurate with their marginal productivities. If this information is available at the outset, and *before* income shares are assigned in any period, no problem arises. Individuals will receive income shares that correspond with those capacities that are inherent in their own endowments. An individual's income share will depend in no way on the inherent capacities-endowments of others than himself.

Assume, however, that neither the entrants themselves nor potential employers have any information about relative individual productivities when persons are hired. Assume, further, however, that each employer knows that the productivities over the whole group of N entrants are distributed as indicated in Figure 1. Assume that information about individual productivities becomes available at the end of the demonstration period of a single-period duration, say, one year. For simplicity in exposition, assume that this information is available to individuals themselves and to *all* potential employers. There is no need to get into problems of firm-specific information, or problems raised by differences in information as between employee and employers.

For the first period, each of the N entrants, no matter where he might stand in the distributional array, can expect to receive the mean expected value of the whole distribution, say, E_m, in Figure 1. At the end of this period, when full information becomes available, wages will be appropriately adjusted, and, from this point in time, all workers will be paid for marginal value productivities.

In this model, note that each person is *treated equally with his equals,* in terms of identification by basic natural talents and capacities. In the first period, all persons, regardless of their capacities, receive equal shares in value. After the first period, persons in each and every position on the capacity-talent scale secure the value of their own inherent contribution to value in the economy.

I want to argue that this precept or principle: *equal treatment for equals* is a necessary element in any set of rules for social order in a community that makes any claim of "fairness" and that such a principle will tend to emerge from the conceptualized contractual agreements among all persons. John Rawls did not specifically discuss this principle, as such, in his formulation of a theory of justice, although we may read the discussion of his criterion "careers open to talents" as indirectly stating such a principle.[7] In one form or another, such a principle is central in normative tax theory, and it is also analogous to the more general principle of equality before the law. But the particular application of the equal-treatment principle to the problems of distributive justice has not, to my knowledge, been fully worked out and analyzed.

In the model described above, the principle of "equal treatment" is met, and no further institutional adjustments are suggested. If, however, the model, as described, should obscure elements of the game as actually played, we may predict violation of the principle through the ordinary workings of the competitive market. As an alternative model, suppose, now, that the inclusive array of expected values of productivities for the N entrants is as depicted in Figure 1. The conditions of the model remain as before with one important exception.

Potential employers are now assumed to have *some* information about individual productivities in a probabilistic sense before persons are hired. As before, there is no information available about individuals, as individuals, but there now are assumed to exist certain identifiable characteristics that enable employers to classify persons within two roughly equal-sized sets for groupings.[8] The mean value of productivity differs as between these two sets. Further, employers are assumed to know the array of values, the distribution, for each of the two sets of potential employees. Figure 2 depicts the situation in this model. Note that the range of the two distributions is the same for the two sets of persons; only the mean values differ. As before, assume that the length of the demonstration period is one year, and that, subsequent to this period, all employees, regardless of their initial classification, secure the full value of their marginal contributions to value.

Figure 2

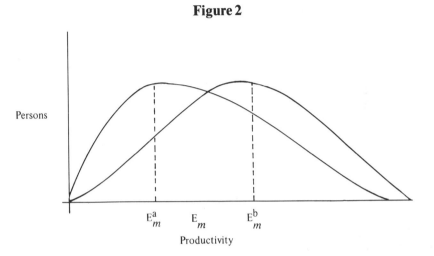

Persons

E^a_m E_m E^b_m

Productivity

For the initial period, employers in this setting will be forced by competitive pressures to offer different wages or incomes to workers from the two sets, A and B. All entrants from the A group will be paid a wage E_m for the first period, regardless of their ultimate productivity. Similarly, all workers from the B group will be paid E_m for the first period. It is clear that the "equal-treatment" norm is violated here by the workings of the competitive market. Workers from the A group, and identified as such, will receive a lower present value of lifetime earnings than their "equals" in the B group, not because of something inherent in their own individualized "luck in the draw" of natural talents and capacities, but, instead, because they happen to be classified as a member of a group with lower mean productivity. To put the same result differently, an entrant from the A group who makes precisely the same choices, who has precisely the same luck in the game itself, who, for a given wage, exerts precisely the same effort, will secure over his lifetime a net claim to final product value lower than his equal from the B group. He is effectively "penalized" by his membership in the group that happens to exhibit the lower average productivity.

I should emphasize that the competitive market process that generates the violation of the "equal-treatment" norm is efficient, by construction. The differentials in present values between any pair of genuine equals, one from each of the two subgroups, do not reflect *market failure* in any meaningful sense of this term.[9] In the competitive market model that I have postulated here, employers act on the basis of the information that is available to them. Their first-period information is, by assumption, limited to identification by class or group. If a single employer chose deliberately to ignore such information, and chose instead to pay all entrants the mean expected value for the whole set of N entrants, he could not hire any of the workers from the B group.[10]

Note also that there is no "discrimination," as such, in the model. Employers are presumably interested solely and exclusively in maximizing profits, and they have no tastes or preferences as to the type of input units employed, either individually or as a mix among the two types. Similarly, employees are exclusively interested in wages, and are totally indifferent as to whom their coworkers might be.

Once the violation of the equal-treatment principle is recognized, a question arises concerning the possible efficiency losses that any interference with the working of competitive markets designed to correct the violation might produce.

Consider the following scenario. Suppose that all potential employers should be required to hire entrants *as if* the initial classification into the A and B groups were not possible. That is to say, suppose that all employers should be constrained to "hire blind," to throw away or ignore information deliberately that had been of potential value to them in the setting described above. Note that, in this new situation, employers could do no more than pay the mean value for the whole set of N entrants for the initial or demonstration period. Despite the fact that all persons in the community, employers and workers alike, recognize that the B workers, as a set, are, on average, more productive than the A workers, as a set, the competitive market will force all wages during the initial period to the level E_m. All workers will be employed, as before, by assumption. Efficiency losses will emerge only to the extent that we allow workers to respond to wage-rate differences by modifying effort (e.g., through changing number of hours worked). If incentives of this sort are allowed, the initial market solution, with mean wages, E_a and E_b for the two classes respectively, the A-class workers will work less than they would under the uniform wage, E_m. The B-class workers, on the other hand, will work more at wage E_b ($> E_m$) than at E_m. Since, by construction, the mean productivity of the B-class workers exceeds that of the A-class workers, there will be *some* efficiency loss involved in the shift to the arrangement where all employers pay all workers in N the uniform initial-period wage, E_m. This efficiency loss may, however, be very small.

IX. IMPLICATIONS FOR POLICY

The analysis in the preceding section demonstrates that it becomes conceptually possible to secure satisfaction of the "equal treatment for equals" or "fair chances" criterion with little minor efficiency losses of the sort ordinarily discussed by welfare economists. There may, however, be significant gaps between conceptual possibility and practical implementation. In the model that was specifically analyzed, I simply assumed that information about individual productivities is not available until after a demonstration period is complete, a period during which some wage-payments scheme must be worked out. Clearly, if potential employers could, in some way, secure accurate information about individual productivity before entrants are taken on as employees, there need be no violation of the equal-treatment criterion, even if the two-group identification with differing average productivities continues to hold. In such a full information setting, employers will be led by their profit-seeking behavior to ignore averages over groups and to look exclusively at prospective individual values. Recognition of this result suggests that policy aimed directly at increasing the flow of relevant information concerning prospective employee productivity before employment commences may be of independent value in terms of promoting a basic sense of "fair chances" in the community.

It should, however, be anticipated that some of the elements isolated by the model analyzed above will remain. The equal-treatment principle will not be fully met with improved information. How and to what extent could constraints be imposed on hiring and wage-setting behavior in a fully competitive economy for the purpose of enhancing "fairness"?

If constraints are to be imposed, note that efficiency in results would require that such constraints be *universally applied*. They must bear on each and every employer who faces the set of entrants into the work force. And note that each of these employers will have a continuing private-profit motivation to use the classificatory information that we presume is available to him. To impose the hiring constraints on some employers but not on others or to impose the constraints so loosely that only some employers will be affected will guarantee net-efficiency losses without accomplishing the results intended. Some minimal steps may be taken to deny the information as to class identification to employers. In this sense, legal and administrative rules that dictate that blanks for identifiable characteristics not be filled out may seem justifiable.

Care must also be taken to note precisely the nature of the constraints that would be required to prove effective in promoting genuine equal treatment of equals. A constraint that merely directs potential employers to pay all entrants *equal wages* would be disastrous for *all* entrants from the class described by the relatively low average productivity. This result emerges because, in such a setting, every employer, having the general classsificatory information, will on probabilistic grounds find it to his interest to hire entrants *only* from the group with the higher average productivity. Regardless of their ultimate contribution to value, individuals from the group with relatively low average productivity will find it difficult if not impossible to find employment in this setting.

If the "equal treatment for equals" criterion is to be satisfied, equal wages for equally productive persons will have to be paid during the initial demonstration periods as well as for all subsequent periods during which individualized contributions are fully known. But this end-result must be produced by the profit-maximizing response of potential employers within the constraint that entrants be chosen as if they are drawn from the inclusive group and not from identifiable classes within the larger set. In more specific terms, the suggested constraints must take the form of *hiring quotas,* with new entrants taken on in proportion to the relative numbers of the identifiable classes in the inclusive set. In my example, if A and B are equal in size, each being of size $N/2$, each employer should be required to hire equal numbers of entrants from A and from B. In this case, competition would prevent employers from paying differential wages to members of the two groups; he will necessarily pay first-period wages equal to the average productivity expected for all entrants from N, and not from A and/or B.

The hiring quota or constraint in this model should be made to apply *only* to initial or demonstration-period hiring. By our assumption, after this period, full information is available concerning individual productivities, not only to the specific firm that employs particular persons but to other potential employees as well. Average productivities of classes or groups, even if these differ substantially by easily identifiable classes, become totally irrelevant to decisions about continuing employment and relative wage scales. Market competition will insure universalized payment in accordance with relative marginal productivities.

In the distribution of actual productivities as indicated in Figure 2, the firms or industries that employ relatively more high-productivity workers would be anticipated to retain relatively more B-class employees in their work force than firms or industries that require less productive workers. This sort of permanent "imbalance" in the ratios between A-class and B-class employees does not imply any violation of the "equal treatment" norm. Indeed, quite the contrary. To require that all firms and industries "balance" the work force between the two classes of workers would require that the equal-treatment norm be violated, with the employees from the relatively more productive group, from B in our example, being subjected to "unfair" treatment.

I have tried to be careful in saying that the implications for policy outlined in the previous section depend strictly on the existence of the parameters of the model that was specified. The assumptions of this model are extremely restrictive, and it need not follow that the policy implications suggested are relevant when and if these assumptions are modified. Recall that I assumed (1) that all N entrants in the inclusive group can produce economic value in the employment categories considered; (2) that potential employers initially possess no information at all about the individual productivities to be expected from any entrant; (3) that employers do possess information that allows the N entrants to be subdivided into two readily identifiable classes, that are known to differ in average productivity; (4) that the demonstration period during which information about individual productivity comes to be available is the same for all entrants; (5) that this productivity information is known to all potential employers at the end of the demonstration period; and finally, (6) that the economy is fully competitive.

It is useful at this point to see just how rigid these assumptions are; how might they be relaxed without destroying the validity of the policy implications that were suggested above? The requirement for competition need not be made overly restrictive; the general competitiveness of the economy in some broadly workable sense seems all that would be necessary here. Nor need there be concern about the subdivision into only two readily identifiable classes or groups or about the uniformity of the demonstration period. These assumptions may be modified to allow for several classes with several lengths of demonstration period without changing the structure of the analysis. The assumptions that remain critical to the analytical implications are those which relate to the *absence* of information on relative individual productivities and the *presence* of information about average productivities for classes or groups smaller than the whole set of entrants prior to the work force. These assumptions are critical because it is only on these assumptions that we get profit-seeking employers in a competitive environment differentiating among entrants on the basis of class in the complete absence of information about individual productivity. It is such differentiation that introduces the "unfairness" in the game, that violates the equal-treatment norm, that insures that persons who ultimately demonstrate equality with others in the "natural draw" secure lower present values of claims to product solely because they are members of a class with relatively low average productivity.

The reader will, of course, have noticed that I have deliberately refrained from attaching labels to the classes, but whatever designations seem fitting can be added, whether these be for male-female, black-white, Protestant-Catholic, short-tall, Yankee-redneck, or what have you. I should argue that in the real world, where the assumptions of the formal model are, of course, not present, the policy implications follow generally with respect to hiring practices, provided that potential employers should be observed to make such differentiation by class, provided that those who do so are observed to survive.

Note what the analysis *does not say.* The *average* present values for claims for members of the "less productive" class will, in any case, be lower than the average for the "more productive" class. Satisfaction of the equal-treatment criterion will not modify this basic result. There is no way that a hiring-quota system could, or should, equalize the differing average productivities of members of the various identifiable classes. A hiring-quota system, ideally administered, should do nothing more than insure that the individual, regardless of his ultimate productivity, is not affected in the value of the claims that he secures by factors *external to his own capacities,* which are not equally applicable to all members of the group, inclusively defined.

X. OBJECTIONS CONSIDERED

Objections can be raised to the policy implications and, by inference, to the analysis itself. In particular, since my whole model allows for separate individual shares in product value to be determined, in part, by "natural capacities," and since these are acknowledged to differ among persons, why have I advanced the argument that the "fair chances" or "equal treatment" criterion requires blindness only with respect to one feature of a person, namely, his identification as a member of a particular class or group? If "luck in the genetic-cultural draw" is to be accepted, and lived with, in terms of basic individual capacities to produce economic value, why should not this same "luck in the genetic draw" be extended to cover membership in the identifiable class or group? If person A_1 is "unlucky" in that his inherent productive capacity, when demonstrated, falls below that of the mean capacity for the community, can he not also be considered, and so consider himself, to be "unlucky" in having been born to membership in the A group, where persons are, on average, less productive than in the B group? Perhaps to some readers this objection is compelling, but to me there is an element of what I should call *perverse handicapping* in the uncorrected operation of competitive markets in the setting postulated in the model. An individual member of the A group, in my example, is forced to start the race behind his equals, behind those whom he later matches in terms of demonstrated capacity. He has to catch up to be equal, which, in my set of values becomes inherently "unfair."

A more specific objection may be raised concerning my argument to the effect that the imposition of initial-period hiring quotas may be accompanied with relatively insignificant welfare or efficiency losses, limited essentially to the slight differences in the product value of the offsetting responses of the members of two groups in the model. In the model itself, I assumed that all of the N entrants can be employed, and can produce value, in the "industry" or "set of employment categories" considered. If, for any reason, some persons who might seek entry into the relevant "industry" cannot be employed, there must be some means of rationing places. In such a setting, a legal requirement for all employers to select entrants proportionately from the A and B groups may introduce an additional efficiency loss. The average productivity of persons employed will be lower than the average productivity under the unencumbered operation of the competitive market.

Too much should not be made of this additional efficiency-loss emendation, provided that the market is assumed to be competitive. To the extent that entrants seek to enter occupational-employment categories, they should be able to do so and to secure employment therein if there are no barriers to entry and if wage levels are competitively determined. Problems arise only with genuinely "noncompeting" groups, where threshold differences in natural talents create sharp dividing lines between those who qualify and those who do not, and where there are no genuinely marginal employees who can readily shift into and out of such groups.

On the other hand, implementation of the equal-treatment criterion may involve efficiency loss in situations where, for any reasons, artificial and nonmarket barriers to entry into occupations and employments have been established. If competitive organization is not allowed to determine the number of medical doctors, for example, there may be many more applicants for medical school than there are places. In such a setting, the introduction of quotas among groups or classes of entrants based on some proportion of identifiable characteristics with distinguishable average productivity differentials will produce a higher fail rate (and hence higher cost) than would be the case without such quotas. This amounts to saying that "fairness" costs less in market than in nonmarket settings.

A much more serious objection than any of these discussed to this point lies in the prospect that the policy implications of the whole analysis may be extended and applied in settings where the assumptions of the model are clearly violated, notably to employment and pay structures in which information about individual productivities *is* known to employers. As noted, there is no implication in my analysis that uniform wages should be paid all entrants, even in the initial period, save as a result of the hiring arrangements that make such uniformity a *result* rather than a specific objective. And there is surely no implication that wage rates should be standardized over groups on the basis of elements other than individual productivities, when the latter are ascertained. And, as I suggested earlier, it is a perversion of my argument to suggest that average wages among groups with differing average productivities should somehow be forcibly equalized. Also, as noted earlier, "equal treatment" in the initial hiring stage does not, and cannot, be perverted to mean the maintenance of "balance" in employment, *after* productivities are known.

We must recognize that any projected interference with the working of the competitive market in hiring must be organized and put into being politically—that is, by persons acting on behalf of governments, persons who have their own self-interest to consider, whether this be tenure in office, electoral success, or their own idealized goal for society. Thus the dangers that the implications derived from basically sound analysis will be perverted for use in situations where they simply do not apply, and where, if applied, they will produce damage, both in terms of efficiency and of fairness, must be acknowledged.

Once again, distrust in the ordinary political arrangements suggests resort to genuinely constitutional rules that will, to an extent at least, be immune from ordinary political pressures. But courts, even if nominally bound by rules, can also get confused, especially since the parameters of the cases at hand rarely, if ever, correspond to the conditions of the models that might have been systematically analyzed. The meanderings of the Supreme Court in the recent Bakke and Weber cases attest to this confusion. I find myself sympathetic to the Court's dilemma in both cases. I would not have had this appreciation of the dilemma facing the Court before I worked out the "equal treatment" principle of this essay. So, at the least, I have learned something.

XI. APPENDIX

In this Appendix I want to extend the basic analysis developed in previous discussion to a setting in which, for some reason, there is an arbitrary limit on the number of applicants who can secure "employment" in an "industry," a limit that is lower than the total number of applicants, and where the competitive forces of the market are not allowed to operate. I shall develop the argument through the use of stylized models, but my aim is to isolate certain features that bear considerable relevance to familiar policy issues.

1. Consider first a model in which there are only 100 "places" to be filled, but where there are 1,000 applicants. Suppose that there is absolutely no information about individual capacities or productivities, but that the distribution of such capacities is known to take the form depicted in Figure 1. How can the 100 "best" applicants be selected? In this model, it is clear that only by sampling the whole population of applicants can this objective be attained. If this sampling takes the form of a required period of demonstration, the selection process will be costly but necessary.

2. Consider, as a second model, a situation where "entrance tests" can be administered cheaply, and where there is a perfect correspondence between scores on these tests and the observed productivities in periods subsequent to the tests. In this case, the indicated policy is simply to select the 100 persons who score highest on the entrance tests. No one is excluded; the game is fair.

3. As a third model, consider a situation where nothing is known about individual capacities, and where a costly demonstration period is required to determine these. Assume, however, that the set of 1,000 applicants may be divided into two classes, A and B, in terms of some readily identifiable characteristic, and that the average productivities of these two classes are known to differ, as depicted in Figure 2. If the range of capacities is the same for both groups, all of the 1,000 applicants must be tested before the 100 best qualified can be chosen. Assume that, if such a testing procedure is done, there will be 90 successful applicants from B and only 10 from A. Note that this apparently biased result does not violate the equal-treatment criterion in any way because, at the level of initial testing, all persons are given fair chances to compete. No arbitrary exclusion based on class is involved.

In the setting of this model, however, the temptation to use the class-identification information may be very strong. By testing only from the B group, known to have the relatively higher mean capacity, 90 of the 100 required applicants may be selected. The costs of locating the remaining 10 applicants from the A class will be equal to the costs of getting the 90 from the B class. Further, the capacities of the 10 "best" from the A class, who might be excluded by a sampling limited to the B class, may be only slightly lower than the additional 10 persons who might qualify under the more restricted testing. The benefit-cost calculus may put great pressures on decision-making authorities to sample only from the B group.

To do so, however, would clearly violate the equal-treatment criterion, as discussed above. Potential applicants from the A class, even if they have full knowledge of the probability coefficients, can properly label the game to be unfair, because they would be prohibited entry, even at the demonstration-testing stage.

4. A more complex model involves a combination of the first and second models above. Suppose that no class identification (Model 2) is possible, and that *some* information about individual capacities can be secured from inexpensive entrance examinations, but that this information will prove accurate only within rather broad prob-

ability limits. All potential applicants may be given the entrance tests, but, differently from Model 2, the selection of the 100 persons with the highest entrance-test scores, will not insure that the 100 "best" persons, in terms of proven capacities, will be chosen. To determine the latter, an additional costly demonstration period must be administered. In this setting, a decision to admit more than 100 persons for the demonstration period may well be warranted. Regardless of the number admitted to the demonstration period, however, so long as scores on the entrance test are used to determine the lower cutoff point, there is no overt violation of the equal-treatment criterion. A person who is excluded because of his low entrance-test score cannot claim unfairness; he is treated equally with his equal at this level.

5. The most complex model of all is attained by adding the possibility of class identification to the partial information model above. In this setting, there is no violation of the equal-treatment criterion *if the class-identification information is not used.* If applicants to be allowed to enter a demonstration or tryout period are selected purely by entrance test scores, even if it is known that these scores are grossly imperfect predictors of ultimate capacities, those excluded cannot be justified in possible claims of unfairness.

6. This result depends, however, on the presumption that scores on the entrance test are not biased by class. Suppose, for example, that the differences in the mean test scores for A and B applicants are significantly larger than the differences in the mean values of capacities, when finally determined, although both means vary in the same way. In this situation, even though the entrance-test scores may be the single best predictor of ultimate capacity, the result of the use of this score as the sole criterion to select applicants for the extended demonstration periods will tend to bias the whole selection process to the disadvantage of members of the A class, which is known to be characterized by lower mean test scores and lower mean productivities.

There is no overt violation of the equal-treatment norm here. A person from the A group is not excluded because he or she is a member of that group. And such a person can observe members of the B group with the same test scores as his or her own also being excluded. However, in an indirect sense, basic unfairness can be claimed here, due to the bias in the test. With observed identical test scores, a rejected member of the A applicants will embody a somewhat higher probability of ultimate success than a member of the rejected B applicants, with an identical test score. If equals are defined by equal probabilities of success in the extended demonstration period, then identical test scores do not meet the definition. In this particular case, there is a logical argument, based on fairness precepts, for putting the cutoff test score somewhat lower for the A applicants.

7. Whether or not the bias suggested exists is, of course, an empirical question to be determined. Unless it can be shown to exist, there can be no alleged unfairness in a system that relies exclusively on entrance-test scores, even when everyone recognizes that these scores are imperfect predictors of ultimate capacities. In the models of this Appendix, as in the body of this chapter, unfairness, in the absence of such a test bias, stems *only* from the use of class-identification information.

8. The extensions of the basic equal-treatment analysis summarized in this Appendix are relevant to some of the problems faced by the Supreme Court in the Bakke and Weber cases, perhaps the most important decisions of the decade of the 1970s.[11]

Allen Bakke was successful in his particular claim that he had suffered "reverse discrimination" in the University of California-Davis practice of selecting medical-school entrants. His evidence was that his score on an entrance test was higher than that of blacks who were admitted under a designated quota system. As the analysis above has suggested, Bakke was justified on the "equal-treatment-for equals" criterion if there was no evidence of the test-score bias discussed in Section 6 above. Even if entrance-test scores could be shown to be quite imperfect predictors of success in medical school, the sole use of such scores to determine success or failure in admission does not violate the fairness precept. In such a setting, there is no argument for the establishment and enforcement of racial quotas, and any attempt to introduce such quotas would violate the fairness norm for members of the relatively high mean-productivity race.

Since no evidence of test-score bias was explicitly introduced, the Court's opinion of the Bakke position seems likely to have been in accordance with applications of the equal-treatment precept. On the other hand, the apparent "hedging" by Justice Powell on the use of race may well have been prompted by considerations of the sort discussed in Section 3 above. The "low-cost" way for a medical school to secure, say, 100 entrants of reasonably high quality, given information about the mean success of persons from identifiable classes, would be to restrict persons by race or class, and to use test scores only within classes. This method of operation would tend to emerge without the slightest preference on the part of anyone for racial or class considerations, per se.

In the Weber case, the majority of a reduced-sized Court found against Weber's claim of unfair or unequal treatment. In this case, Weber's argument was based on the fact that his seniority ranking was above that of a black applicant who was chosen for a training program based on a proportionate white-black quota arrangement.

The issues raised in *Weber* are considerably more complex than those raised in *Bakke.* It will be useful to see if the basic analysis worked out in previous discussion can be applied so as to offer insights into the Court's genuine dilemma. For purposes of discussion, we presume that the mean productivities of the two races, black and white, were estimated by employers to be as depicted above in Figure 2. In this setting, and prior to any program of affirmative action, Kaiser would have been willing, presumably, to hire blacks initially only if they were available at lower wages (for comparable skill categories); or, if wages were equalized, at higher qualification levels for the same categories. This policy would have emerged on the assumption that uncertainty about individual productivities was necessarily present when hiring decisions were made. (No overt racial discrimination at all would have been involved in such a policy.) Union wage standardization would have, presumably, required equalization of wage rates across all workers in a given category. Hence, a black worker, on being hired, would have represented a *higher* level of qualification (on average) than his white-worker counterpart. Seniority records commence, however, only from the date of initial employment, and these records could not, of course, reflect differential qualification levels at point of entry. It might have been argued, therefore, that a black worker was not the "equal" of the white worker who exhibited the same seniority, and that, because of the difference, the seniority records, standing alone, did not reflect the appropriate criterion of legal equality for selection and advancement to a training program. "Equal treatment" at the level of training-program selection, if designed to offset the initial differential in qualification on employment, might require some quota arrangement, and one that might necessarily have been inconsistent with simple seniority.

The majority of the reduced-sized Court would have been on much more secure grounds in its *Weber* opinion had it chosen to use an argument like that sketched out briefly here. Unfortunately, Justice Brennan, for the majority, did not use such an argument, and instead, relied on an internally contradictory argument that seemed to reflect personally biased judicial legislation. As a result, the opinion was highly vulnerable to the scathing dissent of Justice Rehnquist. Neither the majority opinion nor the dissent recognized the potential conflict between the satisfaction of the "equal treatment" criterion and the commitment against quotas in the discussion of the basic legislation.

NOTES

1. James M. Buchanan, *The Limits of Liberty* (Chicago: University of Chicago Press, 1975).

2. I would like to note at this point that I am leaving off the adjective "distributive" before "justice," but I am exclusively discussing "distributive justice" here as opposed to "commutative justice." The latter is, of course, important in its own right. We can attribute "injustice" to any institution or rule that would prevent the bookstore and me from making mutually advantageous trades.

3. Let me add clarification at this point, concerning the indirect constraint that law may exercise on behavior. You may be constrained, not by the law directly, but by the fact of the law itself. You may consider it unethical to violate law, not because the law is just in its object, but simply because it is law.

4. John Rawls, *A Theory of Justice* (Cambridge, Mass: Harvard University Press, 1971).

5. I should add a necessary footnote to the discussion at this point concerning the argument for public or governmental *financing* of education as opposed to the more complex extension of a possible argument for governmental provision and organization of education. I do not propose to discuss such an extension here; I would say only that there are very strong efficiency-based arguments for limiting government's role to financing, although some "fairness" arguments may be adduced for governmental provision.

6. See Dan Usher, "The Problem of Equity," mimeographed, Queens University, 1975.

7. See Rawls, p. 73. "...those who are at the same level of talent and ability, and have the same willingness to use them, should have the same prospects of success regardless of their initial place in the social system, that is, irrespective of the income class into which they are born." In his discussion, however, Rawls seems to think that the institutions of transfer taxation and publicly financed education will suffice to satisfy the equal-chances criterion, in the absence, of course, of discriminatory "tastes."

8. What I call identifiable characteristics are *indices* in the terminology of Michael Spence, which he defines as "unalterably observable char-

acteristics." See Michael Spence, *Market Signaling* (Cambridge, Mass.: Harvard University Press, 1974), chap. 4.

9. Frank Knight often remarked that it is difficult to know whether critics of competitive markets base their criticisms on failures of markets to be competitive or on the very successes of markets in attaining efficiency.

10. Akerlof discusses the market phenomena that I have described under the heading "statistical discrimination," which in itself is somewhat misleading since no "discrimination," as such, is involved. In addition, although his discussion is somewhat unclear in this respect, Akerlof seems to suggest that the existence of such phenomena implies inefficiency through the generation of what he refers to as a "low-level equilibrium trap," one that results from the incentives exerted on the behavior of the members of the class or group with relatively lower average qualifications. See George Akerlof, "The Economics of Caste and the Rat Race and Other Woeful Tales," *Quarterly Journal of Economics,* November 1976.

Such incentive effects may, of course, be present which would imply inefficiency. In my model, however, I have explicitly eliminated these effects to insure that there is no inefficiency in the competitive solution.

In his earlier treatment, Kenneth Arrow refers to the differences in perceived qualifications, based on perceived differences in averages, as one explanation for observed differences in wages among differing racial groups. Arrow's whole analysis is marred, however, by his apparent commitment to the presumption that basic productivities among groups cannot differ, even in average terms. See Kenneth Arrow, "Models of Job Discrimination" (chap. 1), and "Some Mathematical Models of Race in the Labor Market" (chap. 6), in *Racial Discrimination in Economic Life,* ed. Anthony H. Pascal (Lexington, Mass.: D.C. Heath, 1972).

In his book, *Market Signaling,* Michael Spence discusses models in which results analogous to those emerging from the models here seem to be derived. His whole analysis, however, is based on the signaling role of education and on individuals' choices of educational investment. In his discussion Spence, like Arrow, postulates that the actual productivity distributions between the two classes (races in his model) are identical. Differences in treatment of "equals" in separate classes stem from the possible differing levels of educational signals required to establish conditional probabilities for employers. Given an initial, historically determined, "prejudice," the expectations of employers and employees alike, over both classes, may prove to be self-reinforcing. See Spence, chaps. 2 and 3.

By contrast, in my model, which postulates actual differences in the mean or average productivities of the two classes, the differential treatment of "equals" arises with no "prejudice" or "discrimination" present, at *any* point in time. For an earlier, and more formal presentation of the model introduced here, see E. S. Phelps, "The Statistical Theory of Racism and Sexism," *American Economic Review,* September 1972.

11. *Regents of University of California* v. *Bakke,* 98 S. Ct. 2733 (1978); *United Steelworkers, etc.* v. *Weber,* 99 S. Ct. 2721 (1979).

Social Contradictions and the Liberal Theory of Justice

HERBERT GINTIS

I. INTRODUCTION

The liberal theory of justice was conceived in the turmoil of seventeenth-century state formation. For John Locke, its first consistent formulator, as well as his illustrious intellectual forebears Bodin, Pufendorf, and Hobbes, the object of a theory of justice was the securing of domestic peace and national unity. In contrast to the Machiavellian preoccupation with the supreme role of force in the formation of national will, the architects of the liberal theory of justice were always mindful that legitimacy, when attainable, is the most secure, if not the cheapest, instrument of assent.

The liberal theory of justice, with its characteristic emphasis on consent of the governed, has always manifested itself as a *theory of political obligation*. The investigation of justice is neither more nor less than the study of the conditions under which individuals are morally bound to submit to social conventions. Conversely, an unjust society is one in which individuals have the natural right—if not the positive obligation—to oppose and transform these conventions.

As such, the liberal theory of justice has always located itself at the same time in two normally distinct social spheres: the sphere of *science* and the sphere of *culture*. As a rigorous political philosophy, it has been subject to the norms of reason, consistency, and validity. In this respect it is in no way different from the philosophy of natural science, and indeed from scientific investigation itself. As an element of cultural intercourse in capitalist societies—and as a theory of political obligation it is inevitable that it attain this position —the liberal theory of justice is by contrast subject to all the laws of socio-cultural development. These laws, of course, are by no means subject simply to the intellectual canons of reason.

In this paper I shall argue that the liberal theory of justice is internally inconsistent insofar as it attempts to justify the conjoint articulation of the following social institutions: (a) economic activity based on private property in the means of production; (b) governmental forms stressing rights of political participation vested equally in all members of society by virtue of their citizenship; and (c) patriarchal rights of adult males over the control and reproduction of family life. The internal inconsistencies that have arisen, I shall suggest, do not flow from some deficiency inherent in any philosophy of natural rights, but rather in the incompatibility of sustaining a theory in which person rights, property rights, and patriarchal rights enter as equally fundamental and irreducible. Moreover, the need for such a treatment derives not from the *scientific* project of the liberal theory of justice, but from its *cultural* project of legitimating societies in which this diversity of rights does exist and is central to social reproduction. Finally, I shall suggest that a reasonable case can be made for a philosophy of natural rights in which only rights vested in individuals as members of the social community are fundamental. Other rights may be sustained, but only insofar as they reinforce and enhance the rights of persons in the social community. Not being myself a philosopher, I will not even attempt to produce such a philosophy. However, I do believe that a reasonable interpretation of John Rawls's recent reformulation of the liberal theory of justice in fact approximates such a philosophy, although he has not recognized it to be such.

Shorn of details, the argument to be presented can be outlined as follows. I shall begin by suggesting that there is no unique rational critique of a political philosophy. Any critique is inevitably an indictment of one or more of the social forms which it recommends and a program for their reform. The goal of the critique of the liberal theory of justice is the transformation of basic social institutions. In turn, the transformation of society occurs not in thought but through social action. Such action, I will argue, must take the form of exploiting internal contradictions in society itself.

Advanced capitalist social formations must be treated not as harmonious unities, but as contradictory totalities. The most fundamental form of contradiction in these societies lies in the distinct conditions of political participation in its major sites of social practice: state, family, and capitalist production. The state is organized, according to the principles of liberal democracy, by vesting rights of participation in *persons.* The family, by contrast, vests rights in adult male *"heads of household."* Finally, the site of capitalist production vests rights of decision-making and control in *property,* to be exercised by its owners or their duly appointed representatives. These principles of political participation are contradictory in the sense that if transported from their original domain of application, they lead to the failure of reproduction of their new site of exercise.

The liberal theory of justice is internally inconsistent in that it cannot justify the containment of its fundamental categories of natural rights to those social spheres where they avoid mutual conflict. The model of social life that it employs to maintain the isolation and containment of the rights that it affirms to regions of social life where they do not conflict, is rationally indefensible. A more adequate model of social life—which I shall elaborate upon in the course of my argument—does not support the multiplicity of fundamental and irreducible rights. Thus, the liberal theory of justice not only fails to legitimate liberal democratic capitalism; it fails as well as an internally coherent political philosophy.

The strategy of the liberal theory of justice for maintaining the compatibility of rights vested in persons, property, and "heads of household" is to assert the categorical distinctness of the social practices occurring in the sites to which they variously apply. Rights vested in *persons* are deemed to hold in the sphere of the *political, property* rights being reserved for the *economic,* and *patriarchal* privilege in the realm of personal *kinship* relations. We shall see that these categorical distinctions cannot be sustained.

In keeping with the general method of viewing inconsistencies in social philosophy as aspects of contradictions in society, I will then argue that indeed a major systemic problem facing advanced capitalism is that of maintaining the boundaries between the range of application of diverse types of rights. In fact, I shall argue that both class and gender struggles have taken the form, first, of gaining the rights of full citizenship, and then of attempting to *transport* the form of political practices in the state, structured according to the principle of rights vested in persons, to the family and the economy, where they tend to undermine property and patriarchal rights.

It would be foolhardy indeed to predict on the basis of this observed logic of the process of social struggles in advanced capitalism a future involving the total subjugation of property rights and patriarchal privilege in favor of a system in which person rights reign supreme. Another possible outcome is surely the sacrifice of democracy on the altar of hierarchical privilege in economic life. Such has occurred in the past: witness the dramatic collapse of parliamentary regimes throughout Europe in the 1920s and 1930s, in the face of the electoral and organizational power of an increasingly imposing working class.

In more recent times, the conflict between democratic principles of state and the hegemony of property in economic life has emerged in several diverse spheres. First, the demise of parliamentary institutions in the decades of the 1960s and 1970s in a considerable number of Third World countries undergoing capitalist development[1] dramatically illustrates our contention that the link between rights vested in persons and in property is tenuous indeed. The capitalist world economy increasingly boasts of far more "free enterprise" than of "free citizens." Second, the growth of Eurocommunism in Western Europe illustrates the possibility of the exercise of person rights in the form of universal suffrage to overcome, not the system of rights in general, but only that portion inimical to the well-being of the majority—the prerogatives of capital. Nor should this lesson be overlooked in the United States, where popular movements in recent years have dramatically reduced military in favor of social expenditures, brought an end to a war whose main beneficiaries were the exponents of a world economy open to capitalist investment, and succeeded in preventing the disastrous effects of economic slowdown from falling wholly on the shoulders of workers and the poor, at the expense of considerably lower profits and no forseeable end to depressed economic conditions.[2]

In the United States the response to this novel situation among political scientists and philosophers has not yet solidified. However, a move away from the traditional liberal tolerance for democratic principles is clearly drawing some tentative support. Nowhere is this more evident than in the writings of the influential Trilateral Commission, among whose members are numbered David Rockefeller, former President Jimmy Carter, and many of his closest cabinet members and political advisors. The Commission's report *The Crisis of Democracy,* while clearly a tentative testing of opinion, is forthright in attributing the country's ills to the "democratic distemper" of an all too powerful and self-conscious electorate.[3]

Liberal principles, then, are in some need of support. And given their clearly emancipatory content, they are worthy of such support. But not in their current form. To remain relevant in coming years the discourse of natural rights will have to shed its support for patriarchal privilege—which it is now in the process of doing—and for the prerogatives of private property in the means of production. This prospect is a tall order for a political philosophy that has been the mainstay of support for liberal capitalism. Yet it is one which, I shall endeavor to show, is necessary, and warranted by reason and concern for social welfare.

II. METHODOLOGY

Cows moo, beavers build dams, and human beings make theories of the world. The production of social theory is a social act. Nothing could be more inconsistent than the student of society who believes that the object of study is subject to lawlike behavior, but that the observer lies outside these laws. Any consistent social theory must therefore be self-reflexive: it must be able to account for its own appearance and development.

The critique of social theory is also a social act, and must equally be self-reflective. The norms of science demand two properties of any adequate social theory: internal consistency and adequacy toward its object of knowledge. It was Hegel who first noted that since society propels itself forward through its internal contradictions, and since the world of thought is part of social life-space, social theory itself will inevitably contain its characteristic contradictions and dislocations. To note their existence is no great feat and does not define an adequate critique.

It is equally true that to discover particular inadequacies of a social theory toward its object of knowledge does not constitute a valid critique. Again, as Hegel noted in his *Phenomenology of Mind,* there is an independent world of "facts" prior to our theoretical constructions on the basis of which we appropriate these facts.[4] A cogent critique is therefore always at the same time the affirmation of an alternative theory, from whose point of view the discrepant "facts" are culled.

My critique in this paper will be based on Marx's methodology of *theory and practice.* "The philosophers have only interpreted the world," said Marx in his *Thesis on Feuerbach,* "the point however is to change it."[5] The project of social theory is not abstract understanding, but intervention toward the transformation or reproduction of the social relations of everyday life. Fundamental social change takes place, not through acts of intervention outside the laws of social dynamics, but securely within them. It follows logically that a social intervention which transforms some basic social institution can only occur by exploiting contradictions inherent in the structure of society.

The contradiction in liberal democratic capitalism on the basis of which I will critique the liberal theory of justice is that concerning the valid application of rights vested in persons and rights vested in property. A major axis of class struggle in advanced capitalism has concerned precisely this point, yet the liberal theory of justice has been remarkably unaware of its own inconsistent treatment of this issue.

As C.B. Macpherson has shown in his remarkable book *The Political Theory of Possessive Individualism*,[6] this inconsistency appears in the very earliest of its formulations, in the works of John Locke. As he also notes, the inconsistency is a reflection of the major tension in liberal political movements of Locke's day. To achieve its twin goals of national unity and the full establishment of private property and free contract, the emergent bourgeoisies were forced into alliances with the popular classes, and hence to extend to these classes, at least in principle, the rights of citizenship. From this conjunctural situation, liberal theory was forced to accept the principle of inalienable rights, while inherent in the concept of property is freedom to alienate.

III. POSITIVE AND NEGATIVE LIBERTIES

The form of this inconsistency in the early versions of the liberal theory of justice is not difficult to describe. The aim of the social contract on which the formation of civil society is based is the protection of property. Since each individual possesses property in his person, it is in the interest of all that this social contract be effected. As a result, the purpose of the state is the protection of private property, pure and simple. To achieve this end, the state must be *representative* of property owners and hence be subject to their will.

Liberals in the seventeenth and eighteenth centuries were quite united on the claim that the rights of political participation were to be limited to the owners, not of property in general, but *real* property. Their reasoning was straightforward. The mass of peasants, artisans, and workers possessed little or no real property, and were they allowed to participate in the running of the state, it could not be guaranteed that they would refrain from redistributing the real estate of citizens, contrary to the dictates of justice. Conversely, the owners of real property, also having property in their person, could be expected to act consonant with the state's dedication to the preservation of personal liberties.

Thus early political philosophy developed the concept of *negative liberties* to express the rights of individuals as having property in their persons: freedom of speech, movement, thought, and religion were justified as forms of *freedom from outside interference.* Conversely, the *positive liberties* of rights to participation in governance were to be limited to those who had real property to protect.

I shall not dwell on this stage in liberal theory, as it has been quite swamped by the course of history. The American and French Revolutions, the English Reform Bill of 1832, as well as the wave of revolutions of 1848 in Europe all demonstrated the extreme difficulties in restricting rights of political participation to the propertied. Nineteenth-century liberalism witnessed intense debates over the feasibility of political democracy—whence the anguish of even so "enlightened" a thinker as John Stuart Mill in his *On Representative Government*—but the course of events swept away all possible reservations. By the early twentieth century, liberalism was well on its way to accepting political democracy. Ironically, contemporary liberalism invariably presents itself as though it invented the term, conveniently ignoring its ambivalent if not wholly negative attitude toward democracy over the century and a half of popular struggles for full political representation.

As a result of these political developments, the modern liberal theory of justice must affirm at once these distinct and indeed at times incompatible categories of rights: first, property rights, held to be legitimate in the sphere of economic affairs; second, inviolable personal liberties—freedom from unwarranted incursions upon individual choice and action; and third, the inalienable rights of political participation and with them the inalienable privileges and obligations of citizenship.

That these rights are capable of conflicting with one another is clear to all. For instance, the principle of majority rule can be used to infringe upon individual liberties, as in the case of prohibiting forms of religious expression, or penalizing the private sexual practices of consenting adults. Similarly, the positive right of individuals to equal treatment by prospective employers irrespective of race, creed, sex, or ethnicity, can conflict with the employer's right as a property owner to enter freely into contract with other owners (in this case, the prospective worker, as owner of his or her labor services).

What is held, however, is that these basic principles can be drawn upon to justify the organization of distinct spheres of social life: property rights justify the organization of the economy on the principles of free contract, market exchange, and wage labor; personal rights justify noninterference in the private sphere of family, kinship, and friendship; and political rights justify the organization of the state according to the principles of parliamentary democracy, the legitimate exercise of opposition by political parties, universal suffrage, due process, and liberty of association, press, and speech.

While the practical problem of maintaining the hegemony of these principles in their respective spheres may be difficult, the ethical legitimacy of this separation is not doubted in liberal theory. Property owners may attempt to subvert the democratic process, and voters may attempt to violate property rights and personal liberties. But if the basic issue of the justice of this separation can be maintained so that political obligation to the liberal democratic capitalist order can be affirmed, the practical problem of reproducing the conditions of justice can be dealt with on the basis of the goodwill of the body politic.

But can the ethical basis of the liberal theory of justice in fact be maintained? I shall argue that it cannot. This will require a detour from political philosophy through social theory. I shall argue that the partitioning of the social universe into "personal," "political," and "economic" cannot be maintained, and that this partitioning flows from a confusion of social *practices* that occur in all spheres of social life, with social *structures* that articulate the personal, the political, and the economic in whatever sphere of social life in which they prevail.

IV. SITES AND PRACTICES

By a *social practice* I mean an intervention into social life by an individual or group, whose *object* is some aspect of social life and whose *project* is the transformation of this object. Within "transformation" I will also include the project of the *reproduction* of the object in question. Indeed, it is an elemental fact that the conservative force for the maintenance and reproduction of existing social relationships is not automatic, but rather located in individuals and groups.[7]

Several types of practices may be singled out for special treatment, being basic to the transformation of the social totality. An *appropriative practice* is one whose object is the natural world and whose project is the transformation of nature toward the production of useful objects. A *political practice* is one whose object is some social relation and whose project is the transformation of this social relation. A political practice, then, is one oriented toward changing the "rules of the game" in social life.

Individuals may engage in political practices, but in general, effective political practices require the joint activity of many. Toward formulating and executing a political practice, a group must (a) communicate internally; (b) develop a common orientation; (c) legitimate this orientation, and hence create the bonds of solidarity on the basis of which it can be executed with the full support of the group; and (d) communicate with other and perhaps opposing groups. The means to this end is the set of *tools of communicative discourse,* including the demarcation of the terms of discourse and the boundaries of their acceptable usage. We shall call these tools of discourse the *cultural objects* of social life.

A *cultural practice* has as its object the ensemble of cultural objects in society, and as its project the transformation of these objects. Ultimately the goal of a cultural practice is the production of a set of tools of discourse capable of supporting more effective political practices on the part of an interested group. For instance, in the United States Declaration of Independence, the term "men" in the phrase "All men are created equal" originally extended effectively to white male citizens alone. Through a variety of cultural and associated political practices, this cultural object "men" has come to cover nonwhites, and women as well. The outcome of these cultural practices have since often been employed in recent decades as a basis for the solidarity and legitimacy on which the civil rights and women's liberation movements have depended for their power.

As with the social behavior of individuals in general, practices do not take place randomly. Rather, practices are *structured* by the characteristic social relations of the area of social life in which they occur. I shall define a *site* of social practice as a sphere of social activity with a sufficiently cohesive set of social relations to form a coherent and at least partially self-sustaining subsystem of a social formation. Sites, then, structure the practices that occur within them, much as a language structures the acts of communication that take place through it.

We may isolate three sites for special treatment by virtue of their substantive importance for the advanced capitalist social formation and their pertinence to the liberal theory of justice. These are the *family site* of kinship and domesticity, the *state site* of liberal parliamentary democracy, and finally the *site of capitalist production,* comprising the bulk of economic activity. I wish to stress that *each* of these sites articulates and structures *all* the practices occurring within them. Appropriative practices, for instance, occur within the state site (e.g., the provisioning of public goods) and the family (housekeeping, repair, food preparation, and child rearing), as well as within the site of capitalist production. Political practices occur not only within the state but within family and economy as well. Indeed, the division of labor in the capitalist enterprise is an ineluctably political structure in which the capitalist or his representative have control over the stabilization and transformation of all social relationships, and these relationships can be characterized in terms of the political categories of hierarchical authority and bureaucratic order. Similarly, the family site also is the locus of relations of power and control, in which patriarchal privilege is the norm. Finally, cultural practices occur at all sites and are structured differentially according to the requisites of the reproduction of the site in question. The cultural structure of the family involves the demarcation of prerogatives according to age, gender, and kinship. That of the site of capitalist production identifies prerogatives with ownership and contractual obligation, and the state with the status of citizenship.

The following claim will be central to my argument: the internal dynamics of a site cannot be understood without due regard to the *particular way* in which it articulates appropriative, political, and cultural practices. That is, I am claiming the *scientific* rather than the *moral* status of the framework I have just sketched. This bears two implications. First, no practice can be taken as a reflection of the others, and therefore reducible to them. The Parsonian emphasis on the primacy of culture, the traditional Marxian emphasis on the primacy of appropriative practices, and the Weberian stress on the primacy of the political, are all one-sided and incapable of adequate explanatory cogency.

Second, there is no validity to the identification of particular practices with particular sites. The economy is *not* the site where appropriation of nature takes place; the state is *not* the realm of the political; and there is no separate locus of the production or reproduction of culture. This observation will be of central relevance for our critique of the liberal theory of justice, which, I shall argue, depends for its cogency on just such a partitioning of society into the political, the economic, and the personal.

Before turning to this issue, we must outline the way in which sites articulate to provide the dynamics of social life. As I suggested before, these sites articulate both as a *reproductive and a contradictory totality.* First, a brief discussion of these terms is in order.

To say that a social formation is a totality is to suggest that the integrity and development derive from the *structure of the whole.* This in turn involves two affirmations. On the one hand, no part of the system can be understood even roughly outside the particular form of its articulation with its environing subsystems. And on the other, no part is the "essence" or "core" of the system in terms of which the others are reflections or responses. Of course, some sites in society may be more important than others qualitatively, but it remains that *the essence of the system is the structured articulation of the totality.*

To say that a system is a *reproductive totality* is to assert that the various sites in society act in general to supply the conditions of existence of other sites. Without this quality, a system could not for long reproduce itself through time, since by the nature of the totality, autonomous sites cannot supply their own conditions of existence. Finally, to say that a system is a *contradictory* totality is to assert that its normal operation throws up conditions requiring the structural transformation of one or more sites or their articulation. Whether this structural transformation takes place through revolution, reform, crisis, or war, and the content of the structural change will of course depend on the particular configuration of group practices arising in response to the contradictory situation.

It may seem inconsistent to treat a social formation at one and the same time as a reproductive yet contradictory totality. It is not. Just as a biological organism reproduces itself while transforming— often in dramatic ways (the caterpillar/the butterfly)—its basic structure as an organism, so it is with a social system. The biological organism, however, falls short of being a *contradictory* totality because it is not a *dialectical* totality. The key dynamic in a social totality lies in the dialectical relationship between structure and practice: structures exist only in the specific practices they structure, while practices have no existence outside the specific nature of their social structuration. Practices may in fact reproduce the totality, but they are contradictory by their nature as conscious interventions into the world with the project of transforming it—changing it into what it is not.

According to this general principle, all social systems are contradictory totalities. But I shall make the considerably stronger claim that the state site, the family site, and the site of the capitalist production in advanced capitalism *articulate* as a contradictory totality. To motivate this, I shall begin with a general discussion of the articulation of sites in a social formation.

The first major way sites articulate dynamically is through the principle of *structural delimitation.* By virtue of its coherent internal organization, each site undergoes change according to its own laws of development. But each site equally draws its input from environing sites, and outputs to these sites. Thus the forms of development of a site are delimited by its *boundary relations* with other sites, reproducing and changing outside its range of direct control. This is the principle of structural delimitation.

Structural delimitation can take either reproductive or contradictory forms. Reproductive delimitation occurs when a site is induced to develop so as to continue to supply the conditions of existence of environing sites. For instance, the state in capitalist society is structurally constrained to reproduce the conditions of profitability and growth in the economy, quite independent from the political philosophies of voters or officials. For governmental policies which constrain growth and profits will lead to recession, unemployment, and the weakening of a country's international economic position. This in turn will lead to a lack of political support for the governing regime, forcing a shift in economic policy.

As another example of reproductive delimitation, we note that the site of capitalist production is structurally constrained to reproduce the conditions of existence of patriarchy at the family site. One of these conditions is clearly that women not have access to occupational status and income on the same basis as men. For the superior economic position of men—far more than any physical, moral, or legal prerogatives favoring them—is basic to their maintenance of power in family life. Yet patriarchy as a moral system frowns upon the superiority of women over men in *all* relations of authority—including the economic. Thus, employers are constrained, in the interests of maintaining the legitimacy of authority relations in the enterprise, to prefer men to women, even in the face of the higher wage a male must be offered.[8] In this manner, the site of capitalist production is structurally delimited to the reproduction of patriarchy.

The principle of reproductive structural delimitation illustrates a major social mechanism affecting the reproduction of a social formation independent from the projects of actors within it. The principle of contradictory delimitation illustrates the contrary: the failure of reproduction independent from the conscious constitution of group practices. The validity of the concept should be clear from the fact that the laws of development of a site do not include the necessity of their supplying the condition of existence of other sites; unless rigidly constrained by their environments, they will periodically fail to do so.

For instance, the independent development of the capitalist

economy, especially its tendency to replace all social relations with exchange relations, will tend to undermine the family site by replacing its appropriative practices with market-oriented alternatives and by drawing women into the labor force in increasing numbers. Similarly, the development of property law in the state site is likely to develop rights vested in persons over patriarchal privilege, thereby undermining another basis of male domination in the family. Indeed, both of these movements have occurred in the twentieth century.

Were structural delimitation the only form of dynamic articulation of sites, the relevance of the sites/practices framework for the theory of justice would be quite limited. It is not. Indeed, principles of structural causality alone are quite incapable of explaining social regularities. The reason is straightforward: Given the basic structures of society and their boundary relations, we may be able to explain the reproduction of the totality as well as contradictions appearing within it. But by their very nature, structuralist principles cannot explain the reproduction of the boundary lines *between* structures. Moreover, if structures *frame* but do not *determine* practices, and if practices are the direct determinants of structural transformation, the structuralist principles above cannot explain social change. For instance, the principle of structural delimitation can explain the state's tendency to reproduce the conditions of profit and growth *given* that the control over investment lies in the hands of private capital; but why must the control of investment retain this form? Faced with electoral demands conflicting with economic profit, why do elected officials not move to *restrict* the ability of the capitalist to induce recession and unemployment? Clearly no structural argument can answer this question. The answer involves the fact that private control over investment is struggled for by owners, and consented to by the citizenry at large, as part of the overall accord among classes and other affected groups in constituting their political practices. Such an accord, where and when it occurs, and were it to break down what might be its replacement, are not structurally determined. Indeed, the boundaries between structures are themselves the product of such political practices.

Thus, the boundaries between sites are maintained by practices structured but not determined by these sites. It follows then that the *failure* of boundary maintenance between sites is likely to be explicable only in terms of the constitution of practices. I shall argue that this is indeed the case. The major mechanism by which this occurs I shall call the *transportation of practices across sites*. By this I mean that individuals and groups intent on transforming the social relations of a site will draw on whatever political and cultural tools are at hand to this end. Often this will involve drawing on *models* of political and cultural practices operative in other sites.

In contrast to delimitation, which describes the interaction of sites only along their boundaries, the principle of transportation of practices argues that the *internal* functioning of a site can facilitate the transformation of the *internal* functioning of another. The failure of structural theories to recognize this dynamic flows from two aspects of its methodology. First, they must treat practices as *determined* by their structuration[9] so that only boundary relations among sites is possible. Second, they involve a model of the interaction between individual and society in which individual behavior is determined by the structural position one holds within a site. As a result, when an individual moves from one site to another, he or she fully assumes a new role quite independent from those held in other sites. Our model of sites and practices, of course, does not methodologically commit us to this error.

The transportation of practices occurs because (a) individuals and groups preserve a measure of their integrity as social actors when they pass from one site to another, and (b) the tools of communicative discourse, and hence the cultural object-world, is common to all the major sites in advanced capitalism in the form of the liberal discourse of rights. A person may be mother and wife at home, worker in the factory, and Democrat in the state, but she remains a unified human actor, unable to psychotically "disassociate" her history, experience, and behavior from one sphere to another. And her concerns in all these spheres are expressible in terms of the discourse of natural rights. In forming her conception of morality and legitimacy, and in instituting her political and cultural practice, she may be expected to draw on the totality of her experience and resources, from whatever site they may reside. Whence the substance of the articulation of sites as a contradictory totality.

V. THE SOCIAL FORMATION
AS A CONTRADICTORY TOTALITY

I have stressed that each site in a social formation must be viewed as articulating an ensemble of appropriative, political, and cultural practices. In particular, all sites embody a political structure framing the political practices occurring within it. According to the principle of practices, groups in constituting their political practices in one site are capable of drawing on political practices in others to suit their purpose. In advanced capitalist societies this process is facilitated by the fact that while each site has its specific organization of cultural practices, the form of discourse—the liberal discourse of rights—is common to all. Thus, should the structure of political practices in distinct sites be *incompatible,* we immediately deduce the nature of the system as a contradictory totality.

As I suggested, the political structures of family, state, and site of capitalist production are indeed incompatible. The state site recognizes the rights of participation as vested in *persons,* on the basis of citizenship; the site of capitalist production vests rights of participation in terms of *property,* these rights devolving upon individuals and groups insofar as they own property; the family vests rights in adult male heads of households. Yet all do so according to the cultural tools of liberal natural rights.

In these terms, the course of the transportation of practices in the history of capitalist development can be traced as follows.[10] First workers and women contested *in the state* for equal political rights. These were normally not won until well into the twentieth century. Second, workers drew on the discourse of rights to support the transportation of the political practice of *free association* to the economy, where it became the linchpin of industrial unionism. Using their status as full citizens as support, women in contemporary years have struggled for the transportation of rights vested in persons to the family site, where these rights come into conflict with patriarchal privilege. Similarly, in addition to pressing for concrete distributional gains, workers in recent years have struggled for the transportation of person rights to the economy, where they conflict with the prerogatives of property. Clearly, the demands for minimum wage, due process in promotion and firing, the right to adequate health and safety conditions, and the more radical demand for workplace democracy now becoming widespread in Western Europe are of this form. No less are the demands for nondiscrimination in hiring, which pits the rights of citizens to equal treatment in social intercourse against the employer's right as a property owner to contract freely. Women similarly have attempted to transport their political rights in the state to the site of capitalist production in the form of antisexist legislation.

It is no accident that popular groups have consistently attempted to transport political practices from state to these other sites. For the site of capitalist production is rigorously described as a *site of domination,* of capital over labor. The form of domination is not metaphysical or cultural, but directly *political:* property rights vest control over the transformation of the site of capitalist production —control of investment and of the production process in particular. Similarly, the family is a *site of domination,* in this case of adult males over women and children. The liberal democratic state, by contrast, while integral to the reproduction of the conditions of domination in family and society, is itself not such a site. The principle of rights vested in persons, won by popular groups with great struggle, thus has become the basis for incursions upon the privileges of property and gender.

VI. CONTRADICTIONS IN THE
LIBERAL THEORY OF JUSTICE

To this point I have stressed the mutual dependency of three fundamental sites in advanced capitalist social formations: family, state, and economy. In the remainder of this paper I shall abstract from the family and its position in liberal theory in order to focus on the interplay between state and the site of capitalist production. This is not a reflection of a judgment of relative importance, but my particular expertise. Moreover, I shall act as a social scientist viewing political philosophy from the stance of an outsider. I shall provide the substance of a critique the philosophical aspects of which I leave others to develop, should they so desire.

My critique of the liberal theory of justice comprises two assertions. The first is relatively straightforward. A political philosophy that recommends a certain configuration of social institutions can be validated only if in fact the corresponding social formation is *reproducible.* I shall suggest that the social formation envisioned by liberal theory is *not* reproducible, in the sense that according to the actual laws of social life the boundary between person rights and property rights which it suggests can only be maintained under specific and not generally prevailing social circumstances. Second, the liberal theory of justice has not correctly delimited the range of alienable and inalienable rights, as a result of its accepting a version of social theory in which the "political" is identified with the operations of governance, and the "private appropriative" with capitalist production.

These two critiques are not independent. To see this, we must note an ambiguity in the concept of the social actualization of a political philosophy's being reproducible. On the one hand, we may assert reproducibility only if individuals in such a society ascribe to and act upon the general ethical principles according to which it is philosophically justified. On the other hand, we may wish to assert reproducibility of the social totality even if—or perhaps *only when* —individuals are ignorant of these ethical principles.

Several political philosophies have been of the latter sort. Thus, Plato's *Republic* works only when citizens are ignorant of the actual bases for the prerogatives of monarchs, priests, and warriors. Similarly, Enlightenment thought in the age of Voltaire at once maintained an atheist or deist theology, while recommending a traditional and authoritarian religious training for the masses as a basis for social stability.

Liberal social theory has not maintained this position. Indeed it could not without internal inconsistency, given its commitment to consent from an original position prior to social convention as a basis for political obligation. Thus for liberal theory the issue of reproduction must be posed as follows: Can the social formation justified by the liberal theory of justice reproduce itself given that individuals are committed to the liberal conception of justice? It is here that the issue of the inconsistency in the liberal treatment of inalienable rights comes into play. For one cannot demand that individuals remain committed to an inconsistent conception of justice. And as I have suggested, the precise form of inconsistency concerns the defense of the boundaries of application of person and property rights. But this of course is exactly the material problem in the reproduction of liberal democratic capitalism.

As I have suggested above, the problem in the reproduction of advanced capitalist social formation lies in its differential political organization of state, family, and site of capitalist production. Since these sites articulate as a contradictory totality, this social formation is not in general reproducible. Indeed, one can locate the social condition under which the integrity of this contradictory totality might be expected. These include rapid economic growth, a quantitatively small state sector, a multiplicity of cleavages among the electorate, and a relatively weak working class.[11] These conditions are far from general, and indeed scarcely hold in many of the contemporary capitalist social formations.

Moreover, the incursions upon liberal democratic capitalism, taking the form of the demand to extend the domain of application of person rights over diverse spheres of social life, have been undertaken through the application of liberal tools of discourse and not without a general commitment at least to the underlying principle of the liberal theory of justice. The lack of commitment has centered on a rejection of liberalism's philosophical position on boundary specification—that is, precisely at what I have taken as the point of deepest weakness of the liberal conception of justice.

Let us turn, then, to the liberal justification of rights vested in persons in the state and rights vested in property in economic life. I am certain that a variety of liberal sources could be used to this purpose, but I shall limit myself to John Locke's *Second Treatise of Government*.[12] Locke's argument begins quite fundamentally with the notion that "every Man has a *Property* in his own *Person*."[13] Indeed it is from this axiom that he will go on to develop the position that private property exists *prior* to social convention, and hence is inviolable. Yet the peculiar attribute of the property in one's person is that it is *inalienable* in the sense that the individual cannot, *even by consent,* relinquish this right to others. Thus, in discussing the nature of slavery, he notes: "a Man, not having the Power of his own Life, *cannot,* by Compact, or his own Consent, *enslave himself* to anyone, nor put himself under the Absolute, arbitrary Power of another...."[14] Now it might be concluded that Locke considers slavery a wholly unjust institution. Property in one's person, while not alienable, can be justly alienated, as might be done to "Captives taken in a just War."[15] The critical factor here, however, is that such an individual does not possess the status of citizenship: "These Men having ... forfeited their Lives, and with it their Liberties ... cannot in that state be considered any part of *Civil Society*."[16]

Most liberals today would not agree that even a captive in a just war has forfeited his or her life. Therefore, Locke's objection can be ignored, and we may rest content that the rights of persons in their body are inalienable by virtue of the status of membership in civil society—a, broadly speaking, citizenship. The question, then, concerns merely the *extent* of such inalienable rights.

I shall limit myself here to the assertion that all personal rights of political participation are inalienable. No doubt Locke would have disagreed, but the contemporary liberal commitment to political democracy has provided good reasons for accepting this principle (e.g., it is affirmed both by John Rawls and Robert Nozick, however otherwise divergent their views).[17] However, if our analysis of the capitalist social formation as an articulated ensemble of sites is correct, politics cannot be limited to the state, and hence political rights must extend to the site of capitalist production itself. That is, one cannot alienate, in return for money or other emoluments, one's right as a member of civil society to participate equally in the governance of production and investment. But this is exactly the form of capital-labor relations in capitalism: The worker, in return for a wage, agrees to submit to the political authority of the employer for a specified period of time. The worker is thus alienating an inalienable right, and such a system cannot be just.

The reader will note that this is not a general argument concerning the injustice of either property rights or market institutions. It is an argument *only* against property rights in the means of production, and then only insofar as they are exercised in the employment of wage labor. Equally, it is not an argument against the use of market institutions, but only markets in wage-labor and capital. Like slavery, wage-labor is unjust, and markets in wage-labor are ethically akin to markets in human beings themselves.

Now of course there will be counterarguments to the above by those intent on preserving the notion of harmonious relations between the principles of political democracy and private property. I cannot be expected to foresee all such arguments, but one is of sufficient importance to bear serious treatment. This is the view of traditional economic theory, which holds that while it may *appear* that the worker is alienating his or her rights of participation, in fact the whole operation of the capitalist economy acts to render his or her will determinate of economic outcomes. This is the so-called theory of "worker sovereignty."[18]

According to this view labor is a commodity like any other. [19] In a market economy, the forces of competition act to generate a mix of commodities perfectly conformable to the preferences of consumers. Thus the constellation of jobs open to workers will conform to the preferences of workers for income, quality of work, and control over work process. Just as citizens elect representatives to take control of their political affairs by voting with their ballots, workers choose representatives to control their labor according to their wills, but in this case by voting with their feet.

In particular, if workers preferred direct political democracy in the workplace, they would be willing to offer their services to a capitalist who allowed them to organize their own affairs, and indeed at a lower wage in return for the superior working conditions. That this does not often occur is an indication either that workers do not so desire, or that there is no method of production in terms of efficient technology that is compatible with democratic work.

There are deep problems with this traditional theory, not the least of which are empirical.[20] For instance, studies show that workers *do* prefer situations where they participate democratically in their work. Studies also show fairly uniformly that a move toward worker control in production increases both productivity and worker satisfaction. This and other similar empirical findings cast doubt on the representation of labor as a commodity. The basis for the noncommodity status of labor lies precisely in the fact that the exchange of labor for a wage is not the form of a quid pro quo, or as in the case of commodity exchanges. What the worker obtains is a definable quid—a wage. But what the employer obtains in return is *not* a product with definable attributes, but rather merely the willingness of the worker to submit to the political authority of the enterprise. When the buyer of labor services does receive a guaranteed and specified range of services, the contract entered into is *not* one of employer/employee but rather independent agent/independent agent. This exchange does not suffer from the critique presented above.

Moreover, the political power of capital is by no means a peripheral element in the project of capital. Since the labor exchange involves no specifiable pro quo, only the political power of capital is capable of evincing the type and degree of labor ensuring the generation of profits. The configuration of forces is quite distinct from that of commodity exchange, where the guarantee of the integrity of exchange lies not in the power of the exchanging parties, but of the *state,* in the form of the judicial branch of government.

Since labor is not a commodity, it is not surprising that the model of worker sovereignty, as proposed by traditional economics, fails to hold. No form of political organization of production which conflicts with the capitalist's need to control the terms of the labor exchange will emerge through market competition, however productive, however desired by workers, or even however low a wage workers might be willing to accept to enjoy their political rights of participation. For in this latter case, the power given up to workers in exchange for low wages will naturally improve their position vis-à-vis capital in future wage negotiations. Indeed the very legitimacy of profits in a situation where workers are engaged in major decision-making would be quite problematic.

The treatment of labor as a commodity, on a par with others in the system of market exchange, thus complements the implicit claim in the liberal theory of justice that the realm of the political is confined to the state and its organs. In both cases I am asserting the *factual* not *ethical* cogency of this representation. Many have claimed that capitalist social relations indeed reduce labor to a commodity status, a status inadmissible from the point of view of the moral worth of the individual. I have suggested that this is not the case. Were labor a commodity, the traditional economic argument as to the *essential* retention of control of the worker (worker sovereignty) would be correct, save perhaps at one point. This point is one which the concept of worker sovereignty shares with the more general category of consumer sovereignty. The justification of the principle of consumer sovereignty lies in the Pareto principle that an optimal social condition obtains when no individual could be made better off without at the same time rendering another individual worse off. But a Pareto-optimal social configuration is just only if the initial distribution of wealth is itself equitable. Thus, consumer sovereignty plus equitable distribution is sufficient for social justice.

In the case of worker sovereignty, the claim takes the following form: free markets in labor and competition among employers will produce a constellation of jobs exactly reflecting the workers' trade-offs for income and quality of work, and given their technical capacities as producers. But this configuration of jobs will be *just* only if the initial distribution of resources among workers and between workers and capitalists is equitable. Thus, if labor is taken to be a commodity, it follows logically that the issue of the justice of the capitalist system reduces to the issue of the equity of the distribution of resources.

In this case, the political issue of the rectification of injustice becomes that of the redistribution of wealth. Indeed it is in this form that the issue has often appeared in debate concerning the moral superiority of socialism over capitalism in the twentieth century. Thus my claim that labor is *not* a commodity is critical to changing the terrain of this debate. The issue of the justice of a capitalist social formation, I have urged, is one of *control,* not *ownership.* The institution of wage-labor, by subjecting workers to an unjust structure of political practices in the economy, deprives them of their inalienable rights. This condition would hold *whatever* the distribution of formal ownership of the means of production—even social ownership. Thus *if* labor is not a commodity, a liberal theory of justice amended to delineate the proper range of application of person rights to a just social formation would be as critical of state socialism as of capitalism itself. For both systems frame political participation in economic life in terms of property rights, and differ only as to the private versus social nature of these rights. An adequate theory of social justice, I have claimed, would deny the applicability of the concept of property rights altogether in structuring political practices in the economy.

VII. CONCLUSION

Locke's is of course not the last word on the liberal theory of justice; indeed it is perhaps its first coherent formulation. Yet its force derives from a subterfuge which has reappeared in different forms in all subsequent formulations. For Locke civil society arises purely for the protection of property rights. Yet it appears that there are two qualitatively distinct forms of property—roughly speaking, "alienable" and "inalienable." To include both under the common rubric of "property" may lend liberal political philosophy an aura of consistency, but this appearance is misleading. Only by grossly misrepresenting the structure of capitalist social formations can formulas for the domain of application of these two types of "property" be maintained.

More recent formulations, for instance John Rawls's *A Theory of Justice,* began in effect with rights vested in persons (full equality in the original position) and derive from this private property as a possibly just institutional form. This approach may be able to justify contractual exchange and the right to the enjoyment of private real property. But it is no more able to justify wage-labor than was Locke. While contractual services may be exchanged, or services against money, the noncommodity status of labor renders it nonalienable. Thus, I have argued elsewhere that a consistent application of Rawls's principles would suggest a social formation quite distinct from either capitalism or state socialism—a social formation in which the principles of political democracy would govern the structures of political practice in economic life.[21]

I have stressed in this paper that the liberal theory of justice must be *transformed* rather than replaced. This position does not derive from an abstract assessment of its intellectual merits and drawbacks above. Rather, it is informed by my understanding that in fact emancipatory struggles in capitalist social formations have developed through the application and transformation of the tools of liberal discourse. This paper is simply one more intervention in line with this general movement.

NOTES

1. Robert Packenham, *Liberal America and the Third World* (Princeton, N.J.: Princeton University Press, 1973).

2. For a detailed analysis of these trends, see Samuel Bowles and

Herbert Gintis, "Economic Crisis and the Marxian Theory of the State," University of Massachusetts mimeograph, 1980.

3. The Trilateral Commission, *The Crisis of Democracy* (New York: New York University Press, 1975).

4. Georg Hegel, *The Phenomenology of Mind* (New York: Harper & Row, 1967).

5. Karl Marx, "Theses on Feuerbach," in Robert C. Tucker, ed., *The Marx-Engels Reader* (New York: Norton, 1972).

6. C.B. Macpherson, *The Political Theory of Possessive Individualism* (London: Oxford University Press, 1962).

7. Erving Goffman, *The Presentation of Self in Everyday Life* (Garden City, N.Y.: Doubleday, 1959).

8. This dynamic is, of course, quite complex. For a more expansive treatment, see Herbert Gintis, "The Nature of the Labor Exchange," *Review of Radical Political Economics,* Summer 1976, and Samuel Bowles and Herbert Gintis, *Schooling in Capitalist America* (New York: Basic Books, 1976).

9. For a liberal theory of this type, see Talcott Parsons, *The Social System* (New York: Free Press, 1951), and for a Marxian version of the same method, see Louis Althusser, *For Marx* (New York: Vintage, 1970).

10. For details, see Herbert Gintis, "Theory, Practice and the Tools of Political Discourse," *Socialist Review,* Spring 1980.

11. See Herbert Gintis and Samuel Bowles, "The Invisible Fist: Have Capitalism and Democracy Reached a Parting of the Ways?" *American Economic Review,* May 1978.

12. John Locke, *Two Treatises of Government* (New York: New American Library, 1960). For a related critique of John Rawls, see Barry Clark and Herbert Gintis, "Rawlsian Justice and Economic Systems," *Philosophy and Public Affairs,* Summer 1978.

13. Ibid., p. 328.

14. Ibid., p. 325.

15. Ibid., p. 366.

16. Ibid.

17. See John Rawls, *A Theory of Justice* (Cambridge, Mass.: Harvard University Press, 1971), and Robert Nozick, *Anarchy, State and Utopia* (New York: Basic Books, 1974).

18. See Gintis, "Nature of the Labor Exchange," for an extended treatment.

19. See Paul Samuelson, *Foundations of Economic Analysis* (New York: Atheneum, 1972), and Gerard Debreu, "Valuation Equilibrium and Pareto-Optimum," *Proceedings* of the National Academy of Sciences, 1954.

20. For a fuller discussion see Gintis, "Nature of the Labor Exchange," and Bowles and Gintis, *Schooling in Capitalist America,* chap. 3.

21. Clark and Gintis, "Rawlsian Justice and Economic Systems."

Overcoming Injustice: Possibilities and Limits

DENIS GOULET

I. IS ECONOMIC JUSTICE POSSIBLE?

To Don Quixote, the man from La Mancha, nothing appeared impossible. In the real world, however, Quixote stands as a caricature of the idealist who never learns to locate the dividing line between the possible and the impossible. Whenever moral philosophers fall prey to Quixote's illusion, they end up placing inhuman burdens on the consciences of their fellow human beings. Not surprisingly, therefore, most ethical theorists endorse the medieval dictum that *nemo ad impossibile tenetur*—no one has a duty to do what is impossible.

Debates on justice are often flawed because protagonists assume either that social perfection is totally possible or, in contrast, totally impossible. *Both views are wrong, misleading, and dangerous.* Indeed the most important, and perhaps the most difficult, task faced by moralists is to delineate the boundaries of possibility. One part of the task is easy, of course, since whatever exists is clearly possible. What exists may not be very good, moral, or just, but it certainly is possible. But students of social change must also grapple with competing images of human improvement or preferred structures which to some appear possible, to others unattainable. Ultimately, the difference between conservatives and radicals may well be their contrary assumptions regarding what is possible in social arenas. Sound development, the elimination of misery, injustice, repression and exploitation are all projective images of goods whose feasibility is inherently open to debate. Prevailing attitudes toward such goals have changed greatly in the last thirty years: after World War II prospects for making the world better—around such institutions as the United Nations, the World Bank, the General Agreement on

113

Tariffs and Trade, and the International Monetary Fund—seemed hopeful. But thirty years and many failures later, development experts have grown pessimistic: they no longer confidently recommend economic planning, social engineering, resource transfers, and policy research on the dynamics of social change. They sadly admit that there is more underdevelopment and oppressive poverty in 1980 than in 1945. One also finds greater cultural dependency, technological drift, and political oppression than before. Recently Robert McNamara, president of the World Bank, warned that "we are going to have to decide—and decide soon—if we can really afford to continue temporizing with severe development problems that are getting worse rather than better."[1] Are we to conclude, then, that promises made in the name of development are impossible dreams, mere illusions, mechanical rabbits set in front of racing greyhounds simply to egg them on in a futile race after unreachable prizes?

Not only development specialists, but social critics as well speak in a chorus of doomsday voices. Thus in *Pyramids of Sacrifice*[2] sociologist Peter Berger accuses scholars, politicians, and problem-solving activists of immolating new victims on the altar of a better future—under a variety of banners: revolution, development, growth, capitalism, socialism. And Harvard historian Barrington Moore, author of a landmark study on the *Social Origins of Dictatorship and Democracy,* changes his tune in a later book, *Reflections on the Causes of Human Misery.*

In *Social Origins* Moore argued that:

> For a Western scholar to say a good word on behalf of revolutionary radicalism is not easy because it runs counter to deeply grooved mental reflexes. The assumption that gradual and piecemeal reform has demonstrated its superiority over violent revolution as a way to advance human freedom is so pervasive that even to question such an assumption seems strange. In closing this book I should like to draw attention for the last time to what the evidence from the comparative history of modernization may tell us about this issue. As I have reluctantly come to read this evidence, the costs of moderation have been at least as atrocious as those of revolution, perhaps a great deal more.[3]

But a few years later Moore observes that:

> Why is it that revolutionaries sooner or later adopt, and sometimes intensify, the cruelties of the regimes against which they fight? Why is it that revolutionaries begin with camaraderie

and end with fratricide? Why do revolutionaries start by proclaiming the brotherhood of man, the end of lies, deceit, and secrecy, and culminate in tyranny whose victims are overwhelmingly the little people for whom the revolution was proclaimed as the advent of a happier life? To raise these questions is not to deny that revolutions have been among the most significant ways in which modern men—and in many crucial situations modern women—have managed to sweep aside some of the institutional causes of human suffering. But an impartial outlook and the plain facts of revolutionary change compel the raising of these questions as well. In my estimation the essence of the answer rests in this fundamental contradiction between the effectiveness of immoral political methods and the necessity for morality in any social order. Against his opponents, whether they be a compelling revolutionary faction or the leaders of the existing government, a revolutionary cannot be scrupulous about the means that he uses, if he is serious about his objectives and not merely an oratorical promoter of edifying illusions. If he refrains from using unscrupulous means, the enemy may use them first and destroy the revolution itself. [4]

Moore places us on guard against a double illusion, "the defeatist illusion of impotence within a permanent present or the opposite one of romantic utopianism." The most sobering fact, however, is that these two illusions, he adds, "themselves have been among the major sources of human misery." [5]

An equally chastening message issues from Robert Heilbroner's probing *Inquiry Into the Human Prospect.* "Is there hope for Man?" Heilbroner asks.

In another era such a question might have raised thoughts of man's ultimate salvation or damnation. But today the brooding doubts that it arouses have to do with life on earth, now, and in the relatively few generations that constitute the limit of our capacity to imagine the future. For the question asks whether we can imagine the future other than as a continuation of the darkness, cruelty, and disorder of the past; worse, whether we do not foresee in the human prospect a deterioration of things, even an impending catastrophe of fearful dimensions.

That such a question is in the air, hovering in the background of our minds, is a proposition that I shall not defend by citing bits of evidence from books, articles, and the like. I will rest my case on the reader's own response, gambling that my

initial assertion does not generate in him or her the incredulity
I should feel were I to open a book whose first statement was
that the prevailing mood of our times was one of widely shared
optimism. Thus I shall simply start by assuming that the reader
shares with me an awareness of an oppressive anticipation of
the future.[6]

The same theme—namely, a future of probable catastrophe—
is echoed by growing numbers of social analysts in the U.S. Among
the most influential are those men so brilliantly portrayed by Peter
Steinfels in his book *The Neo-Conservatives:*[7] Patrick Moynihan,
Nathan Glazer, Daniel Bell, Irving Kristol, Norman Podhoretz,
Peter Berger, Michael Novak, and others.

An alarming trend is, in short, discernible: students of social
dynamics tell us to trim our aspirational sails. Trying to do too much
good in society, they argue, can cause more harm than deliberately
setting out to exploit others.

A vital question thrusts itself upon us, therefore: How is our
calculus of possibility to be shaped? For purposes of clarity, let me
split the question into two parts: (1) What view do we have of the
trajectory of history, what earlier scholars like Spengler, Toynbee,
Dawson, and Edward Hallett Carr called the "laws" of history?
And (2) Can politics, which deals with power, and ethics, which
speaks of the good that ought to be, influence one another?

With these questions as background, I shall now explore four
points:

    A. competing images of history;
    B. two views of politics;
    C. whether the U.S. is a special or a general case of a na-
        tion at work in history; and
    D. the specific contribution, if there is one, of Christian
        ethics to global justice.

A. Competing Images of History

I shall focus here on the impact that three different readings of
history have on the boundaries of possibility. First let us consider
existentialism as an adventure in absurdity.

1. Absurdity

Sartre and his disciples see human existence as cruel folly: you
and I are thrown irrationally into existence like projectiles hurled

randomly into cosmic space. No meaningful purposes or benevolent designs govern our destiny: in final analysis, all we do is pointless. Camus gives poignant expression to pervasive meaninglessness in *The Myth of Sisyphus:* "There is but one truly serious philosophical problem, and that is suicide. Judging whether life is or is not worth living amounts to answering the fundamental question of philosophy."[8]

No contemporary thinker is more biting and sarcastic in analyzing futility than the Romanian philosopher, E. Cioran, author of such cheerful works as *The Trouble with Being Born, The Fall into Time, The New Gods, A Short History of Decay,* and *The Courage to Exist.* For Cioran, it takes great courage simply to be, to accept our birth, our life, and our very selves as worthless ephemeral entities adrift in existential space. Cioran writes: "We hear on all sides that if everything is pointless, to do well whatever it is you're doing is not. Yet it is, even so."[9] Sartre retorts that human dignity resides in our freedom: we have it in our power to endorse our absurd condition freely and lucidly, thereby creating meaning. Sartre grants that there is no ultimate value to our creation, yet he insists that nobility resides in the courageous effort itself. Indeed, it is the only nobility of which humans are capable.

Although some critics accuse existentialists of narcissistic obsession with their subjective selves, the two giants of the movement, Sartre and Camus, have always struggled mightily to formulate an ethic of political responsibility. And the personal lives of both men bear witness to the personal duty of solidarity they felt toward oppressed victims throughout the world.

Nevertheless, a dark cloud hangs over existentialism as a philosophy of history. The Brazilian Marxist philosopher, Alvaro Vieira Pinto, calls existentialism a bourgeois luxury found only in rich and exploitative countries: existentialism is inherently alienating, he claims, and has nothing to say to the struggling poor of the Third World.[10]

Obviously this harsh judgment must be mitigated in the light of the Christian-Marxist dialogue that has flourished intermittently since the early 1950s. Over twenty years ago, the then-orthodox Polish Marxist Adam Schaff (in *A Philosophy of Man*) conceded that existentialism did pose valid questions about conscience and ethical responsibility even though he rejected its answers. All the same, existentialism lives under the curse of being a philosophy for only a very small number. Its view of life is too far removed from the daily experience of the masses, who refuse to believe that their struggles for dignity mean nothing. Consequently, the potential impact of existentialism on historical possibilities for change is severely limited.

Far more prevalent than existentialism in Third World nations are cyclical views of history.

2. The Endless Circle

For many hundreds of millions of impoverished peoples in Asia, history is pictured as Karma: the wheel of destiny turning round upon itself, without end and with monotonous repetition. Karma, the law of life, is an endless cycle of births, deaths, rebirths, and new deaths. History has no immanent value other than as a staging ground for personal efforts of individuals striving to break the Karmic circle by suppressing desire and gaining release from rebirth. The ultimate purpose of time is to escape from time.

The general effect of this world-view—shared by Hindus, Buddhists, and some nature religions—is to lead people to pay little attention to secular historical tasks. Obviously, we must beware of oversimplifications here. Gandhi, after all, stands as living proof that traditional Hindu values can carry a potent political charge. But Gandhi was deeply influenced by his reading of the Christian scriptures and his practice of British law in South Africa. Ariyaratne, the Sri Lankan leader of the Sarvodaya movement, is another contemporary Asian leader who revitalizes Karmic traditions into a socially dynamic force. And scholars like Dissanayake remind us that Buddha himself was indifferent neither to political justice nor to social order.[11] Nonetheless, it remains true that Hindu and Buddhist world-views, in nations where they are culturally dominant, have generally exercised little dynamic impact on political and economic organization, except perhaps to legitimize a hierarchical stratification system. My point here is that, within cyclical perspectives of history, periods of greater justice are followed by eras of injustice, and so on forever. Just and unjust social orders alike are mere epiphenomenal whims of destiny; and the supreme wisdom lies in gaining release from time and from repetition.

The very notion of social justice is now closely tied to the concept of development. Yet, as Myrdal wrote more than twenty years ago:

> It becomes very uncertain whether and in what sense it can be
> held that there has in recent decades been any economic prog-
> ress at all for mankind as a whole.

Increasing Awareness

Other facts basic to our problem are political ones:

(i) the people in the under-developed countries are becoming increasingly aware of these huge international inequalities and the danger that they will continue to grow; and

(ii) these peoples and their spokesmen show an inclination to put part of the blame for their poverty on the rest of the world and, in particular, on the countries which are better off— or rather, they attribute the inequalities to the world economic system which keeps them so poor while other nations are so rich and becoming richer.

The Second World War helped to release many checks and controls upholding the established power system in the world, and one of its results was the liberation on a vast scale of subject peoples from colonial rule. An important characteristic of the new nationalism which was born in this process is, however, that the demand of the peoples is for equality of opportunity with other peoples, as well as for liberty. All these very poor nations, as they are touched by the Great Awakening, crave economic development as well as national independence.[12]

To crave development, however, or to engineer social change by deliberate interventions of will implies a reading of history that is neither absurd nor cyclical but teleological. In other words, the development quest points to goals in history.

3. History with a Goal

Teleological readings see purpose and meaning in historical processes. They postulate a historical trajectory which leaves room for qualitative changes—for better or for worse—and not merely repetition. Most Westerners hold teleological views, whether they embrace religious or secular philosophical outlooks. More importantly, the belief in historical goals has been diffused throughout the world as part of a cultural package that includes such notions as the scientific approach to evidence, the theory of evolution in nature, the attainability of progress, and a preference for technological modes of rationality.

In recent decades the teleological image of history is usually enshrined in aspirations after development, whether they are to be achieved through revolutionary or gradualist change strategies. Expressed in secular terms, teleology declares that human intelligence and will, if effectively harnessed to rational and concerted action, can decisively shape history. By their effort societies can gain mastery over nature, control over their own social structures, and even alter the patterns of biological growth (whether through genetic engineering or by applying psychologically tested rewards and punishments).

Secular humanists in 1980 doubtless reject the euphoric belief in the inevitability of progress which marked their nineteenth-century forebears: too many wars, and too many tragedies under banners of reason and progress render naive optimism untenable. Nevertheless, secular humanists still believe that social injustice is a reversible human creation: and if it was caused by human actions, it can also be eliminated, or at least attenuated, by human effort. Revolutionaries, progressives, liberals, and conservatives disagree over which specific goals are realistic, but all concur that the institutionalization of justice is both a possible and a worthwhile human endeavor. Conservatives seek, above all, to preserve that modicum of justice that may have feebly emerged from centuries of social experimentation, struggle, and consolidation. Revolutionaries, in turn, push frontiers of possibility outward and marshal human will and organization in the fight to produce greater justice. Neither camp assumes, however, that present levels of justice are either permanently frozen or subject to impersonal laws that escape human control. Conservatives resist change because they think it will lead to less justice in society; revolutionaries embrace risk because they hope it will create more justice.

Jews, Christians, and Muslims worship a God who acts in and upon history, while they appeal to values outside history to ground their belief in its purposefulness. They invoke doctrines of benevolent creation, of a divine vocation for human beings, individually and collectively, of God's purposes in time, or the responsibility men and women have to act as co-creators of a livable world, where justice, love, peace, loyalty, and truthfulness may flourish. Most religious believers embrace an ethical system that posits a connection between what is done to others in society and the final destiny of individual persons. For the most part, they also accept the notion that historical time as a totality points to some ultimate goal or crowning achievement. Hence religious teleological outlooks not only admit progressively wider possibilities of societal justice but also impose on their adherents the duty to make those possibilities actual.

Later I shall examine the different coefficients of secular commitment, or insertion in history, attaching to competing world-views.

But one point is already clear, namely, that one has higher or lower expectations regarding how much social justice is possible in accord with one's view of the dynamics of history. And secular teleological views about human mastery of nature and purpose in social processes have affected all belief systems. To this extent, at least, have the boundaries of historical possibility regarding economic justice been widened.

Images of history, however, are very abstract things and do not guide action directly: we must also examine which conception of politics prevails in any society.

B. Two Views of Politics

An old Western tradition, already explicit in Aristotle and Plato, defines the mission of politics as the wise and just management of society's common welfare. Similar notions can also be found in Chinese and Indian thought. Modern political discourse, however, no longer uses categories like the common good or wisdom and virtue in leaders. To students of modern politics, the defining category is power: its conquest and exercise. And popular wisdom, understanding that compromises are unavoidable in political arenas, views politics as the art of the possible.

But two contrasting interpretations of this saying vie for acceptance and, if we are to make an accurate calculus of possibility, it matters greatly which one we endorse.

1. The Static Interpretation

Most politicians assume given limits of possibility when they speak of the "art of the possible." Competing interests cannot be accommodated, and no decisive action can result except from compromise, what Lyndon B. Johnson fondly called "horse-trading." Whenever opposing claims have to be reconciled, rules must be followed. These rules are usually dictated by electoral considerations and assessments of the relative power of one's adversaries. Most people assume that political skill consists in knowing how to manipulate a limited pool of resources or favors so as to maximize one's power leverage. Within this framework, all pressures or claims are treated as *inputs* to political decision making, and final allocations of resources or influence are considered as *outputs.* Basically, this engineering model of politics is based on bargaining and on a belief in the need to be efficient.

In this view of things, the boundaries of the possible are limited and not subject to great elasticity. And there is no room for sharp breaks with existing rules or radical departures from loyalty systems: one must endlessly adjust, accommodate, and maneuver within set limits. Shrewd conventional politicians become expert at judging how palatable to different constituencies are all laws, planned reforms, or specific policy measures. They rebuff attempts to introduce quantum leaps in social justice as impossible, on the grounds that the required trade-offs are unacceptable to interest groups wielding effective power.

This exegesis of the dictum "politics is the art of the possible" is essentially conservative, or at best, cautiously reformist. It is a posture that does not help much, however, when societies are plagued with chronic unjust structures.

2. A Dynamic Alternative

Many students of development have concluded that the only brand of politics worth pursuing is one which defines its task as the creation of new possibilities. Inertia, hopelessness, and the inability to improve conditions of life by means of small, piecemeal measures— all these are part of the legacy of underdevelopment. Therefore, development politics needs to change the ground rules governing access to resources, influence, and power. Development politics is the art of rendering new things possible, not of manipulating variables within a closed circle of initial possibilities.

To illustrate, China under Mao broke radically with its past and launched a revolution to destroy unequal systems of land tenure and job opportunity. Even within a capitalistic framework, Juscelino Kubitschek (president 1954-60) moved Brazil several discontinuous strides forward by building a new capital, Brasilia, far from population centers on the coast. He deliberately provoked imbalances in transportation and in the flow of skills and money to stimulate rapid development.

My point is that development politics requires leaders who devise strategies for creating new possibilities and for overcoming resistance to their innovations. At times explosions from outside a system are needed to "open things up." More frequently, however, a strategy of "implosion" must be practiced. "Implosion" demands constant pressure applied from within the boundaries of existing possibilities to expand their range and shatter their limits.

If one wants to know how much justice is possible in any society, one must first ask whether power-wielders take politics as the manipulation of fixed possibilities or as the creation of new ones.

Within this dynamic perspective of politics as the art of creating new possibilities, ethics plays four related roles: evaluative, critical, pedagogical, and normative. Ethical judgments applied by persons having effective power in society influence events differently from those applied by persons lacking such power. In terms of immediate results, ethical norms are influential only if they are acted upon by persons wielding power. Nevertheless, those lacking power may influence decisions if they can pressure power-holders to accept their ethical judgments as normative. More importantly, if the governed reject rulers' norms, and if the express their rejection collectively through strong organizations, their counter-norms can play an indirect role in decision-making.

The main lesson drawn from the interplay between power and normative values is that power without legitimacy must ultimately perish. Indeed, legitimacy itself must be founded on perceived ethical merit if it is to endure. As he reflects upon his long struggle with the Mafia in Sicily, Danilo Dolci concludes "that in order to change a situation one must appeal, whether explicitly or tacitly, to moral rather than material considerations, for they take precedence.... Revolutionary action is, therefore, also that which helps to evolve a new sensitivity, a new capacity, a new culture, new instincts—human nature remade."[13]

In his study of bereavement and social uprooting, *Loss and Change,*[14] the British sociologist Peter Marris contends that people need familiar values and continuity in their social identity if they are to be receptive to change. Both individuals and societies must have secure moorings to which to return before sailing into the unknown waters of change programs that appear risky or threatening. If Marris is right, we should ask ourselves if the U.S. defines its own identity and historical role in ways compatible with the requirements of global justice. To pose the question differently: Do Americans have a self-image of a nation having a unique role in history, or of one that obeys the general laws of history?

C. Is U.S. Society Unique?

Notwithstanding the view held by many American historians, I maintain that this country has no special role to play in world history. The nation's Founding Fathers and its early essayists called America a city set on a hill, a New Jerusalem, a beacon of freedom to light up the entire world.[15]   But whatever may have been the basis for this grandiose view in past centuries, today's Americans should bend their self-images to another reality. The star of nations, as of empires, rises and falls. And every great power—Spain in the Golden Century, Britain under Victoria, France at the height of its cultural prestige—whose star is on the rise, arrogates to itself a special civilizing mission or manifest destiny. Conversely, when their civilizational star is on the wane, great powers depict their decline as apocalyptic catastrophe.

The British economist John White comments on the decline of the West and the ascent of Asian nations in these terms:

> Why is historical method so little in evidence in the international development industry?
>
> By all historical parallels, development in the so-called Third World ought to take the form of the rise of new and competing cultures to contend with the old and dying civilisation which is coterminous with the white western world stretching from California to the Urals. The obvious candidates are in Asia, especially in East Asia, where two societies have succeeded in modernizing on the basis of models of social organization which are historically specific and owe little to the international development industry.
>
> Yet two new factors cast doubt on the relevance of the Toynbee-esque model of the challenge and response of competing cultures:
>
> (1) technology;
> (2) telecommunications.
>
> These factors open the anti-developmental and rather depressing possibility of a single and unchallengable global culture. Can there ever again be a new civilisation?[16]

Those who believe in the uniqueness of the U.S. historical experience also assign general validity to its development model. Paradoxically, the very society said to have a special mission in history is presented as the model for others to imitate. Most American prescriptions for development in the 1950s and 1960s assumed that what worked for the U.S. would also work for Indonesia, Kenya, and Peru. Robert Packenham, in *Liberal America and the Third World*,[17] formulates the value premise underlying America's Third World outreach: that political democracy could be fostered by opening up educational, occupational, and social mobility to lower classes, transforming them thereby into productive and affluent middle classes having a stake in a stable political system friendly to the U.S. Thousands of American agricultural extension agents, road engineers, and industrial project managers fanned out throughout the Third World secure in their conviction that higher productivity was the key to development and that modern institutions could lead to higher productivity. Thus if Thailand was to become modern it should have a graduate school of public administration patterned after those found in Big Ten universities. Or if Brazilian economic planners were to succeed, they must create statistical services like those used by the U.S. Department of Labor's manpower division. The same expert who advised Brazil on labor statistics could then be dispatched to Tunisia to repeat the operation. Or the investment specialist who gave financial counsel to Taiwan could then be flown to Colombia. In short, all societies could learn from the U.S. success story.

This approach has now been consigned to the ashcan: AID and Peace Corps now favor development models drawn from the specific conditions—cultural and political—of each Third World nation. Nevertheless, a residual belief in America's unique position in history continues to shape the development thinking of many policymakers, editorialists, and the public at large.

These people still assume that Third World nations should pursue economic prosperity as a goal and mold their social institutions as a means to that end. One still meets American technicians, bureaucrats, and educators in Asia, Africa, and Latin America who complain that things don't get done because their counterparts do not resemble Americans enough: they are not practical, energetic, punctual, efficient; they are not no-nonsense problem-solvers. One reason why so few qualified American professionals work smoothly with their Third World counterparts—in terms of their own values —is that our own nation's cultural experience has been so homogeneous. With our dream of melting-pots and of "entering the American mainstream"—the recent glorification of ethnic differences notwithstanding—we Americans have not had to become familiar with several languages or cultural frameworks to function successfully within our society. Yet our counterparts in India, Lebanon, Tanzania, and elsewhere have had to do precisely this. Their heterogeneous cultural experience helps immunize them against the illusion that economic, technological, or military superiority can ever mean cultural superiority.

Bluntly put, my point is that the U.S. enjoys no superiority vis-à-vis other nations except in such purely relative domains as technology and managerial practices. More importantly, this nation possesses no special moral wisdom about human rights, democracy, or political maturity which can justify its playing some unique prescriptive role in world affairs. The severe tensions, not to mention contradictions, between our government's rhetoric on human rights and its support of regimes whose loyalty it thinks it "needs" for security reasons is clear evidence that the U.S. behaves like any other power. For too long Americans have naively denied that this country produced "imperialistic" results as it impinged on weaker nations. There is no way to avoid being imperialistic when one is richer, larger, and stronger than others, particularly if one is also monumentally ignorant of others' values.

A more modest appraisal of our country's historical accomplishments might help us render the North-South debates on the New International Economic Order less acrimonious. The U.S. can lay no special claims on the world's resources, has no unique right to decide how the bipolar division of geostrategic influence is to be transformed into a pluripolar redistribution of power. The two superpowers can no longer define the rules of global politics. Some analysts urge that global decisions be vested in an expanded club of "big boys"—the U.S., the Soviet Union, the European Community, Japan, the OPEC nations, and China. This prescription, however, sits ill with over 140 other nations, most of them "developing" countries. According to Roger Fisher, a Harvard law scholar, as he comments on the Iranian hostage issue, "The cure to an international conflict is to understand our interests and those of our adversary, and then to find measures that will solve their problem in a way that solves ours. Punishing governments has not worked in the past and will not work now."[18]

The wider problem is this: global interdependence can be accepted as a positive value by all nations only if it is based on mutuality, not on domination. The quality of interdependence sought is that of two oarsmen rowing their boat together, not that of a rider atop a horse.[19] If the U.S. is to contribute to a new global order founded on reciprocity, it will have to purge its self-image as a unique society with a special mission in history. Unless it does so, the most promising new possibilities in international governance will be eliminated.

Now that Western development models are increasingly criticized, specialists show a new interest in the impact of religious values on social change. Recent events in Iran, Afghanistan, and Saudi Arabia dramatically seize the attention even of secular observers to the role of Islam on political life. The issue is larger than Islam, however: at stake is a new appreciation of the importance of all traditional values in shaping autonomous models of societal development. In most Third World countries traditional and indigenous values bear a religious coloration. Hence it is no idle endeavor to ask whether the attachment of the masses to traditional religion facilitates or hinders development.

D. Does Religion Favor More Global Justice?

Richard Falk, professor of international law at Princeton University, asserts that "awe and mystery are as integral to human experience as bread and reason." After noting the failures of most efforts at global problem-solving, Falk concludes that "[N]o amount of tinkering can fix up the present international system...the future prospects of the human species depend upon internalizing an essentially religious perspective, sufficient to transform secular outlooks that now dominate the destiny of the planet."[20] The editorial writers on London's prestigious journal, *The Economist*, enjoy a reputation as hardheaded, sophisticated analysts of current affairs. Yet they, too, urge us to transcend purely secular viewpoints on history and politics. Writing on the conclave convened to elect Paul VI's successor in August 1978, these editorialists pleaded for the church to stand out "as a Christian beacon in a secular world which may be starting to re-examine its wish to be secular." Three weeks later, a second editorial in *The Economist* observed that the

> late-twentieth century world, with its urge to openness and equality, is also a world which is starting to think that its recent preoccupation with the material aspects of life may be incomplete. It therefore needs a church, Catholic, Orthodox, Protestant, or whatever, prepared to carry the banner for the non-material aspects, and to insist that some kinds of truth—the non-political kinds—are objective and permanent.[21]

In a similar vein Godfrey Gunatilleke, director of Sri Lanka's Centre for Development Studies, laments that "political and religio-cultural components are not kept in the field of vision" of experts and are left outside the "development strategy itself." Gunatilleke blames this omission on "European ideologies of social change and the cognitive system which grew out of the industrial revolution and enthroned the economistic view of society and man."[22]

Finally, let me cite the conservative American sociologist Daniel Bell for whom "The real problem of *modernity* is the problem of belief. To use an unfashionable term, it is a spiritual crisis, since the new anchorages have proved illusory and the old ones have become submerged."[23]

Thus even "experts" now belatedly admit that development entails far more than self-sustained economic growth, modern institutions, or the mastery of new technologies. Development calls for new meaning systems to be created, new bonds of solidarity to be forged. Hence the crucial question: Do religions impede necessary change, or do they, on the contrary, provide dynamism for the development process?

Liberation theologies in Latin America prove that religion need not be the servant of an exploitative status quo. In too many societies, however, religion does operate as "the opium of the masses." Marx, who coined the phrase, was convinced that religious alienation turned men away from the tasks of building history on earth. Otherworldly gods and paradises, he jeered, poison men's minds by garnishing them with dreams of celestial bliss. Religion, in short, abolishes history by making human destiny reside outside history. Religious doctrines, Marx added, negate humanism and perpetuate injustice by promising happiness to people who remain alienated in the real world. The same passion displayed by Marx led André Breton, the French surrealist poet, to stigmatize Jesus Christ as "that eternal thief of human energies." No community of religious believers can ignore the challenge posed to its values today, not only by Marx or Breton, but by secularization processes everywhere. Can any religion offer a convincing rationale why men and women should build history even as they strive to bear witness to transcendence?[24] Can any religion hold to a humanistic philosophy of history that incites faith in the future of the world while making commitment to today's historical tasks an inescapable duty?

As we try to answer these questions, may I suggest a comparison between the "coefficient of secular commitment" found in Marxism and that attaching to Teilhard de Chardin's version of Christianity. It is not necessary to repeat here the argument I have made in an earlier essay.[25] But two points are worth noting: (1) that the coefficient of secular commitment can be applied to *all* religions, and (2) that a few key doctrines of religion can be fruitfully examined to determine how "serious" that religion is about insertion in history.

One vital arena is the way in which any religion values time itself: is earthly life simply a means to some paradise beyond this world, or is it rather some end having its own dignity and worth? Throughout his long life the Christian philosopher Jacques Maritain struggled to define, for pluralistic and secular twentieth-century societies, a model of humanism that treats achievements in art, politics, culture, and science as "infra-valent" ends.[26] Infra-valent ends are not simply means to other-worldly ends; they are goals having their own final value, even though these goals rank lower in the order of being than the absolute ultimate goal (eternal blissful union with a loving God). Maritain distinguished two brands of humanism: anthropocentric (man-centered), and theocentric (God-centered). Both forms see human achievements as worthy in themselves and not merely as means serving higher purposes. Historical time and material life are valuable for their own sake, not merely as stepping-stones to celestial rewards. Therefore, the ethical "goodness" of persons is judged not primarily in terms of their subjective intentions, but according to their objective contributions to the betterment of human societies. Theocentric humanists—be they Hindus, Buddhists, Christians, or Muslims—are called to work on behalf of greater economic justice, not because this is a precondition for God's triumph, but because social improvement is an urgent human duty in its own right. To scorn creatures is, in short, to despise their creator.

Teilhard de Chardin once contrasted the pagan with the true Christian humanist. The pagan, he says, loves the earth in order to enjoy it; the Christian, *loving it no less,* does so in order to make it purer and draw from it the strength to escape from it. For Teilhard, however, escape is not a flight from reality but the transcendental opening or "issue" which alone confers final meaning on the cosmos.[27] Chardin finds no pretext, however subtle or "spiritual," which justifies inertia in religious believers confronted with pressing secular tasks to accomplish: knowledge and wisdom to be won, justice to be forged, creativity to be unleashed, political friendship to be instituted, authentic human development to be achieved.

A second arena in which a religion's coefficient of insertion in secular affairs may be judged is eschatology—the realm of "last things" or the final destiny of human effort. If gods are portrayed as dramatic saviors who "bail humanity out" in spite of its sins and errors, human beings will be tempted to "sin by omission" in the face of their ecological responsibilities, their political duty to reduce armaments, their social vocation to abolish misery. A crucial link exists between a religiously inspired commitment to human tasks and whatever "final redemption," "nirvana," or "paradise" is postulated. In religions with a high coefficient of insertion in history, that link is intrinsic and essential, not extrinsic or accidental. We must, as Kazantzakis was fond of saying, help God save us; and by helping Him save us, we also save Him.

Latin American "theologians of liberation"[28] reject purely spiritual views of religion which legitimize passivity in the face of oppressive social structures. Their writings and social experiments interest students of development because these theologians embrace creative tensions between fidelity to the demands of religious mystery and of making history. To make history is to engage in scientific and artistic work, political struggles, efforts to achieve justice and prosperity for all, to alter social structures to meet human needs, and to formulate new moral norms in the face of rapidly changing conditions. Making history and witnessing to transcendence: these are the two dimensions of comprehensive human development.

An important conclusion flows from these reflections: religions, in their triple character as belief systems, ethical codes, and cultural legitimizers, must openly face the new challenges posed to them by the bureaucratization and secularization of human existence. If religions fail to meet these challenges, they become vectors of injustice, not carriers of justice.

Conclusion

"Is Economic Justice Possible?" Greater economic justice *IS* possible, but only at great cost. There are no painless shortcuts to authentic development, no magic buttons we can press to get rid of oppressive structures or generate new wisdoms to match our sciences. And justice itself is a relative moral value, to be pursued in fragile harmony with other moral goods—peace, love, compassion, ecological responsibility, and the political defense of human rights. As history teaches, it is dangerous to reduce morality to one dimension, to the fanatical pursuit of a single virtue—justice, courage, moderation, faith, freedom, tolerance, or social order. As Camus warns, "the long fight for justice exhausts the love that nevertheless gave birth to it. In the clamor in which we live, love is impossible and *justice does not suffice.*"[29]

The central moral tension of the twentieth century lies at the intersection of justice and freedom. George Orwell in *1984,* B.F. Skinner in *Walden Two,* and Ursula K. LeGuin in *The Dispossessed* depict utopias in which one-dimensional quests for justice at the expense of freedom, or freedom at the expense of justice, lead to hellish paradises for depersonalized robots or to somber cosmic catastrophes.

The task of reconciling conflicts between freedom and justice is a delicate one. Equally difficult is that of harmonizing the demands of justice with the requirements of peace. Ancient philosophers called justice one of the four hinges, or cardinal virtues upon which all others hang. Justice shared honors with prudence, fortitude, and temperance: all four had to be present in the right balance for integral moral life to exist.

Yet, although justice is not the only ethical value to be realized in the world, there is a sense in which the thirst for justice is the touchstone of any person's commitment to integral moral goodness. The Greek word for justice, *dikeia,* signifies wholeness, the totality of what is right and just as established by custom, legal sanction, and correct judgment. A just person was one who displayed *all* ethical qualities; the term corresponded to the Latin notion of a virtuous individual—one who allies moral rectitude with strength of character. And when André Schwartz-Bart, in his moving novel *The Last of the Just,* evokes the Just One—the Lamed Vov—he resurrects a centuries-old Hasidic tradition about men who incarnate total human goodness (piety, courage, love, wisdom, compassion, etc.), not simply the virtue of "justice" in the restricted sense. Schwartz-Bart writes: "if just one of them were lacking, the sufferings of mankind would poison even the souls of the newborn, and humanity would suffocate with a single cry."[30]

May we properly conclude, then, that justice is only a tiny stone in the larger mosaic of essential ethical values? No, for if justice is absent, life in society becomes unlivable. Justice ranks highest in the constellation of ethical goals because it is a platform of convergence around which other values coalesce. In this sense, then, the term "social justice" can express all that is implied in the word "authentic development."

Let me now summarize my argument. The creation of justice, and of sound development, is possible only if we hold certain conceptions of history and of politics, if we abandon the illusion that the U.S. holds a unique place in the history of human societies, if we pursue justice in delicate balance with other relative ethical values, and if we fully commit religion to secular tasks.

This, you will say, is a tall order. Indeed it is: but to strive for anything less is to condemn ourselves to one of the twin illusions denounced by Barrington Moore earlier—the impotence of clinging to a permanent status quo, or the opposite folly of romantic utopianism. We need a creative utopianism which accepts politics as the art of creating new possibilities.

The chorus of pessimistic voices around us might well dissuade us from trying to change history. Perhaps so, but Joan Robinson pointedly reminds us that "Anyone who writes a book, however gloomy its message might be, is necessarily an optimist. If the pessimists really believed what they were saying there would be no point in saying it."[31]

Economic justice, in the U.S. and in the world at large, will be possible if we make it possible. Ultimately, we have no choice but to try to make it possible. Henry Miller, author of *Sexus, Plexus, Nexus,* and other delightfully shocking novels, is no dreamy-eyed Utopian or naive moralist. Yet, when he was interviewed twenty years ago on the future of human history, Miller replied that "it is not our religious convictions but the very conditions of our life on earth which will make angels of us."[32] Realism, in other words, obliges us to forge new possibilities.

Social activists readily despair when, after repeated failures, they keep discovering how difficult it is to change any society's basic institutions. Yet E.M. Cioran, our old pessimistic and cynical philosopher friend, tells us that "paradise was unendurable, otherwise the first man would have adapted to it."[33]

As we struggle to build a better earth we should get rid of images of paradise. Our earth to be built—to be made fraternal and just—is far more endurable to us, ambiguous beings and feeble emergences of the spirit, than any Utopian paradise could be.

It does not suffice, however, to show that greater economic justice is a possibility, given the dynamics of history. We must also inquire concretely into a second question: "Can the United States help build a just world?" This is the topic of the second half of this chapter, which is now addressed.

II. CAN THE U.S. HELP BUILD A JUST WORLD?

David Noble, economist and social critic, calls the United States "a remarkably dynamic society that goes nowhere." He observes that

> [M]odern Americans confront a world in which everything changes, yet nothing moves. The perpetual rush to novelty that characterizes the modern marketplace, with its escalating promise of technological transcendence, is matched by the persistence of pre-formed patterns of life which promise merely more of the same.... Every new, seemingly bold departure ends by following an already familiar path.[34]

Noble probably exaggerates; yet change agents should ask themselves not only how the United States can make its own social order more humane, but whether it can help build a just world. If we are to succeed, writes John Gardner, founder of Common Cause:

> We must encompass all of American life in our vision; and, what is more, the vision can't be limited to our nation. Unless there's a destiny for the planet, there isn't a destiny for any of us. We're going to have to fashion a world in which each group is free to develop its own variations on a universal value system that honors justice, peace, and the worth of each person.[35]

Gardner, in effect, pleads for a world of authentic development when he calls for "a universal value system that honors justice, peace, and the worth of each person." Authentic development

> aims at the full realization of human capabilities: men and women become makers of their own histories, personal and societal. They free themselves from every servitude imposed by nature or by oppressive systems, they achieve wisdom in their mastery over nature and over their own wants, they create new webs of solidarity based not on domination but on reciprocity among themselves, they achieve a rich symbiosis between contemplation and transforming action, between efficiency and free expression. This total concept of development can perhaps best be expressed as "human ascent"—the ascent of all men in their integral humanity, including the economic, biological, psychological, social, cultural, ideological, spiritual, mystical, and transcendental dimensions.[36]

This normative conception of development goes far beyond economic performance, or purely social and political achievements: it deals head-on with the underlying values of the good life and the just society. Such a humanistic approach can be found in the pioneer work of L. J. Lebret, creator of the "Economy and Humanism" movement in 1942, as in Gandhi's campaign for indigenous Indian patterns of modernity around production by the masses instead of mass production.

Fortunately, development experts now confess the bankruptcy of their earlier views.[37] No longer do they speak of stages of growth: instead they seek alternative strategies that combine equity with growth, cultural creativity over standard solutions to problems, and resource transfers that promote self-reliance instead of perpetuating dependency. The main components of these new strategies are:

meeting basic needs as a first priority, promoting self-reliance, and building on the latent dynamisms present in traditional value systems.[38] Those elements do not necessarily coexist in harmony, however: on the contrary, they are usually found in a state of tension one with another. As I have noted elsewhere: "Self-reliance can be an obstacle to meeting basic needs when available resources are few. Similarly, building on local values can strengthen counterdevelopmental tendencies rooted in hierarchical privilege systems which still enjoy cultural legitimacy."[39] What ties these disparate elements together, making of them a coherent strategy, is political leadership committed to changing institutions in society to make its development goals attainable. But leaders will retain their developmental mandate only if they keep in touch with the hopes of the people at the base. (I avoid the term "masses" because it connotes an impersonal, amorphous collection of people, not living persons and communities with a wide range of values and aspirations.)

In every international development forum—the United Nations, the World Bank, the OECD, GATT, the Group of 77, etc.—we hear ringing endorsements of growth with equity. But a growth-with-equity strategy cannot be sustained in most fragile Third World nations unless global institutions support their efforts. In 1980 a conference was held in Nairobi on this very theme: international support systems for the basic-human-need strategies in developing countries. [40] Admittedly, the circulation systems that now govern resource flows across national boundaries—flows of goods, capital, technology, and information—are neither as equitable nor as efficient as they should be. The present international order, in other words, is simultaneously unjust and dysfunctional; hence the Third World's demand for a new International Economic Order.[41] It is not enough, however, merely to urge new development models upon poor nations or to plead for a new international order: we also need to raise basic questions about the validity of our own society's development.

With these queries as background, I should now like to address two questions:

    A. Is the U.S. a genuinely developed nation? and,
    B. What measures should this country take to make the
       world more just?

A. Is the U.S. a Genuinely Developed Nation?

World Bank publications rank the United States among the world's most advanced countries, with the fifth highest GNP per capita in the world, after Kuwait, Switzerland, Sweden and Denmark. Yet 99 percent of U.S. adults are literate, in contrast to 60 percent for Kuwait. And the annual per capita consumption of energy for the U.S., measured in kilograms of coal equivalent, is 11,554 as compared with 3,342 for Switzerland and 6,046 for Sweden. [42] Americans own more cars, telephones, and stereo sets than citizens of any other country, but are they more developed than others? The answer depends on how one measures development. While writing about North American Indians, Barry Lopez notes that:

> A psychiatrist who for the past several years has worked with Navajo singers (medicine men) claims that their medicine is more complex than any of ours—with the possible exception of open-heart surgery—and as efficacious in many instances.
>
> Some native ideas could serve us well in this historical moment: that a concept of wealth should be founded in physical health and spiritual well-being, not material possessions; that to be "poor" is to be without a family, without a tribe—without people who care deeply for you. [43]

Even Zbigniew Brzezinski, President Carter's national security advisor, admits that material goods are not enough. In his interview with James Reston in December, 1978, Brzezinski stated that:

> The crisis of contemporary democracy associated with inflation is a product of a culture in which 5 per cent more of material goods per annum is the definition of happiness. People are discovering that it isn't.... Ultimately, every human being, once he reaches the stage of self-consciousness, wants to feel that there is some inner and deeper meaning to his existence than just being and consuming, and once he begins to feel that way, he wants his social organization to correspond to that feeling; whereas some aspects of our social organization, the vulgar and crass commercialism, correspond largely only to the desires of the stomach, in a figurative sense, to the consumptive [sic!] ethic. I think modern man is discovering this isn't enough. [44]

Many American social critics likewise question whether prosperity or technological advance can define development. One thinks here of Galbraith's *The Affluent Society* and *The New Industrial State,* Erich Fromm's *To Have or to Be?,* Daniel Bell's *The Cultural Contradictions of Capitalism,* John Friedmann's *Retracking America,* Edgar Friedenberg's *The Disposal of Liberty and Other Industrial*

Wastes, the book by Peter Berger and Richard Neuhaus, *To Em-power People,* and Hazel Henderson's *Creating Alternative Futures: The End of Economics.* Across all ideological, professional, and age boundaries Americans yearn to find a better image of what the good life—or genuine development—is.

In his novel *The Plague* Camus wrote that he knew all that was important about a city if he learned how its people worked, loved, and died. Similarly, Freud observed late in life that the best sign of a healthy personality is that one can love and work with pleasure— *lieben und arbeiten!* These criteria do not match what Studs Terkel reported in his book *Working.*[45]   In hundreds of interviews with American workers, from coal-miners to waiters and hookers, Terkel learned that most people derived little pleasure from their jobs. They were resigned to work as a necessary evil, simply a means to earn money which they would then spend, often in fatiguing and boring ways which brought them no deep satisfactions. The prolif-eration of ego-stroking institutes—Esalen, EST, TM, Arica, etc.— is evidence enough that affluence in America bears little relation to the good life or to genuine human development.[46] Luxury, comfort, and new gadgets are so unrewarding because material wealth and technological mastery are instrumental goods. Their value rests on two criteria: how well they serve as means to obtain more basic goods, and whether they are bought at too high a price.

I cannot here review the vast literature on the good life, new cultural styles, and sources of meaning which now abounds in the United States. One conclusion stands out sharply in all these writ-ings: namely, that abundant goods do not necessarily confer the fullness of good. Erich Fromm is right to remind us that "'affluent alienation' is no less dehumanizing than 'impoverished aliena-tion.'"[47]

In his suggestive novel *Things,* Georges Perenc traces the des-tiny of an upwardly mobile young married couple who end up de-stroying themselves by their attachment to things and to the social status they derive from possessions.

A truly developed society provides a decent sufficiency of essential goods to all its members, and it offers support structures for human interactions which facilitate exchanges that are just, reciprocal, and fulfilling. This it does while creating a new symbiosis with nature in ways that are ecologically sound. Development of this type is impossible in the absence of a sound theory of needs, what Galbraith calls a "view of what the production is ultimately for."[48]

The late social psychologist, Abraham Maslow, perhaps America's best-known need theorist, posits a hierarchy in which higher needs— spiritual, intellectual, and aesthetic—can only be felt and satisfied after lower ones are met.[49] In real-life conditions of underdevelopment, however, poor people spend considerable resources on celebration, ritual, and gratuitous pleasures long before they have gotten enough of the essential goods. Life must be lived to the fullest even by those who have nothing. I recall an incident while living in a slum quarter of Madrid in 1957 in which a penniless factory worker's wife bitterly complained to me that well-meaning helpers deprive poor helpees of the pleasure of giving.

It helps, I think, to classify needs into three categories: subsistence needs, or those of the first order; enhancement needs; and luxury needs.

1. Needs of the First Order

Food, clothing, and shelter are required for survival. Also included in this category of goods are those without which protection and security against nature and hostile organisms are impossible. Other kinds of first-order goods enable members of society to accomplish mandatory tasks: thus fishermen need boats, nets, and bait, and chefs need cooking utensils. One's working tools, in short, are goods of first necessity. So, too, are training and education, at least to the extent required for survival and mutual protection.

The first regulatory principle, therefore, is that major productive energies in all economies should be harnessed to satisfy first-order needs before being diverted to goods that meet other needs.

2. Enhancement Needs

All individuals and societies seek to express themselves in diverse ways: through language, gesture, symbolic activity, silence, and display. Beyond expression, however, men and women need to create and to actualize their latent capacities. In order to do so they must have access to goods that enable them to invent, explore, and bring their capacities to maturity. Such needs are called enhancement needs because they are not directly ordered to utilitarian functions except insofar as they contribute to expression and creation. Enhancement needs are of two general types: what psychologists call "actualization needs," and what philosophers term "needs of transcendence." For Herbert Marcuse transcendence means the sustained capacity of human communities to choose futures that are not merely the logical outcome or extrapolated projection of their present. Transcendence is the creation of alternatives to what has to be in virtue of what has already been. Whatever may be the ultimate meaning of human life, it is more than simple existence. Beyond subsistence, survival, and utility, human beings have an endless range of enhancement needs, the satisfaction of which perfects them and thrusts them beyond perceived limits.

Hence the second rule: after needs of the first order have been met the major productive energies of society ought to provide goods and services that best satisfy the actualization and transcendence needs of all.

3. Luxury Needs

While commenting on wasteful display and luxury, Thorsten Veblen noted that "In view of economic theory the expenditure in question is no more and no less legitimate than any other expenditure. It is here called 'waste' because this expenditure does not serve human life or human well-being on the whole, not because it is waste or misdirection of effort or expenditure as viewed from the standpoint of the individual consumer who chooses it."[50] Although economists often treat the distinction between objective and subjective need as unscientific, because it involves value judgments that go beyond the simple analysis of preference or demand, they nevertheless must help determine themselves what is "reasonable" expenditure and what is "waste." Paul Baran claims that if society forbids the economy to cater to the tastes of drug addicts, it should logically and rationally overrule consumer preferences, even when they are expressed with effective purchasing power, if these are foolish, frivolous, or wasteful. According to Baran, soundly focused research can lead to objective judgments on cultural requirements as well as on biological needs.[51]

Luxury does not always exercise a debilitating effect on human virtue. Historians of culture describe the great contribution to all civilizations made by wasteful luxurious expenditures.[52] Moralists sometimes exaggerate the merits of poverty and overestimate the dangers inherent in wealth.

Apologists of luxury usually err at the other extreme by overlooking two important facts—one psychological, the other political. Psychologically, it is a sign of shallowness, perhaps even of pathology, for individuals to ground their identity and sense of importance on having luxury goods rather than goods that enhance their actualization and transcendence needs. Toynbee insists that the Gospel injunction "What does it profit a man to gain the whole world and all the riches thereof, if he lose his own soul?" applies to societies as well as to persons. If all people living on earth were adequately fed, clothed, and housed, some individuals might perhaps be allowed to indulge in their luxury fantasies. But massive wastefulness and luxurious display coexist alongside dehumanizing need: a relative superfluity of goods is enjoyed by a tiny minority while the majority suffers from an absolute insufficiency of goods. Political realism and moral objectivity alike dictate new priorities in production.

A third general principle derived from this brief classification of needs condemns as irrational and immoral the use of large portions of a society's production capabilities for luxury goods while more essential needs of large numbers remain unsatisfied. Luxury goods can improve the quality of human life for some, but no moral, political, or psychological justification exists for granting luxury needs equal or higher priority than the global satisfaction of survival and enhancement needs.[53] As Gandhi used to say: "There are enough resources to meet the needs of all, but not enough to satisfy the wants of each one."

The ancient Fathers of the Christian church were fond of pointing out that material goods do not satisfy us because they simply generate more desires, whereas spiritual goods satisfy us more deeply and free us from new desires. This doctrine runs directly counter to David McClelland's assertion that "achievement motivation" is the key to bringing satisfactions to people.[54] He says that passive Third World people must be taught to desire more.

Beyond the level of individual psychology, we should question the capacity of markets to respond to true needs. Barbara Ward judges that "A market system, wholly uncorrected by institutions of justice, sharing, and solidarity, makes the strong stronger and the weak weaker.... Markets as masters of society enrich the rich and pauperize the poor."[55] Although a want is not necessarily a true need, to the pure market economist an effective want is simply what somebody is willing and able to pay for.

Yet competition among unequals necessarily stigmatizes weaker players. Accordingly, as Mannheim wrote almost thirty years ago, a qualitative difference exists between market competition as the organizing principle of an economy and as a regulatory mechanism.[56] Markets should play a role as a subordinate mechanism to stimulate and rationalize supply and demand, but they cannot assure equitable distribution if they serve as the organizing principle of economic life. To state the point differently, in competitive arenas equality of opportunity cannot assure equality of results.[57]

Given the great resiliency of American society, one can plausibly argue that the trade-off in this land is between social efficiency and welfare, and that structural injustices wrought by market forces can be offset by political action, legislation, and income distribution. [58]

Indeed the failure of socialist appeals to win popular support in the 1930s is largely traceable to this resiliency in American society: labor unions won legal rights to conduct collective bargaining, and Roosevelt's New Deal provided economic protection to workers victimized by the capitalist system. In the 1980s the functional equivalent of legitimizing labor unions in the 1930s is worker management. As recently as the fall of 1979, James O'Toole, director of the Center for Future Research at the University of Southern California, pleaded once again the case for worker-management in U.S. workplaces. O'Toole is the social anthropologist who created shock waves in American academic circles by voluntarily renouncing his tenure at the University of Southern California, preferring to work on a year-by-year basis.[59] Writing in the Op-Ed page of the *New York Times,*[60] O'Toole states that what ails the American economy is a declining national productivity/labor-cost ratio, "that is, the total compensation of workers is rising faster than their output of goods and services." But international competition is so keen, he adds, that "Americans cannot continue to demand more from work while producing less." His solution is to give new incentives to workers, only 20 percent of whom are engaged in directly productive tasks, with the remaining 80 percent assigned to managerial, clerical, sales, technical, and other service jobs. O'Toole wants workers to have high compensation and a generous package of social entitlements, but these rewards should be tied to their productivity levels. The way to tie the two, he explains, is to let workers manage their firms, decide on salary scales, levels and types of output, work rules, and even marketing strategies. He applauds the example of a small company in Holland, Michigan—Donnelly Mirrors—which provides managerial information to its workers to aid their decisions and commits itself to a policy of long-term full employment. This company's pilot experience convinces O'Toole of the viability of a system, quite widespread in Europe, in which "workers don't demand or get pay or benefits that exceed the productive capacity to pay for them."[61]

My intent here is not to debate the merits of the Donnelly Mirror model, or to assess the pros and cons of the workers' capitalism scheme advanced by Louis Kelso who promotes his book, *Two-Factor Theory*,[62] with the colorful phrase: How To Turn Eighty Million Workers into Capitalists on Borrowed Money. The great popularity of schemes like Kelso's testifies to their appeal to large numbers of blue- and white-collar workers. This very popularity, however, warns social analysts that the United States will not necessarily embrace socialism even if the collective consciousness of its citizens regarding the structural defects of capitalism becomes more acute and widespread. As I have written elsewhere:

> Italian author Guido Piovene once compared the United States to a huge digestive system. All kinds of abrasives can be introduced into it. But, like the oyster, it has an infinite capacity to secrete social gastric juices which transform the rough stones of dissent into smooth pearls of conformity.[63]

There are no neat, easy-change strategies for the United States, a big, diverse, and sprawling society whose tolerance for contradictions is enormous. In my opinion, American capitalism will undergo profound changes. The main reason is that, as Daniel Bell observes in *The Cultural Contradictions of Capitalism*,[64] our society is torn apart by a "disjunction" of the political, economic, and cultural realms: each obeys a different set of ground rules or what Bell calls "axial principles." That the system must change drastically is granted even by so conservative an economist as Henry Wallich, formerly of Yale and now on the Federal Reserve Board of Governors. Wallich concludes that capitalism can survive and that corporations can remain profitable even if a widespread nationalization of corporate productive assets takes place.[65] Does this mean that America is moving toward socialism? If so, it certainly is creeping at a snail's pace.

In my view, the transformations now occurring in the U.S. economic system are leading not to socialism but to new hybrids that combine elements of socialism with functional residues drawn from several phases of evolutionary capitalism. New hybrid patterns will continue to take shape from the dialectical interplay—in theory, in political debate, and in social experimentation—which will, I believe, grow more pronounced and more intense in this country.

In questions of development, it is the better part of wisdom not to apply models derived elsewhere to one's own country. Those models that work best always come from critical reflection on the social experimentation conducted within the specific conditions of a particular society. As the dialectical processes—ideological, technological, political, educational and mythical (through media images and fads, both so much a part of American life)—work themselves out over time, and as new approaches are tried in concrete policy arenas—energy, new blends of work and recreation, new patterns of social auditing, approaches to housing[66]—there may emerge in the U.S. a qualitatively different system that is neither capitalism nor socialism. And indeed, given the atrocious performance of socialist societies in the domain of political liberties, and socialism's resultant "bad image" for most Americans, there are distinct advantages to not posing alternatives to present patterns under the banner of socialism. Change agents who do so carry a dead, and deadly, linguistic albatross around their necks. Similar considerations have led leaders in newly independent Guinea-Bissau to avoid labeling their own experiments with political labels drawn from outside their own specific conditions.[67]

My tentative predictions about U.S. society do not rest on the assumption that only small incremental changes can take place. On the contrary, severe disruptions in the world's economic and political arenas may well prepare the way for abrupt discontinuous social mutations within U.S. society. This cumbersome phrase—abrupt discontinuous social mutations—suggests revolutionary change. It is intended to do so, for it reflects the view that needed revolutionary changes can only occur in the United States in the wake of dramatic breakdowns in our present system of social accommodation by innovation, critique, absorption, and partial repudiation.

We have asked ourselves a question: "Is the U.S. a genuinely developed nation?" The answer is: No, but it must strive to become one. We now move to our second query: Can the U.S. help make the world more just?

B. How Can the U.S. Help to Make the World More Just?

Wide agreement now exists over the main values to be promoted in a new world order: universal economic justice (providing the basic needs of all as the first priority of economic effort), a minimum of violence in the conduct of societal affairs (this refers to war, to the systemic violence of exploitation, and to terroristic counter-violence), broad popular participation in important decisions affecting people, and ecological responsibility.[68] But very little agreement exists regarding how international systems must be changed in order to arrive at structures supportive of these four values.[69] As we narrow the issue still further, we are led to ask: What should the U.S. do to help correct structural inequities in the world? As we approach this question we are nearly paralyzed by the conflicting interests and values that influence foreign-policy decisions in this nation. Nevertheless, we may fruitfully organize diverse information and competing analyses around two unifying principles: first, the concept of targeting resources to eliminate the worst aspects of absolute poverty by the year 2000, and second, a three-fold scenario of alternative policies in North-South relations. A brief comment on each is now in order.

1. Eliminating Absolute Poverty

The World Bank's *1979 World Development Report* declares that

> Absolute poverty is not likely to be eliminated by the year 2000. Nonetheless, substantial progress could be achieved through a combination of higher growth, improved income distribution, and reduced fertility. These projections emphasize the need to seek every possible means to support the future growth of developing countries.[70]

And World Bank President Robert McNamara placed absolute poverty at the center of the development problem in these words:

> If we focus on the ultimate objectives of development, it is obvious that an essential one must be the liberation of the 800 million individuals in the developing world who are trapped in absolute poverty—a condition of life so limited by malnutrition, illiteracy, disease, high infant-mortality, and low life-expectancy as to be below any rational definition of human decency.
>
> As I have argued before, this requires that the traditional growth approach be supplemented by a direct concern with the basic needs of the poor.[71]

The first quotation states that "absolute poverty is not likely to be eliminated by the year 2000." This does not mean, however, that substantial progress is beyond our reach. On the contrary, elimination of the worst aspects of absolute poverty by the year 2000 has been set as a goal by many people and agencies working in the field of development. What, in concrete terms, does such targeting comprise?

The Overseas Development Council (ODC), a nongovernmental research institute in Washington, D.C., proposes common goals to be pursued by all countries:

- raising the life-expectancy of all persons in the world from the present level of 48 years to 65
- bringing the world's literacy rate from 34 percent to 75 percent
- reducing infant-mortality rates from the present 125 per 1,000 births to 50
- lowering the birth rate from the current 39 per 1,000 to 25 [72]

Obviously these targets, which all relate to the physical and social quality of life, cannot be reached unless goals of increased production and greater resource transfers are also defined. These goals center on:

- increasing food production capacities
- creating large numbers of paid jobs for people with few skills
- providing basic goods and services at low cost to people lacking buying power
- creating incentive systems that quickly give poor masses a stake in higher productivity for their economic systems

It is also widely agreed that if these objectives are to be reached three related growth goals must also be met. These are:

- doubling food production in poor countries (by capitalizing presently underutilized human and physical resources)
- doubling per capita incomes (through investment, tax, credit, and employment policies)
- reducing the social disparities between rich and poor countries and regions by one half (as measured by the Physical Quality of Life Index and the Disparity Reduction Rate, two instruments devised by the Overseas Development Council as social indicators of progress) [73]

After calculating the probable costs of such an ambitious program, ODC concludes that eliminating the worst features of absolute poverty by the year 2000 is a feasible goal for most developing countries on two conditions: (1) that their leaders be truly committed to meeting the basic needs of their poor; and (2) that these countries be reasonably assured at the outset of receiving sustained outside support. [74] Appropriate outside support means, more concretely, a two-pronged strategy in which rich industrial countries: (a) provide much more financial aid to low-income countries; and (b) adopt a package of coherent measures aimed at developing the economic potential of middle-income countries. This package would include increased opportunities in international trade, better access to private financial markets, expanded credit from international financial institutions, improved scientific and technological cooperation from the North, and major changes in the international division of labor in the global economy. The strategy also calls for a doubling of aid from rich nations, targeted in ways which are not interventionist, yet which meet basic need priorities of the poorest populations. Part of the additional resource flows are also intended to benefit the economics of rich countries: to provide them with jobs, to help fight global inflation, and to create a climate of better political collaboration across all national boundaries.

The vital issue in all this is linkage between a basic human needs (BHN) strategy for the world's poor and the precise contours to be given to the New International Economic Order (NIEO) now being urged by the Third World. The African scholar Alfred Tévoédjrè suggests using "contracts of solidarity," an idea which now has gained considerable support in Third World circles.[75] These contracts, to be practiced or desired, are instruments specifically designed to offset the weaker bargaining power of poor nations and institutions. In January 1980 in Dakar, the first Congress of the World Social Prospects Study Association founded by Tévoédjrè, a historian and social scientist, assigned one of its four commissions to study the contract idea further. The concept is new and requires more operational research; yet even at this early stage it represents a valuable attempt to establish new models of international exchange marked by reciprocity, not domination. Contracts of solidarity are seen by their proponents as useful ways to break the logjam between the North and South over how to reconcile NIEO themes and advocacy of a BHN strategy. Regarding this logjam, the Pakistani economist Mahbub ul Haq, now a policy advisor to the World Bank, complains that the

> real disappointment of the first phase of these negotiations is not that the North has not accepted the specific proposals put forward by the South. The real disappointment has been that the North has not put forward any counterproposals that it considered more reasonable. The North has been content to remain frozen in an essentially defensive posture.[76]

Because the posture of the United States, the main Northern interlocutor in the North-South dialogue, is so crucial, it is worth analyzing here. Roger Hansen, a political scientist at Johns Hopkins University and former advisor to Zbigniew Brzezinski, identifies three alternative postures the U.S. might take in responding to Third World demands.[77] He calls them: the graduation scenario, the global reform model, and the Basic Needs formula.

2. The Graduation Scenario

Under the graduation scenario the U.S. would seek to ease North-South tensions by welcoming into the select club of global decision-makers a few "responsible" new members, who would thereby acquire a greater stake in making the present international system work better. The technique is one of selective co-optation; likely candidates for membership include Brazil, Mexico, Venezuela, Nigeria, Saudi Arabia, India, Algeria, and perhaps a few others. Hansen identifies four criteria[78] that render "upper-tier" countries eligible for "graduation" into the club of influential decision-makers in global arenas:

- rapidly growing industrial strength
- emerging financial importance
- actual or potential nuclear power with significant regional military potential
- natural resource abundance

Other elements, like strategic location, may sometimes qualify a country, but the "upper-tier" label is reserved, for the most part, for the four categories just noted.

Graduation, with its correlative integration, implies a bargain of some kind. Advantages accruing to new members of the Northern Club include membership in the OECD, increased voting power in the World Bank and other international financial institutions, more prior consultation by the U.S. and other Northern powers in bilateral and multilateral forums. In exchange, new members in the club of "major league" stewards of the international system are expected to help maintain the system by shoring up the "free world" against Soviet encroachments, by contributing to underwrite the system-maintenance costs of international monetary arrangements, and by helping shape the course of economic development and political evolution in their respective regions in ways compatible with the objectives of the countries of the North. Such authors as Thomas Farer,

C. Fred Bergsten,[79] and Hansen may disagree over the concrete economic, political, and institutional measures required by the graduation or integration model. But all concede that the graduation scenario overlaps with other approaches and that it does not necessarily exclude the integration of all Third World countries over a longer time span. The central premise of the graduation model, however, is that special attention has to be paid by rich countries to understanding the trade and investment needs of upper-tier developing countries, to increasing their global status in international organizations, and to giving them greater freedom from interference in defining their own domestic policies and modalities of exercising regional influence.

Central to the graduation scenario is the belief that crises can be solved without basically changing the present international system: minor adjustments here and there will suffice.

3. The Global Reform Model

Those who criticize the graduation/integration model, however, say that it is naive and founded on the false premise that the present global system can correct itself: that is, that it can generate widespread development in the Third World and greater global economic efficiency as measured by reduced inflation, the avoidance of recession, relative stabilization of prices in the major sectors of international trade, and a high degree of satisfaction in the world at large with the international division of labor which emerges from the market system. These critics judge present structures to be incapable of assuring development for most nations, equity in global exchanges, and a credible political stake in world stability. Therefore, they plead for far-reaching changes, a complete overhaul of the system. Nevertheless, since many of them are realistic negotiators, they concede that the reform process must somehow meet the essential interests of rich and poor countries alike. Hence they seek to overcome the blockages created by two conflicting emphases in reform proposals. Poor countries call for a NIEO and stress the interstate equity issue: parity and fairness among nations. In contrast, most suggestions emanating from rich countries—often from nongovernmental groups sympathetic to Third World demands—stress equity inside national boundaries, that is, getting resources transferred and the benefits issuing from growth to reach the poorest masses. They favor a Basic Human Needs and Human Rights approach to problems of absolute poverty.

The G-77 Arusha statement of 1979 warns us not to use the BHN approach as a substitute for global reform. We are told that

> While the satisfaction of basic human needs of the people, and the eradication of mass poverty have a high priority in economic and social development, the idea is unacceptable and erroneous that these goals can be achieved without the all-round and comprehensive economic development of the developing countries and the establishment of the New International Economic Order. It is necessary for developing countries to guard against the introduction of new concepts by developed countries, norms and principles, such as "basic needs," access to supplies, graduation, selectivity, etc., which are being suggested but are in fact totally incompatible with the development requirements and aspirations of developing countries.[80]

Structural reforms demanded by champions of a NIEO bear on six domains: liberalization of trade, the strengthening of international financial institutions, foreign economic assistance, automatic resource transfers, the institution of global regimes, and pleas for a holistic approach to population stabilization. Trade reform centers on tariffs, export and import quotas, credits and other instruments of global commerce, the aim being to create conditions enabling poor countries to compete on equal terms with developed nations. In international finance, the main issues are debt burdens, democratization of the capital base of financial institutions, and shifts in voting power to Third World members. Under the rubric of "assistance," reformists demand that Northern countries truly meet whatever aid targets are agreed upon internationally—0.7 percent of GNP, or 1 percent, or whatever. A far more crucial instrument of change is automatic transfer of resources, in effect, a binding tax on certain resources that Third World countries can count on receiving uninterruptedly. Among devices to be used to secure automatic resource transfers to poorer countries, Mahbub ul Haq suggests: larger shares of liquid capital generated by the IMF through Special Drawing Rights on the sale of gold, international taxes on nonrenewable resources, pollutants, multinational corporate activities, and commercial activities arising out of international commons like the ocean beds, outer space, the Antarctic, etc.; taxes on armaments expenditures and international civil servants, and rebates to country of origin of taxes collected on earnings of trained immigrants from poor countries.[81] The rubric "global regimes" refers to new ground rules for assuring enough food for everyone, for allocating ocean-bed and space resources to those most in need, and for rendering technology available to poor countries on other than purely commercial terms. All these measures are intended to compensate for the weak competitive position of developing countries.

Robert McNamara has recently repeated his long-held view that "short of nuclear war itself it [i.e., population] is the gravest issue that the world faces over the decades immediately ahead."[82] Increasingly, however, consensus is forming, within development circles, over the need to achieve comprehensive socioeconomic improvement if population stabilization measures are to be adopted by interested couples. The three key linkage points between fertility reduction and socioeconomic development are: basic health care and education, economic growth aimed at raising the living standards of society's poorest members, and upgrading the status of women. The role Northern countries should play in this holistic approach to the population question is to support decisions taken by Southern nations on the basis of clearly perceived interest. Only thus can new modes of North-South cooperation be generated around demographic issues.

These remarks show how far the global reform model takes us beyond the graduation scenario. Let us now turn to the examination of the third policy alternative listed by Roger Hansen, the Basic Needs approach.

4. Abolishing Absolute Poverty/Meeting Basic Needs

In 1977, the Secretary of State, Cyrus Vance, made the case for a Basic Needs approach in these terms:

> Almost one billion people live in absolute poverty. The problem is growing. Increases in GNP for many developing countries have *not* meant increased benefits for the poor. For many, in fact, life is worse. Development has too often not "trickled down."
>
> ..."equality of opportunity" for a fuller life makes sense for *people,* not just states.[83]

Yet the relative importance to be attached to a BHN strategy remains widely debated. As noted, many Third World leaders see the BHN strategy as a stratagem for the rich to prescribe once again the development path to be followed by poor nations. This suspicion is what lies behind the title of a recent essay by one British author: "Basic Human Needs: Concept or Slogan, Synthesis or Smokescreen?"[84] U.S. specialists like Harlan Cleveland, John McHale, and Thomas Wilson speak in terms of a "planetary bargain" or a new "global compact" binding rich and poor nations in new webs of mutual obligations.[85] According to this plan rich nations would support global reforms in the world's circulation systems and commit themselves to certain levels of automatic resource transfers in exchange for guarantees obtained from poor nations that they would use the resources to meet the basic needs of their absolute poor.

Third World leaders fear intervention (the setting of conditions by donors) and reject any insinuation of two-tiered images of a future world: on the one hand, a rich and technologically competitive cluster of nations and, on the other, a larger array of poor countries barely surviving on handouts. Conversely, rich nations, and many nongovernmental aid agencies, suspect that increased resource transfers, and more importantly, the relinquishment of donor control over resources by the mechanism of automaticity, will benefit not the poorest masses but the privileged groups in poor countries.

New negotiating processes are needed if we are gradually to overcome obstacles impeding a global bargain that satisfies Third World demands for a new international division of labor, while sufficiently assuring industrial powers that as John Sewell puts it, "the rich cannot prosper without the poor."[86] Sewell asserts that the U.S. can best solve its domestic problems of inflation, unemployment, and wasteful subsidization of technologically unproductive sectors by creating parity with developing nations and working out with them a mutually satisfactory new division of international labor.

Some of the difficulties behind the Basic Human Needs concept are neither political nor economic, but methodological. To what extent can basic needs be defined in ways that are not ethnocentric or culturally biased? More importantly, should planning experts or model-builders monopolize the task of defining the needs of others? Even if agreement is reached over which goods and services are required, how do "needs" get translated into quantified targets amenable to rational treatment by investors and planners? More fundamentally, to what extent does the very concept of "need" get distorted, as Ivan Illich claims,[87] by those very institutions that have a vested interest in satisfying needs by providing certain commercial packages?

As yet the U.S. has not clearly opted for any of the three scenarios just described. Some decisive strategy is urgently needed. In my opinion, the U.S. should unequivocally support global reform. Yet, as Hansen rightly points out, the reform scenario can include important elements contained in the other two models, that is, the graduation approach and the attack on absolute poverty's worst aspects via a BHN strategy.

The question before us now is: Can the U.S. help to make the world more just? My answer is Yes, but if it is to help the world become more just, the U.S. will have to change its own social order and style of living quite drastically; it must also accept the prospect of living in a different kind of world from the one it has known.[88]

III. GENERAL CONCLUSION

The overall title of this paper is: "Overcoming Injustice: Possibilities and Limits." Let me now briefly summarize the position I have advanced here. The burden of my argument is this:

- that possibilities for greater economic justice can be expanded and limits overcome if we adopt certain viewpoints on the meaning of history
- that a creative Utopianism that defines politics as the art of creating new possibilities is necessary
- that we must purge ourselves of the illusion that the United States has a special mission to play in the world which sets it outside the general laws of history
- that we need to cleanse religion of all elements of alienation from human tasks
- that we must view the progressive achievement of genuine development in the U.S. as part of the larger development process
- that this nation should adopt a global-reform strategy aimed at creating reciprocity and partnership in the governance of world affairs

In other words: "Yes, economic justice is possible, but only under certain conditions." And, "Yes, the U.S. can help build a more just world order, but only if it changes itself and its posture toward the outside world."

One may object that I have not offered a strategy for change or spelled out the steps that can get us from here to there. There are two reasons for this omission: the first is that, in the main, I agree with the procedural strategies outlined by two other writers in this volume—Gar Alperovitz and Herbert Gintis. My purpose has been to complement their contributions, by clearing away some of the myths, erroneous models, and terminological debris that so often paralyze our efforts to obtain greater justice. The second reason is that strategies for achieving global justice cannot emerge from mere intellectualizing: they must arise from the living praxis of all societal actors as they struggle to create new paradigms of problem-solving. The inadequacies of present global structures are obvious. So are the terminal values we ought to promote in a better world: essential goods for all, minimal violence, nonelitist governance systems, and ecological soundness. What we must do is work backward from our critique and our vision of the preferred future, to formulate a strategy for the transition. The first component of this strategy is public education to build up the critical mass of people who are knowledgeably motivated to work for desired change. But we also need qualitatively different modes of problem-solving around immediate, concrete issues like energy, employment, armaments, aid, etc. We must invent nonpalliative ways of dealing with these front-burner problems so as to open up new possibilities facilitating the eventual implantation of the desired terminal values. This is not something that can be mapped out ahead of time, however, for as I stated earlier, we must test out new possibilities through dialectical interplay and social experimentation in multiple arenas.

The late L. J. Lebret never tired of repeating that the central development task is to build a new civilization founded on true solidarity.[89] Genuine solidarity, however, is not the demeaning interdependence of rider and horse but the common effort of two oarsmen rowing the same boat against a swift current.[90] Creating more justice in the world is doubtless a monumental task. In order to succeed we must navigate a treacherous passage between the Scylla of ahistorical Utopias, and the Charibdis of complicity with the mediocre images of human possibility defended by the status quo. The biologist René Dubos often declares in public lectures that only 10 percent or 15 percent of the human brain's creative power is ever put to use. He blames an overspecialized, urban, industrial mode of existence for this atrophy of human imagination. I believe Dubos is right: it is atrophy, paralysis, and inability to exercise our creative powers that are the greatest obstacles to creating new social possibilities. And it is precisely because we face such a long haul that the time to start the journey is now. After spending thirty years to "pacify" rebel tribes in North Africa in the nineteenth century, the French general, Lyautey, eagerly looked forward to rest and to retirement in a pleasant Moroccan villa. He asked his servant-boy what kind of tree provided the best shade for his garden. The Arab lad gave him the name of the tree, but added, hesitantly, "but, *mon général,* the tree takes 80 years to reach maturity." To which Lyautey answered: "Hurry, then, and plant the seed right away: we don't have a minute to lose."

With our escalating and interlocking global problems, we don't have a minute to lose either. A humane world must be built by our efforts—our unceasing, repeated efforts. Success is neither certain nor even probable. But it is worth making the supreme sacrifice for the sake of the possible. For, as Camus wrote, "the only genuine form of generosity toward the future is to give one's all to the present."[91]

NOTES

1. Robert S. McNamara, *Address to the Board of Governors,* World Bank, Belgrade, October 2, 1979, p. 1.

2. Peter L. Berger, *Pyramids of Sacrifice* (New York: Basic Books, 1974).

3. Barrington Moore, Jr., *Social Origins of Dictatorship and Democracy* (Boston: Beacon Press, 1967), p. 505.

4. Barrington Moore, Jr., *Reflections on the Causes of Human Misery* (Boston: Beacon Press, 1970), p. 13.

5. Ibid., pp. 38-39.

6. Robert L. Heilbroner, *An Inquiry Into the Human Prospect* (New York: Norton, 1974), pp. 13-14.

7. Peter Steinfels, *The Neo-Conservatives* (New York: Simon & Schuster, 1979).

8. Albert Camus, *The Myth of Sisyphus and Other Essays* (New York: Knopf, 1961), p. 3.

9. E.M. Cioran, *The Trouble with Being Born* (New York: Viking, 1976), p.12.

10. Alvaro Vieira Pinto, *Consciencia e Realidade Nacional* (Rio de Janeiro: Instituto Superior de Estudos Brasileiros, 1960), I: 65-66.

11. Piyasena Dissanayake, *Political Thoughts of the Buddha* (Colombo, Department of Cultural Affairs, 1977).

12. Gunnar Myrdal, *Economic Theory and Under-developed Regions* (London: Duckworth, 1957), p. 7.

13. Danilo Doci, "Mafia-Client Politics," *Saturday Review,* July 6, 1968, p. 11.

14. Peter Marris, *Loss and Change* (Garden City, N.Y.: Doubleday, 1975).

15. On this see Sydney E. Ahlstrom, *A Religious History of the American People* (New Haven, Conn.: Yale University Press, 1973), pp. 1-13. Cf. Jonathan Edwards, *Thoughts on the Revival in New England,* in the *Works of President Edwards,* 4 vols. (New York: Robert Carter, 1979), 3:313; George Bancroft, *History of the United States,* 6 vols., 2d ed. rev. (Boston: Little, Brown, 1876), 1:3; Robert Baird, *Religion in America*

(1843; New York: Arno Press, 1969); Leonard Woolsey Bacon, *History of American Christianity* (1897; Ann Arbor, Mich.: University Microfilms, 1982), pp. 2, 419; and Frederick Jackson Turner, *The Frontier in American History* (1920; New York: Krieger, 1976).

16. John White, "What is Development? And for Whom?" from unpublished paper delivered at Quaker Conference on "Motive Force in Development," Hammamet, Tunisia, April 1972.

17. Robert A. Packenham, *Liberal America and the Third World* (Princeton, N.J.: Princeton University Press, 1973), pp. 123-129.

18. Roger Fisher, "Sanctions Won't Work," from "My Turn," *Newsweek*, January 14, 1980, p. 21.

19. On this see Denis Goulet, "World Interdependence: Verbal Smokescreen or New Ethic?" *Development Paper*, Overseas Development Council (New York: Praeger, 1976).

20. Richard Falk, "Satisfying Human Needs in a World of Sovereign States: Rhetoric, Reality, and Vision," in Joseph Gremillion and William Ryan, eds., *World Faiths and the New World Order* (Washington, D.C.: Interreligious Peace Colloquium, 1978), pp. 134, 136.

21. *The Economist*, Editorials of August 12, 1978, p. 9, and September 2, 1978, p. 13.

22. Godfrey Gunatilleke, "The Interior Dimension," *International Development Review*, 1979/1, p. 4.

23. Daniel Bell, *The Cultural Contradictions of Capitalism* (New York: Basic Books, 1976), pp. 28-29.

24. Denis Goulet, *A New Moral Order* (Maryknoll, N.Y.: Orbis Books, 1974), final chapter entitled "Makers of History or Witnesses to Transcendence?"

25. Denis Goulet, "Secular History and Teleology," *World Justice*, September 1966, pp. 5-18.

26. Especially in *True Humanism*, first published in 1936.

27. Madeleine Barthelemy Madaule, "La Personne dans la perspective Teilhardienne," in *Essais sur Teilhard de Chardin* (Paris: Fayard, 1962), p. 76.

28. Gustavo Gutierres, *A Theology of Liberation* (Maryknoll, N.Y.: Orbis Books, 1973); see also Juan Luis Segundo, *The Liberation of Theology* (Maryknoll, N.Y.: Orbis Books, 1976).

29. Albert Camus, *The Myth of Sisyphus* (New York: Knopf, 1955), p. 201.

30. André Schwartz-Bart, *The Last of the Just* (New York: Bantam Books, 1961), p. 5.

31. Cited by Moore in the Frontispiece to *Reflections*. The source is Robinson's *Freedom and Necessity*.

32. Claude Sarraute, "Un Entretien avec Henry Miller," in *Le Monde*, April 20, 1960, p. 8.

33. Cioran, *The Trouble with Being Born*, p. 13.

34. David Noble, *America by Design: Science, Technology, and the*

Rise of Corporate Capitalism (New York: Knopf, 1977), p. xvii.

35. John W. Gardner, *Morale* (New York: Norton, 1978), p. 52.

36. Denis Goulet, "An Ethical Model for the Study of Values," *Harvard Educational Review,* May 1971, pp. 206-7.

37. See, e.g., Mahbub ul Haq, *The Poverty Curtain* (New York: Columbia University Press, 1976). Cf. Marc Nerfin, ed., *Another Development: Approaches and Strategies* (Uppsala, Sweden: Dag Hammarskjold Foundation, 1977).

38. For more on this see Mary Evelyn Jegen and Charles K. Wilber, eds., *Growth with Equity* (New York: Paulist Press, 1979). Cf. Harlan Cleveland and Thomas W. Wilson, Jr., *Human Growth: An Essay on Growth, Values and the Quality of Life* (Palo Alto: California Aspen Institute Publications, 1978); and John McHale and Magda Cordell McHale, *Basic Human Needs, A Framework for Action* (New Brunswick, N.J.: Transaction Books, 1978).

39. Denis Goulet, *Looking at Guinea-Bissau: A New Nation's Development Strategy* (Washington, D.C.: Overseas Development Council), Occasional Paper No. 9, 1978, p. 4.

40. The conference was sponsored jointly by the United Nations Environmental Programme, the Arab League Educational, Scientific, and Cultural Organization, and the Aspen Institute for Humanistic Studies, March 31-April 3, 1980.

41. On this see Jan Tinbergen, ed., *RIO: Reshaping the International Order* (New York: Dutton, 1976). See also G. Adler-Karlsson, *The Political Economy of East-West-South Co-Operation* (New York: Springer-Verlag, 1976); and William R. Cline, ed., *Policy Alternatives for a New International Economic Order* (New York: Praeger, 1979).

42. Sources: World Bank, *1979 World Development Report,* pp. 127 ff., and *1979 World Bank Atlas,* passim.

43. Barry Lopez, "The American Indian Mind," *Quest/78,* September-October, 1978, p. 109.

44. James Reston, "Interview with Brzezinski," *Washington Star,* Sunday, December 31, 1978, Section E, page E-4.

45. Studs Terkel, *Working,* (New York: Avon Books, 1975).

46. On this see Peter Marin, "The New Narcissism," *Harper's Magazine,* October 1975, pp. 45-56. Cf. Christopher Lasch, *The Culture of Narcissism* (New York: Warner Books, 1979).

47. Erich Fromm, ed., "Introduction" to *Socialist Humanism* (New York: Anchor Books, 1966), p. ix.

48. John Kenneth Galbraith, *Economic Development in Perspective* (Cambridge, Mass.: Harvard University Press, 1962), p. 43.

49. See especially Abraham Maslow, *Toward a Psychology of Being* (New York: Van Nostrand, 1962).

50. Thornstein Veblen, *The Theory of the Leisure Class* (New York: Mentor Books, 1963), p. 78.

51. Baran's position is reported in Tibor Scitovsky, *Papers on Wel-*

fare and Growth (Palo Alto, Calif.: Stanford University Press, 1964), p. 240.

52. On this, cf., e.g., UNESCO's multivolume *History of Mankind, Cultural and Scientific Development;* or Josef Pieper, *Leisure, The Basis of Culture* (New York: Pantheon, 1963).

53. Denis Goulet, *The Cruel Choice* (New York: Atheneum, 1977), pp. 240-49.

54. David C. McClelland, *The Achieving Society* (Princeton, N.J.: Van Nostrand, 1961).

55. Cf. Barbara Ward, Foreword to Mahbub ul Haq, *The Poverty Curtain,* (New York: Columbia University Press, 1976), p. xii.

56. Karl Manneheim, *Freedom, Power and Democratic Planning* (London: Routledge & Kegan Paul, 1951), p. 191.

57. On this see Edgar Z. Friedenberg, *The Disposal of Liberty and Other Industrial Wastes* (Garden City, N.Y.: Doubleday, 1975).

58. Cf. Arthur Okun, *Equality and Efficiency: The Big Tradeoff* (Washington, D.C.: The Brookings Institution, 1975).

59. See James O'Toole, "Academic Tenure," *Center Magazine,* September/October 1979, pp. 53-60.

60. James O'Toole, "Listen Workers, Managers," *New York Times,* Monday, January 7, 1980, p. A-19.

61. See *Industrial Democracy in Europe, The Challenge and Management Responses* (Geneva: A Business International European Research Report, 1974).

62. Louis O. Kelso and Patricia Hetter, *Two-Factor Theory: The Economics of Reality* (New York: Vintage Books, 1967).

63. Goulet, *The Cruel Choice,* p. 324.

64. Daniel Bell, *The Cultural Contradictions of Capitalism* (New York: Basic Books, 1976).

65. Henry C. Wallich, "The Future of Capitalism," *Newsweek,* January 22, 1973, p. 62.

66. See, e.g., *Experimental Housing Allowance Program, A 1979 Report of Findings,* U.S. Department of Housing and Urban Development, Office of Policy Development and Research, Division of Housing Research, April 1979, 114 pages. Also *Fifth Annual Report of the Housing Assistance Supply Experiment,* October 1977-September 1978 (Santa Monica, Calif.: The Rand Corporation, Document R-2434-HUD dated June 1979).

67. On this see Denis Goulet, *Looking at Guinea-Bissau.*

68. On this see such works as Saul H. Mendlovitz, ed., *On the Creation of a Just World Order: Preferred Worlds for the 1990's* (New York: Free Press, 1975); Richard A. Falk, *A Study of Future Worlds* (New York: Free Press, 1975); Mihalo Mesarovic and Eduard Pestel, *Mankind at the Turning Point* (New York: Dutton, 1974); Gerald and Patricia Mische, *Toward a Human World Order* (New York: Paulist Press, 1977); and Amilcar O. Herrera et al., *Catastrophe or New Society? A Latin American*

World Model (Ottawa: International Development Research Center, 1976).

69. C. Fred Bergsten, *The Future of the International Economic Order: An Agenda for Research* (Lexington, Mass.: D.C. Heath, 1973).

70. *1979 World Development Report,* The World Bank, August 1979, p. 19.

71. Robert McNamara, *Address to the Board of Governors of the World Bank,* Belgrade, October 2, 1979, p. 19.

72. Martin M. McLaughlin, ed., *The United States and World Development Agenda, 1979* (New York: Praeger, 1979), pp. 6-7.

73. See Morris David Morris, *Measuring the Condition of the World's Poor, The Physical Quality of Life Index* (New York: Pergamon Press, 1979); and James P. Grant, *Disparity Reduction Rates in Social Indicators* (Washington, D.C.: Overseas Development Council), Monograph No. 11, September 1978.

74. McLaughlin, *Agenda 1979,* p. 8.

75. See Albert Tévoédjrè, "Contracts of Solidarity," *Labor and Society,* July 1978, pp. 267-77. Cf. Tévoédjrè, *La Pauvreté, richesses des peuples* (Paris: Les editions ouvrières, 1978), pp. 141-200.

76. Mahbub ul Haq, "View from the South: The Second Phase of the North-South Dialogue," in *Agenda 1979,* p. 115.

77. Roger D. Hansen, *Beyond the North-South Stalemate* (New York: McGraw-Hill, 1979), pp. 173 ff.

78. Ibid., pp. 173-74.

79. Writing mainly in such reviews as *Foreign Policy* and *Foreign Affairs.*

80. *Arusha Programme for Collective Self-Reliance and Framework for Negotiations,* UNCTAD V, Manila, May 1979, p. 28. UN DOCUMENT TD/236, February 28, 1979.

81. Mahbub ul Haq, *The Poverty Curtain,* p. 207.

82. Robert S. McNamara, *Address to the Board of Governors,* p. 7.

83. Statement of U.S. Secretary of State Cyrus Vance at meeting of the OECD Ministerial Council, Paris, June 23, 1977. Cited by Hansen, p. 247.

84. Reginald Herbold Green, "Basic Human Needs: Concept or Slogan, Synthesis or Smokescreen?" in Alan Rew, ed., *Down to Basics, Reflections on the Basic Needs Debate, IDS Bulletin,* Sussex, Eng., June 1978, pp. 7-11.

85. Harlan Cleveland, ed., *The Planetary Bargain, Proposals for a New International Economic Order to Meet Human Needs* (Aspen, Colo.: Aspen Institute, 1975); John McHale and Magda C. McHale, *Human Requirements, Supply Levels and Outer Bounds: A Framework for Thinking about the Planetary Bargain* (Aspen, Colo.: Aspen Institute, 1975).

86. John W. Sewell, "Can the North Prosper Without Growth and Progress in the South?" in McLaughlin, pp. 45-76.

87. Ivan Illich, *Toward a History of Needs* (New York: Pantheon Books, 1978).

88. For more on this see Steven H. Arnold and Denis Goulet, "The Abundant Society and World Order," *Alternatives,* August 1979, pp. 213-52.

89. L. J. Lebret, *Developpement—Revolution solidaire* (Paris: Les Editions ouvrières, 1967).

90. On this see Denis Goulet, "World Interdependence: Verbal Smokescreen or New Ethic?"

91. Albert Camus, *L'Homme révolté* (Paris: Gallimard, 1951), p. 375. Translation mine.

Social Justice and the New Inflation

GAR ALPEROVITZ

I. INTRODUCTION

Modern economists usually address questions of social justice in terms of the distributional impact of such policy measures as taxes and transfer payments. To a substantial degree the notion of the price system as a register of social justice has been treated as secondary, if at all.[1] Specific prices are considered to be largely the result of market forces. To be sure, in analyses of monopoly and oligopoly, the problem of economic justice (as distinct from the problem of economic efficiency) has occasionally been confronted. And to a certain degree—especially in connection with food-stamp programs and housing subsidies to low-income groups—the issue of prices as they are experienced by various income categories has entered into the dialogue.

As the United States confronts the difficulties of the final decades of the twentieth century, it is apparent that consideration of the issue of social justice must be broadened. The problem of prices—and especially prices for necessities—is likely to be of growing concern. New forms of inflation in key necessity-related areas are likely to require quite different approaches, both in theory and in practice; the new inflation is not socially neutral. Questions of social justice may accordingly shift from the sidelines of government tax and transfer programs into the marketplace itself.

The issues that must be considered in any serious review are much broader than those usually dealt with by traditional economic analysis. The first is straightforward: To what degree do particular

---

The author wishes to acknowledge the help of Joseph Bowring, David Jones, Mary Saville, and Pat Simms in the preparation of this essay.

kinds of inflation affect different income groups differently? A second has to do with the impact of specific kinds of inflation on macro management of the economy—and the resulting levels of employment for particular income groups. The third and the broadest category involves the impact of price changes—and inflation in general —on the overall social/political context that defines larger economic policy choices.

II. THE NEW INFLATION

The starting point for an analysis of the impact of inflation on social justice in the coming period is recognition that in the 1970s we encountered a substantially different kind of inflation than that which has previously dominated much of the intellectual debate. Inflation is commonly viewed as mainly monetary-based (as a result of overly accommodating Federal Reserve Board policy, for example), demand-induced (too much purchasing power chasing too few goods), or "wage-push" (e.g., wage increases touching off a general spiral).

Though each of the above factors played some role, a significant portion of the inflation that emerged in the 1970s—and promises to resume in the 1980s and beyond—is quite different. At its root, it is not generalized. It was extremely concentrated in a few key sectors of the economy. Figures for 1979, for instance, showed that virtually all the increase in the inflation rate that year was caused by increasing prices in goods and services that may loosely be defined as necessity-related—food, housing, energy, and medical-care costs. The combined rate for these items was 10.9 percent in 1978 and 17.4 percent in 1979. In 1976, when Jimmy Carter was elected, inflation in the above four sectors stood at 3.6 percent. In 1977 it rose to 8.2 percent. The escalation in 1978 to 10.9 percent, and in 1979 to 17.4 percent, was unyielding. Meanwhile, for everything else measured by the CPI (which for the purpose of this essay will be broadly termed nonnecessity related) the inflation rate was in the range 6.5 percent to 6.7 percent from 1976 to 1979—except for 1977 when it was 4.6 percent.[2]

To be sure, there are both measurement and definitional problems that must be faced in any inquiry into the new kind of inflation. Some of these will be reviewed below.[3] The important point, however, is that sector-specific factors caused the main problems in the leading areas. By and large price rises in the remainder of the economy were relatively modest except as a secondary price-wage spiral following upon initial sectoral pressures.

To what degree is the pattern illustrated by the 1976-80 period representative of the 1970s? There is debate as to the degree to which the way the Vietnam War was financed contributed to inflation in the late 1960s and very early 1970s. The unusual pattern of sectoral inflation thereafter, however, is not in dispute. It began in 1973 when major food-price jolts hit the United States. These were compounded by the surge in energy prices starting at the end of the year. Both price increases were symptomatic of a new era in which global markets for these commodities (with the exception of temporary gluts) have become increasingly tight. In 1973 simultaneous poor harvests in several parts of the world (especially in the Soviet Union) led to heavy demands on U.S. grain supplies. Because the United States—unlike virtually every other major industrialized country—did not have a serious policy of insulating the domestic food economy from the effects of short-term world shortages, U.S. food prices rose 20 percent between 1972 and 1973. In 1973-74 the Organization of Petroleum Exporting Countries quadrupled crude oil prices and sent U.S. energy inflation from 2.8 percent in 1972 to 21.6 percent in 1974. Much of the subsequent price-wage spiral grew out of these two jolts in the energy and food sectors. In 1978, the Council of Economic Advisors stated the linkage thus:

> The dominant influence was the rise in fuel and food prices. Its force was not limited to direct effects. The pass-through of cost increases into other prices broadened the inflation, and the rise in consumer prices led to efforts by wage earners to recover lost real income.[4]

In 1975 the worst recession since the 1930s somewhat moderated that portion of inflation attributable to the cycle of wages chasing prices chasing wages, but what is sometimes loosely termed the "momentum" of the underlying rate has continued to the present day. More importantly, with occasional temporary lapses, it has been supplemented by additional special-factor increases in all four necessity-related sectors.

In the last years of the decade energy and food prices were again major contributors. Energy rose 37.4 percent in 1979—and an additional 18.1 percent in 1980—while food prices rose 30 percent in the three-year period 1978-80. (A significant portion of the price rise in beef can be traced to the earlier feed-grain run-up that exacerbated the cattle cycle.)

The result of the food and energy jolts of 1973-74 and 1978-79, plus inflation in the medical-care and housing sectors (to be discussed below), was a rate of inflation in these four areas of 139 percent from 1972 through 1980. In that period, energy prices rose 227 percent, food prices 88 percent, housing costs 127 percent, and medical care 112 percent. During the same period, in contrast to the 138 percent necessity-related increase, the combined price of nonnecessity-related items rose 73 percent.

Much current economic thinking has tended to view inflation in the key sectors as "temporary aberrations," or an inevitable result of continuously changing market prices. On this theory, wage earners are supposed to absorb the special-factor increases and then the economy will resume its normal path. This was the meaning of Carter Administration inflation-chief Alfred Kahn's oft-repeated argument that although "the desire to keep pace by catch-up increases is certainly understandable;...unfortunately it is not possible." Federal Reserve Board Chairman Paul Volcker put the case more bluntly: "The standard of living of the average American has to decline."[5]

The difficulty is that the policy of ignoring the special problems, quite simply, does not seem to work. By one estimate, the necessities-related sectors account for 60 to 70 percent of the spending of four out of five families. By another, the lowest 20 percent of the income distribution spend some 90 percent of their income on the necessity-related items, while the very poor must go in debt to pay their bills.[6] There may be some modest fat in family budgets. Leaving aside the equity question, however, it is economically unwise to expect wage earners to absorb major increases in necessity-related inflation. If they refuse, the inflation momentum simply continues. To ignore the new problems—or to be lulled by a temporary oil glut or food-price hesitation—is to ignore pressures which can undermine economic performance, and which are not likely to go away.

A. Sectoral Problems in the 1980s and Beyond

While the recent massive recession and temporary food and energy surpluses moderated inflation in 1981 and especially in 1982, there is very little likelihood that the upward pressure on key sectoral prices (and the related phenomenon of periodic jolts) will abate for any sustained period; a return to the "normalcy" of the pre-1970s era is extremely doubtful. The new forms of inflation are likely to grow in coming decades. This is most obvious in connection with food and energy, but it is also true, for specific reasons, for housing and health care.

In the food sector, for instance, the precipitating events of 1972-73 almost repeated themselves in 1979. Again, a substantial crop failure in the Soviet Union sent the Russians to the U.S. market, but better regulation of their purchases and record crops in the U.S. moderated the impact. The embargo also helped. In broader perspective, increasing population and affluence in other parts of the world are leading to a steady increase in pressures on U.S. food resources. The U.S. exports roughly half of all grain in world trade. Agricultural experts point out that weather conditions in the "bread basket" areas of the world have been unusually good for much of the past decade. For the future the best judgment we can make is that repeated instances of weather-related crop failures in other countries will cause tight markets to experience recurrent price jolts. We are particularly vulnerable, ironically, to Soviet agricultural difficulties. More broadly, we are seeing what Lester Brown describes as a "fundamental shift in the structure of the world food economy ... [toward an era] of more or less chronic scarcity and higher prices...."[7] In the emerging context, without new policies, a major crop failure anywhere in the globe can mean massive price increases in the United States.

In terms of energy, in an almost infinite number of ways, our economic system has been built upon a foundation of cheap energy. With our rail and mass-transit systems decimated, our tax and housing policies still subsidizing suburban sprawl, and our cities full of sealed-glass office buildings, we remain extremely dependent upon OPEC-produced petroleum. U.S. oil and petroleum product imports totaled $86 billion in 1980, more than ten times what they were in 1973.[8] Again, we may experience temporary gluts—particularly in times of global recession—but for the future, the world price trend is almost certain to continue upward. When the global economy resumes significant growth, energy markets are again likely to tighten. More important, there are enough political problems in the Middle East to make a prediction of occasional chaos the most reasonable forecast, despite our inability to build this self-evident factor neatly into our statistical models. Given the record of the 1970s, the extraordinary dangers in the Middle East and Persian Gulf, and the underlying supply difficulties, a period of continued, and possibly dramatic, price instability is all but certain in the 1980s and beyond.

As for housing, although speculative factors (and tax provisions that intensify them) are important, there has been an underlying surge in demand resulting significantly from demographic factors. The bulge of baby-boom children of the late forties and fifties that is now reaching prime home-buying age is the major factor. In addition to sheer numbers, there are changes in life-style that continue to increase the number of new households (including numbers of divorces, young people marrying at a later age, and elderly people living alone rather than with their children). Expanding demand has come up against a chronic inadequacy of supply in several markets, especially of units geared to low- and middle-income families. Unbalanced regional growth has also intensified pressures in certain areas while leaving vacant housing in others. Monthly costs have also been inflated by speculation based upon overall inflationary expectations and by monetary policies which lead to high interest rates.

A major historical development that has set the stage for accelerating inflation in connection with health care has been the development of various forms of private and public insurance. Blue Cross and Blue Shield, still the major private insurers, have been dominated in their administration over the years by the providers, doctors, and hospital administrators. Furthermore, the "fee-for-service" structure of financing health care has built into it numerous incentives for overconsumption of various services. Not surprisingly, the Blues have not been notable in resisting price increases, in monitoring treatments to prevent waste, or in questioning hospital expansion. Quite the contrary, the reimbursement system established by the Blues has been cost-plus, and when Medicare and Medicaid were proposed, a continuation of fee-for-service, cost-plus reimbursement was the price extracted for medical-establishment support. Unless major structural changes are accomplished in this sector, we can expect further inflationary pressures here as well.

B. The Social Impact of Sectoral Inflation

If the necessity-related areas are (with occasional temporary lapses) likely to continue to generate sector-specific forms of inflation (and help set off secondary, more generalized price-wage increases), a particular issue of social justice is posed because of the differential impact of the new inflation on different groups. Data on this is very thin, and several problems are masked by the usual statistical indicators of apparent "relative" impact. However, common experience is confirmed by the information we now have, and it strongly suggests that the new inflation, as one might expect, affects low- and moderate-income groups in an extremely powerful way.

Data developed for the National Advisory Council on Economic Opportunity, for instance, indicates that the bottom 20 percent—roughly the official poverty population—spends close to 90 percent of their income on food, energy, housing, and medical care.[9] We also know a fair amount about certain key issues. The CPI substantially understates the impact of food inflation on low-income households because it is based on a 1972-73 survey of consumer expenditures. The CPI currently incorporates food expenditures at 18.7 percent of the average family's income. The percentage for low-income families is much higher than average; data from the U.S. Department of Agriculture show that the lowest 20 percent of the income distribution spent almost twice as much as average, or 34.8 percent, in 1979.[10] An increase in food prices hits low-income families much harder than is commonly acknowledged.

The standard CPI even more dramatically underestimates the impact of energy inflation on low- and moderate-income families. It includes household and transportation energy as 10.3 percent of the average family budget in 1979. Low- and moderate-income families actually spend a much larger proportion of their income on energy. The U.S. Department of Energy's Fuel Oil Marketing Advisory Committee estimates that the poor who did not drive spent just under 20 percent on energy in 1979 while those who drove spent about 30 percent of their income on energy.[11] The impact of higher energy prices is particularly severe for the poor who have less of a discretionary budget to cushion the blow.

Whatever the "relative" statistical impact of the new inflation on low- and moderate-income groups, the question of real burden and real equity must be carefully formulated to understand the human, social, and policy consequences: Even if inflation affected the poor and rich by the same percentage of their income, it would not hurt them equally. For the rich, a loss of real income may mean a reduction in luxury spending or in savings. For the poor it often means serious hardship. Nor do relative indicators tell us much about a critical policy choice—whether moderate-income wage earners can, in fact, be forced to reduce their real-income levels further as a principal strategy to reduce overall inflation.

There has been some controversy on these issues recently, particularly as related to the 1970s. For instance, Joseph Minarik of the Brookings Institution, focusing especially on well-known CPI housing-measurement problems, has argued that inflation in the necessities is less than inflation as measured by the overall Consumer Price Index. Joseph Bowring, exploring alternative measures using a variety of experimental indexes, and incorporating new data on

the food and energy expenditures discussed above, has shown Minarik's approach to be seriously flawed; necessity-related inflation is
higher than measured by the CPI in all instances.[12] Lester Thurow
has argued that inflation during the 1970s has hurt virtually all income classes about the same. Aside from the fact that his argument
ignores the distinction between the poor who are intensely burdened
by an "equivalent" relative loss in real income as compared with the
rich, Bowring shows that low- and moderate-income families actually suffered a larger relative loss in real income when the effects of
expenditures on energy and food are accounted for. Thurow agrees,
however, that inflation is likely to intensify the relative burden of
low- and moderate-income families during the 1980s—the issue of
the future we all now face.[13]

Numerous commentators have pointed out that family income
was significantly sustained in the 1970s by large numbers of women
entering the labor force—but that this phenomenon cannot continue
at current rates. In March 1978, 58 percent of all husband-wife families had more than one income earner, an increase of more than two
million such families from March 1970. In 1978 the labor-force participation rates for all wives was 47.6 percent, an increase of 6.8
percent over 1970.[14] The critical situation for the years ahead is much
more important than the precise issue of measurement for the 1970s.
We can expect more, not less, special-sector inflation in the 1980s
and beyond. And we can expect less relief to low- and moderate-
income families from working wives. Family real income is, accordingly, likely to weaken under the assault of inflation in general, basic
necessity-related sectoral inflation in particular, and the absence of
large numbers of women who can add their work to bail out family
budgets.[15]

C. Transfer Programs and Social Justice

If sectoral inflation is both likely to resume its growth and affect low- and moderate-income groups intensely, we must face a
critical political-economic issue directly: Do our adjustment mechanisms alleviate the new burdens? Is equity for the future a thing of
theory but not of practice? If we are interested in social justice and
wish to deal with the reality we are likely to face, we will have to go
well beyond traditional economic thinking.

An important aspect of the problem has to do with the impact
of transfer payments—or subsidies—to remedy difficulties at the
lower end of the income distribution. In theory distributional justice

could be achieved by "after-the-fact" remedies, e.g., an expansion of programs to help the poor. The problem is that in practice this strategy is very weak. Well before the advent of the Reagan Administration, the National Advisory Council on Economic Opportunity, pointing to the weakness of such efforts, urged a shift "from programs that try to reduce the impact of inflation on the poor to focus on policies that begin to deal with the problem directly."[16] To be sure, Social Security is indexed, as are some other transfer programs. But (contrary to a commonly held view) Social Security indexation, far from being excessive due to an exaggeration of housing costs, is probably on balance inadequate because of the understatement of food and energy costs.[17] And there is growing political pressure to reduce benefits. Welfare payments have not been indexed adequately by any measure.[18] Benefit levels for AFDC general assistance and Medicaid are subject to the whim of state legislatures. Predictably, several states have reduced benefits (Georgia by as much as 33 percent between 1974 and 1978). Economist Michael Mazerov and social commentator Robert Howard note that "between January 1970 and April 1979, the CPI rose 82 percent and prices in the necessities doubled. But the average AFDC benefit rose (from $228 per month to $331) only 45 percent.[19] In a recent study of 26 representative occupations, Paul Blumberg found that between 1967 and 1978, welfare recipients had lost the most real income, 16.5 percent.[20]

The inadequacy of transfer programs in specific areas is also illustrated by energy. Rising energy prices have had a devastating impact on poor families during the last decade. The cost to the poor of energy price increases between 1978 and 1980 has been estimated to be about 14 billion dollars—a massive loss of purchasing power by those who can least afford it.[21] Income-support programs to provide compensation for energy price increases supplied only 4 billion dollars between 1976 and 1980. Even after taking this into account, the poor lost about 10 billion in purchasing power between 1978 and 1980 through higher energy prices.[22]

The poor have faced even greater hardship since the Reagan administration came into power. In 1982, Congress voted to cut food-stamp benefits by $1.66 million, child nutrition programs by $1.5 billion. Four hundred thousand families currently receiving welfare lost their eligibility, and another 250,000 families had their benefits reduced. Cuts in Medicaid, health-care, and subsidized housing-construction programs will also hurt the poor.

For all these reasons, in practice it is extremely unlikely that we will be able to keep the poor from falling further behind via the transfer and subsidy route. How far is the question: A sense of the orders of magnitude is given by a Congressional Budget Office estimate that each of the 15 million poor households is likely to experience roughly $1,000 in additional energy costs alone over the next decade. Even if transfer programs were on the increase, to compensate fully would require a $15 billion welfare contribution. There appears to be no political strategy available which is likely to compensate this loss even partially. As we enter a period of conservative politics and budget cutting, only the naive can believe that significant increases in transfer programs will be seen as a serious approach to social justice.

III. UNEMPLOYMENT AND INFLATION

It is not simply that there is little prospect that transfer mechanisms will maintain existing levels of social justice in the 1980s, however. Our difficulties are compounded because the result of our inability to deal with new forms of inflation undercuts—and cannot be separated from—other policy and equity issues. Our second major point has to do with the fact that in practice continued inflation regularly leads to policies to slow the economy—and this further weakens the overall economic position of low- and moderate-income groups.

Over the last decade, a wide range of anti-inflation measures have been tried. Besides the direct creation of recession, these include slow growth, budget cutting, restrictive monetary policies, and attacks on health and safety regulation. A combination of several of the above is now national policy, but except for short periods, each approach has failed to have a sustained impact on inflation. Since none is targeted to the special problems of the key sectors, this is not surprising. Consider budget cutting: There is little doubt that there are times when inflation results from excess demand aggravated by large budget deficits. In such times, reducing the federal deficit by cutting government spending (or raising taxes) can make sense. However, this has not been the major problem in recent years.

The U.S. economy has operated at levels of 70-80 percent of capacity for a substantial period. A massive recession can obviously temporarily hold down wages and costs, but there is little reason to believe that cutting Social Security benefits further or laying off CETA jobholders will significantly alter longer-term inflation. The Congressional Budget Office estimated in 1980 that a $20 billion cut in the federal budget would reduce the rate of inflation by only one-tenth of one percentage point by the end of 1980.[23] Nor can budget cuts hold down natural gas prices, or reduce rising mortgage-interest rates if major lenders continue to doubt policy. Comparisons of the U.S. budget deficit with those of other major industrial nations also remind us that other countries have run larger deficits than the U.S. but have had lower inflation rates. From 1977 to 1979 the U.S. had an average inflation rate of 8.4 percent while the public-sector deficit was .1 percent of the GNP. In contrast, West Germany had an inflation rate of 3.5 percent, though the public-sector deficit was 2.7 percent of the GNP; Japan's inflation rate was 5.1 percent with a deficit of 4.8 percent of its GNP.[24]

Ironically, many government programs now being cut in the name of fighting inflation are the very kinds of sector-related public investment needed to expand supply to bring down prices in the long run (housing, alternative energy, and insulation, for example); or to provide public information and competition to reduce inflation (cooperatives, health programs, etc.).

The approach of fighting inflation through weakening environmental, health, and safety regulations has long been a favorite of many corporations. While, of course, the reduction of nit-picking rules is to be welcomed, cutting regulations as an anti-inflation strategy has at least two major limitations. First, the total effect of regulations on the CPI is relatively small. A Data Resources study for the Environmental Protection Agency, for example, estimated that air- and water-pollution-control costs contribute only two-tenths of a point to the inflation rate each year.[25] Barry P. Bosworth, former director of the Council on Wage and Price stability, estimated that *all* government regulations contributed *three-fourths* of a percentage point.[26] Such estimates suggest that grossly cutting regulations by, say *one-fourth*—a very drastic propsal—would, at best, only cut two-tenths of one point off overall recent inflation rates in the 9 to 13 percent range. Though others have urged that more significant savings are possible, none is major compared with our current inflation rates. And there are other effects. The relaxation of EPA controls on utilities or USDA efforts to remove cancer-causing substances from food can lead to higher medical costs. As we saw in the 1970s rash of DC-10 accidents, and most dramatically at Three-Mile Island, the direct human and financial costs of lax regulation can be staggering. The Three-Mile Island disaster alone will cost hundreds of millions of dollars.

Finally, the Reagan Administration's proclaimed theory that tight money or high interest rates can actually significantly alter inflation *without recession* has been challenged by events and by many economists, ranging from liberal to conservative. The Administration had hoped to avoid the ultimate resort of failed anti-inflation policy—direct creation of recession—through a combination of tax cuts, budget cuts, and tight money. Writing in *Fortune* Magazine in early 1981, the respected conservative former chairman of the Council of Economic Advisors, Herbert Stein, argued that it would ultimately squeeze demand out of the economy—and that higher unemployment was a "predictable by-product" of this process. The task for the president was to stand firm and above all stop promising that unemployment would not increase.

Stein's argument not only illustrated traditional conservative economic policy, and proved correct, but it illuminated a clearly recognizable political-economic sequence that begins with sectoral price jolts and ends with a reluctant decision to slow the overall economy—at tremendous cost in lost output and social welfare. Twice during the last decade, in 1969-70 and 1973-75, policymakers concluded that the only answer to inflation was recession (the latter the worst economic downturn since the Great Depression). With 10.4 percent of the labor force out of work in late 1982, we have bested this record.

The intransigence of continuing inflation suggests that even the so-called solution of recession, though it can close down the housing industry and increase unemployment, cannot in fact "wring inflation out of the economy" *without* extraordinarily *high costs.* How great are the costs of significantly effecting inflation via recession? The question is disputed. Bosworth has estimated "it would require about one million additional unemployed and a loss of $100 billion in output to lower the rate of inflation by one percentage point."[27] The late Arthur Okun estimated the cost of recession to be $200 billion of real GNP lost for each percentage point decrease in the long-term underlying inflation rate.[28] Such estimates can be debated, but even if reduced, recession is obviously a tremendous price to pay for small impact. Moreover, after each recent recession, inflation has increased when the economy recovered. In other words, only a permanent recession would bring a permanent solution. As Lester Thurow has written: "These findings do tell us that some of the suggested cures are worse than the disease."[29]

Much economic theory misses the chain of policy that repeatedly translates inflation into recession in the real political world. It has, however, an extraordinary additional impact on social justice. The consequences of unemployment for low-income groups, and of subemployment, have been well documented. In July 1981, for instance, this was the unemployment picture:

- 7.5 million Americans unemployed
- one of every seven black workers unemployed (14.4%)
- one of every ten Hispanic workers unemployed (9.9%)
- one of every six teenagers unemployed (18.1%)
- one of every eleven blue-collar workers unemployed (9.4%)
- two of every five black teenagers unemployed (40%)[30]

By late 1982, there were 11 million people out of work; and each of the above categories increased. The impact of unemployment on human lives is tragic. M. Harvey Brenner of Johns Hopkins University has found that "virtually all major illnesses, virtually all major causes of death are affected" by unemployment. Brenner estimates that each increase of one percent in unemployment during a recession causes about 37,000 deaths over the succeeding six years. More than 20,000 come from cardiovascular problems, which are aggravated during unemployment by stress and poor diet. More than 900 are suicides, and 648 are homicides, also products of increased stress. Another 495 are attributed to cirrhosis of the liver, an outgrowth of alcohol abuse.[31]

IV. THE SOCIAL-POLITICAL FACTOR

If traditional measures not only fail to deal with the initiating causes of the new inflation, but often in practice lead to greater unemployment, and further exacerbate social injustice, we must face a still more fundamental issue: Larger social/political trends are not unrelated to our failure to deal with economic problems, a fact that has been clearly recognized by social observers and social scientists in general. The relationship between inflation and strictly political attacks on the budget, for instance, is obvious to political scientists; as is the implicit "feedback loop" between economic and political factors. With few exceptions, the economics profession has failed to incorporate this kind of knowledge into theory. It is not simply that we regularly choose economic policies that result in unemployment as a *political-economic* consequence of inflation. It is also that —in a situation when families are under unyielding inflationary pressures—our culture seems to search out political-economic scapegoats that narrow the real-world constraints in which economic policy operates.

The third major question we defined at the outset must accordingly be reviewed in its broadest implications: unchecked inflation fosters a cycle of budget-cutting politics, growing unemployment, and the reduction of health and safety regulations—whether or not these can actually significantly reduce long-term inflation. It has also traditionally led to political attacks on labor. Although we have as yet no comprehensive theory, these political facts cannot be isolated from our analysis of both economic and social-justice issues. An economics that abstracts from such issues moves further and further from reality. Though at present our knowledge is sketchy, in the new economic era economic and social-justice issues must clearly be analyzed together—as intimately related, not separate, phenomena.

We have now reached an impasse. If sectoral inflation is likely to resume in the coming decade, and if traditional approaches are not likely to solve the problem, and if a vicious cycle of continued inflation fosters a culture that further weakens social justice, a minimal conclusion must be faced: *unless new approaches are developed,* problems of social justice, quite simply, will increase.

To some, such side effects may be acceptable, but for those interested in the issue of equity, the fundamental question is: What are the scope and range of appropriate explorations in search of an alternative strategic approach?

Enough has been said to suggest the importance of structural problems in the inflation-initiating sectors. Given the likelihood that such problems will grow, not diminish, in the 1980s—and that very little attention, relatively speaking, has been given them—it is important to ask what can be done, instance by instance, to deal with each sector. We are currently in the midst of an extremely conservative period in American political and economic history. Our own past and the experience of other advanced industrial nations suggest, however, that the "pendulum of politics" can swing— sometimes quickly—as economic difficulties persist. Are there approaches which—in combination with others—might be investigated, now, so as to begin to attack some of the sources of the new inflation directly?

V. THE NECESSITY OF DIRECT SECTORAL STRATEGIES

If economists are to contribute to the solution of some of the difficult paradoxes before us, we shall have to undertake new research and experimentation with direct sectoral strategies. Some must be approached on their own merits, some (as we shall discuss) might be linked with income policies and other strategies. And, as we shall explore below, each of the sectors interacts with each other. (For instance, reducing interest rates and energy-output costs will impact upon food prices.) What follows are a range of policy proposals drawn from a variety of sources. The list constitutes a preliminary overview of measures to be reviewed and refined in the development of a longer-term policy-research agenda.

A. Food

Greater stabilization of U.S. food prices in the new era of shortages and disruptions will ultimately require greater insulation of the American market from increasingly unstable international market conditions. So long as temporary shortages in world grain markets are translated rapidly into high, unstable domestic food prices, the U.S. economy will be hostage to world conditions and to major grain dealers. Agricultural failures and shortages in other nations, especially the Soviet Union, will dominate a significant part of the economy.

America is still the breadbasket of the world. But, archaically, it is also still the "shock absorber" of variations in world food demand. Unlike Japan and the Common Market, the U.S. has not adopted a policy of significantly managing grain trade to ease the shock of abrupt increases in world demand. To be sure, in recent years we have increased reserves. But the size of our reserves is still limited compared with the scale of potential demand—a fact masked by temporary global gluts in 1981 and 1982. Expanding U.S. reserves and toughening our stance in negotiations to force others to participate in international reserve efforts are part of the solution. But these are only first steps; the instabilities we are likely to face in the 1980s and 1990s will require further measures to protect the U.S. consumer and interrupt this portion of the inflation cycle. This means much more direct management of grain exports to insure adequate buffering. In one way or another, it also ultimately means supplanting the current intermediary between the domestic and international marketplace, the multinational grain companies (five of which control 85 percent of U.S. grain exports). While there are a number of possible arrangements, most other major exporting nations have established public corporations to achieve more accountable public control over food trade.[32]

There are a variety of ways in which a public corporation or grain board could be integrated into existing farm policy to achieve greater long-run price stability; each, however, inevitably establishes a two-tier pricing system. The price domestic consumers pay for grains is fixed at a level high enough (together with direct payments) to give farmers an adequate net income. Feed-grain prices are also stabilized to reduce the volatility of meat and dairy costs. Surpluses are sold on the international market at the world price. Profits from international sales could in some proposed variations be used to add supplementary income payments to family farmers, to assist Third World countries to attain greater agricultural self-sufficiency, to accumulate reserves, etc.[33] Finally, bilateral measures are likely to be necessary to insure adequate supply to some Third World consuming nations.

Traditional American policy has aimed at maintaining farm income by supporting prices. This has been accomplished by limiting production, by supplementary payments, by providing price floors through the purchase of surpluses when prices threaten to fall below a given level, and by restricting the flow of commodities to market at certain times in certain geographic areas. As a result, farmers have been guaranteed (often inadequate) price floors, while consumers (and taxpayers) have had to pay for unnecessarily high prices. At the same time the economy remains vulnerable to shortages because there is no price ceiling or overall grain-management strategy to reduce costs. Large farms have also obtained a disproportionate share of government benefits. The general strategy here proposed would reorient farm policy toward the goal of maintaining farm net income at adequate levels through direct supplements when necessary, a goal that is likely to be easier to achieve in the new era of food shortages than in the past era of surpluses.[34] The aim should be an adequate target level of income, with limits on the total payments any one farmer could receive. Reserves and supply flows should be managed to keep commodity prices within a narrow range, supplemented with price ceilings where necessary. By reducing output restrictions on acreage, such a policy could help assure consumers low—and more importantly—more stable prices while contributing to a productive system of efficient small and medium-sized family farms.

Though direct management of grain exports has been opposed by interested farm groups and grain traders, their political power has decreased significantly in recent years. The need for a new compromise with consumers and with overall anti-inflation strategies is likely to grow as both price and production problems increase. The argument for reducing unlimited grain exports has also been strengthened as expert studies have demonstrated the enormous land and water costs of current policies.[35]

There is plenty of room for debate and research about the most effective way to achieve such goals. Note carefully, however, that if *overall inflation* can be reduced by reducing the power of this initiating sectoral source of inflation, general stimulative economic policies might be free to increase overall economic growth and general tax revenues. If a 1 percent increase in GNP were facilitated by a direct sectoral strategy to cap inflation in this area, production increases of the order of $60 to $80 billion would yield federal tax revenues of the order of $25 billion per year. Possible efficiency losses at the micro-sectoral level are likely to be compensated if large-order gains can be achieved at the macro level. So, too, are the carrying costs of large reserves in surplus years. The linking of agricultural price goals with macro inflation and employment strategy could, in short, help generate additional tax flows—which in turn could assist in the achievement of sectoral goals.[36] Linking sectoral and macro strategies could also facilitate legislative compromises that aim to stabilize both farm-income and consumer prices. A careful assessment of trade-offs between macro and micro policies is necessary; such an assessment is likely to produce increasingly refined judgments of the costs and benefits of alternative approaches to replace the often one-sided criticism of sectoral strategies in isolation from their potential positive impact on macro strategies.

Tackling the problem of food-price inflation requires more than changing farm policy. The structure of the industry is characterized by increasing concentration in the first stage of production as well as in the processing, packaging, and distribution of food after it leaves the farm. It has, in fact, been in the post-farm phases of the process that added costs have been greatest.[37]

Concentration and monopoly power contribute to increasing consumers' costs in at least two ways. On the one hand, consumers must pay for higher profit margins, cost-inefficient operations, excessive advertising, and costly promotional campaigns. FTC economist Russell Parker and Department of Agriculture economist John M. Conner estimate that monopoly power in the food industry cost consumers $10-15 billion in 1975, 5 to 8 percent of what they spent in that year for food.[38] Additionally, consumers pay for concentration through its effect on the pass-through of farm commodity prices: corporations quickly pass on price rises, but downward adjustments are much less rapid and sure. Stabilization of food prices and of the general inflationary spiral would contribute to stabilizing inflation in the marketing sector, but measures to increase the competitive structure of the industry must be developed as well.[39]

B. Energy

Let us focus first on supply. If the energy component of general inflationary ratcheting is to be reduced over time, the U.S. must ultimately challenge the stranglehold of the OPEC cartel. A fundamental precondition is a major expansion of global exploration and the development of oil reserves in non-OPEC countries. A decade-long "proliferation" strategy could alter the basic context which allows OPEC to maintain high prices beyond situations of temporary glut or during global economic downturns.

The potential for new oil and natural-gas discoveries in the non-OPEC developing countries is much greater than is commonly recognized.[40] Estimates of ultimate worldwide crude-oil recovery, ranging from those of the Mobil and Exxon corporations to the Congressional Research Service, are in the 1.9 to 2 trillion barrel range.[41] Bernardo Grossling of the U.S. Geological Service estimates worldwide oil recovery to be between 2.6 and 6.5 trillion barrels.[42] "Published Proved Oil Reserves"—the volume of oil remaining in the ground which geological information and engineering information indicate to be recoverable in the future from known reserves, under existing economic and operating conditions—were 559 billion barrels in 1979, excluding reserves in the Soviet Union, Eastern Europe, and China.[43]

Proliferation options include U.S. financial-investment contributions, special Third World oil-development funds set up by multilateral development agencies, and direct international exploration by a U.S. public-energy corporation. Long-term bilateral purchase agreements with particular nations (e.g., Venezuela, for heavy crude) could also expand exploration and production, and thereby help stabilize prices.[44]

Beyond the strategic decision to expand world supplies, longer-term U.S. policy should aim to inject more competition into the world oil market. One method, proposed by MIT oil economist M.A. Adelman, involves the regular auctioning to lowest bidders of rights to export to the United States market. Each month import-authorization tickets would be printed based on an estimate of U.S. oil demand. The tickets would be sold at auction by sealed bid; no oil could be imported without a ticket. Foreign countries would pay a small fee for the right to sell in the U.S. market.[45] The cartel would, of course, attempt to get members to submit uniform fixed bids. But the temptation to cheat—to sell oil at beneath the OPEC price— would be high. A related possibility proposed by some forty members of Congress[46] would be to shift responsibility for buying foreign oil for the American market from the multinationals to an importing institution with a mandate to get the best bargain for the U.S.—a common practice in many other countries. So long as major oil companies are the de facto bargaining agent for the United States in negotiations with OPEC, there is little hope that the U.S. interest in breaking the cartel will be primary. Not only is there little incentive to weaken prices; there is every incentive to keep them high.

A further step toward improving domestic price stability would be to provide the public sector with an independent source of expertise and a capacity to increase competition directly by establishing a so-called yardstick public corporation. The U.S. is one of the few advanced industrial nations which does not have such a capacity. Canada, Italy, France, Great Britain, Mexico, and Norway have each had substantial experience with public energy corporations. Legislation to establish a Federal Energy Corporation modeled on the TVA was originally introduced by Senators Magnuson and Stevenson in 1973. It would have combined both domestic and importing functions, and could also have exploited energy resources on public lands (including offshore tracts), where 14 percent of oil production and 28 percent of gas production already take place, and where the vast majority of new discoveries are likely to be made.

Expansion of global supply, greater leverage in bargaining with OPEC, and strengthening competitive pricing at home, taken together, suggest long-term strategic policy directions. A second major strategy, obviously, is to achieve greater independence through more efficient use of energy via conservation and the expansion of renewable energy supplies (e.g., solar and geothermal).

Conservation viewed as an alternative energy source is highly competitive with more traditional sources; many options are within the $15 per barrel equivalent range. The Harvard Energy Project estimated in 1979 that the United States "might use 30 to 40 percent less energy than it does now, with virtually no penalty for the way Americans live."[47]

The cumulative fuel savings, for instance, resulting from improved automobile efficiency standards (as they exist up to 1985) could be as high as 20 billion barrels over the years 1975-2000—

twice the reserves on the North Slope of Alaska.[48] Note that conservation in this area may be at less cost, not more: The average miles per gallon (MPG) of the U.S. fleet is currently approximately 15— yet the Volkswagen diesel Rabbit gets 42 MPG, the Ford Fiesta and Honda Civic about 35-40 MPG. More rapid movement toward higher efficiency standards offers a very large area for potential savings. A National Highway Traffic Safety Administration report notes: "Domestic manufacturers probably can have the technological capability to increase average fuel economy of passenger autos by 1995 to the neighborhood of 45-50 MPG; light trucks should be capable of achieving 23-30 MPG."[49]

Conservation within the industrial sector can also be significant. Various companies have found that small investments in conservation are often extremely rewarding. Energy consumption at a large American Can facility in New Jersey was reduced by 55 percent with an investment of $73,000 producing an annual savings of $700,000. The Parker Company, a manufacturer of automobile parts, saved $1.2 million a year after investing $50,000 in energy conservation.[50] Through cogeneration—the combined production of electricity and heat—much less fuel is used to produce electricity and steam than is needed to produce the two separately. In the 1930s over half of all American industries used cogeneration (the figure is only 4 percent today). Sweden and Western Germany produce almost 30 percent of their electricity through cogeneration. Robert Williams of Princeton University has calculated that cogeneration could supply 208,000 megawatts of power (the production equivalent of 200 large nuclear power plants)—enough energy so that no new power plants (aside from those under construction) would be needed until the year 2000.[51] The Harvard Energy Project summarizes: "Altogether, it may be economically possible to cut industrial energy use by more than a third through cogeneration and conservation efforts."[52]

The American home also offers especially significant possibilities. The Center for Environmental Studies at Princeton found that up to a 67 percent reduction in energy for space heating in homes is possible with a simple package of window, basement, and attic insulation and the plugging of air leaks. Other studies estimate that if simple insulation were aggressively promoted through a strong national program, total energy use in the residential sector could be cut in half.[53] Beyond the home is the office. The tall skyscrapers of the 1960s were energy disasters and need not be repeated in new construction. New office buildings can be built to use only one-fifth of the energy used in the 1960s to heat and cool average office space.[54]

The potential of renewable energy sources is also well established. The President's Council on Environmental Quality calculated in 1978 that solar power could provide the equivalent of 12 million barrels of oil per day—23 percent of our energy consumption by the year 2000.[55] Many solar technologies are already economically competitive with fossil fuels and nuclear resources; others, like photovoltaics, are likely only to require a relatively small public investment to achieve efficiencies of scale and commercial viability.

Summarizing a massive study of various proven existing options, Roger Sant of the Carnegie Mellon Institute, suggests: "The United States could be using almost the same amount of energy in 1990 that we use today, while satisfying a much larger demand for energy services."[56]

If a strategic decision to maximize world supplies over the coming decade were coupled with an all-out "Manhattan Project" to conserve energy *directly* (through regulation, loan, subsidy, and other targeted programs)—and to expand renewable energy programs—the role of unregulated (and volatile) prices in the energy sector would obviously be far less significant. It is apparent, in fact, that *beyond the very high levels already achieved* further general price increases are likely to yield only small production gains.[57] Nor are they likely to induce major additional conservation. This is particularly true in such necessity areas as heating oil, and particularly for low- and moderate-income groups. By definition, these are areas where price influences are the least significant. Accordingly, a direct approach to reducing the inflationary impulse of sectoral-energy jolts becomes increasingly feasible.

In the context of a major global-supply expansion and targeted domestic conservation and renewable energy effort, a clear policy decision to recontrol energy prices (with special attention to necessity-related costs such as heating oil) in the event of new price pressures would be of substantial interest. A careful evaluation of the costs and benefits of two broad strategies should be undertaken: continued jolts and related additions to overall inflation versus targeted programs and controls (or possibly, a predictable price ceiling triggered by price levels specified in advance). Despite well-known objections to controls, the cost of not achieving stability on the "macro" inflation and growth fronts, as we have seen, is very high. A recontrol strategy biased toward the necessity-related areas could be coupled with consumption taxes for nonnecessity or luxury uses of energy (e.g., private jet fuel, heating oil for second homes, etc.). In any event, recontrol of energy prices may well be an inevitability

in the 1980s: A major Arab-Israeli blowup, the resumption in force
of the Iran-Iraq war, an Iran-type revolution overthrowing the existing government of one or another major producer (especially Saudi
Arabia) could all disrupt supplies. Beyond temporary gluts, stability, in fact, is the least likely scenario in the Middle East for the
1980s. And in a situation of major supply disruption, any U.S. government in power will be forced to draw the line.[58]

Controls, it should be recalled, are not simply a liberal device;
the 1970s controls were imposed by the Nixon Administration to
prevent economic chaos and to keep domestic prices below the cartel
price. The question about controls in the 1980s may well be whether
they are part of a coordinated policy or imposed "helter-skelter"
when costs become absolutely intolerable. The advance exploration
of efficient and equitable mechanisms to replace the clumsy bureaucratic system of the 1970s is an important area for applied research,
as is the refinement of rationing schemes which might be imposed in
the event of significant disruption.

C. Health Care

Health-care costs, though not part of the jolt syndrome, constitute nearly 10 percent of the U.S. GNP; they rose from 6.2 percent
of the GNP in 1965 to 9.5 percent in 1980.[59] As we have discussed,
though there are other factors, a substantial part of the problem derives from the fact that the U.S. health system promotes excessive
costs and treatment through reliance on third-party payments by
government agencies and insurance companies. Neither the patient
nor the provider bears the true cost of treatment decisions; neither
party has an incentive to balance costs against benefits. In fact,
health-care institutions that seek to minimize costs risk reducing
current and future income, since reimbursements often reflect the
record of past costs, particularly capital expenditures.[60]

Hospital cost-containment strategies can help in the short run.
This simply means putting a lid on expenditures, thereby forcing
cost cutting. The process is not without difficulties, however; as
Karen Davis points out, "maintaining rigorous controls over prices
for long periods of time may require excessive administrative ma-
chinery... [and] even if price controls are effective, hospitals may
find other socially undesirable methods of increasing revenues, as
by placing pressures on physicians for lengthened stays."[61] Containment strategies can also result in rationing of care rather than in
greater efficiency.

Nevertheless, there are several successful experiences in localities around the nation where controls have significantly reduced spending without depriving patients of needed care. Maryland, for example, has adopted a "public utility approach" to cost controls; hospital rate increases must be approved by the Maryland Health Services Cost Review Commission. The commission applies different rate-regulation methods to individual hospitals at different times. An analysis of the Maryland program by the federal Health Care Financing Administration concluded:

> While some elements of arbitrariness and uncertainty do exist for hospitals, their rights are guarded by the Hospital Association, Blue Cross and ultimately the court system, as well as by the very open and public nature of the process. The consensus among the participants on both sides seems to be that the system is fair and reasonable. For most of them, the system as it has evolved is a source of considerable pride.[62]

Beyond containment strategies, it is clear that only a longer-term restructuring of the industry to reduce incentives for excessive treatment can reduce the underlying sources of health-care inflation. One approach is to reform the Blue Cross/Blue Shield system. Michigan recently enacted a sweeping reform law which will reduce the boards of directors of the Blues in the state and require that three-quarters of the board members be subscribers. Reimbursement rates to doctors and hospitals will be tied to increases in the inflation rate and the Gross National Product. State regulators are empowered to act to control hospital costs if the Blues have not done so voluntarily by 1983.

Health Maintenance Organizations (HMOs) offer approaches to health delivery which eliminate some pseudo-market distortions. HMO doctors are salaried, and members receive services needed for a fixed per-person or family fee. Because "fee-for-service" payment is eliminated, no one loses when illness is prevented, and no one gains by providing unnecessary treatment. HMOs have had impressive results in reducing costs. Members of the Med Center Health Plan, a Minneapolis-St. Paul HMO, receive service that would cost 15 to 20 percent more under conventional health insurance.[63] Hospitalization rates for HMO members are about 30 percent lower than for people covered by fee-for-service insurance.[64] HMOs have their critics. Some fault prepaid plans for impersonal "assembly line" health care, for delays some patients have experienced before seeing physicians, and for changes in the physicians seen, a practice that raises the chances for inconsistent or insufficient diagnosis.[65]

Imbedded as they are in the surrounding fee-for-service environment, moreover, HMOs as individual institutions are victims of many of the problems of the system as a whole. For example, because doctors have the option of practicing in more lucrative private practices, HMOs must pay nearly comparable salaries. Likewise, existing HMOs rarely own their own hospitals and must pay the going rate in the private sector.

Over the coming decade the system as a whole must be addressed if costs are to be reduced substantially. One proposed longer-term remedy is to establish a National Health Service in which all health workers are salaried and care is delivered through community-controlled HMOs. Legislation to accomplish this and supplement it with resources at the national, regional, and community levels and with provisions for worker and consumer control is pending in the U.S. House of Representatives.[66] Another commonly discussed strategy is national health insurance. The U.S., Australia and South Africa are the only advanced industrial nations that still do not have some form of such a system.

As a society we will ultimately have to decide explicitly what proportion of our total resources we can afford to devote to health care. Most proposals for national health insurance contain explicit expenditure ceilings, but it is illogical to assume that the macro-goals can be reached if all the micro-incentives remain unchanged. It is possible that over the coming two decades comprehensive national health insurance might be a transitional phase toward a national health service.

Virtually all longer-term solutions to the health-care and cost crisis involve planning. At the local level an assessment of specific needs is necessary: Are we dealing with a rural area with an elderly population? A suburb with a disproportionate number of young families needing pediatric services? A mill town where the emphasis needs to be on occupational health? Longer-range manpower and womanpower issues also require planning to determine types of training (medical or paramedical), types of facilities (should hospitals be converted into nursing homes?), and the proportion of resources allocated to medical care and other health-related uses (are more doctors needed or would it be a better use of resources to train more OSHA inspectors or other nonmedical personnel?).

A number of short-term reforms have also been proposed. For instance, evidence presented over the past few years to both Congress and the Department of Health and Human Services has demonstrated that clinical laboratories, including those regulated by federal law, often have high error rates; estimates have ranged from 20 to 50 percent. Both the human costs and the economic costs of such errors are, of course, enormous. False negative test results can leave illness undetected, making expensive treatment necessary that might well have been avoided. False positive test results can cause costly and unnecessary therapeutic programs, such as surgery. Uniform national standards should be set to improve quality and control. According to the Congressional Budget Office, a clinical-laboratory regulation bill which would have saved $251.6 million over a four-year period passed the House Commerce Committee in 1976.

Another problem is unnecessary surgery and hospital stays. Approximately 2 million unnecessary surgeries were performed in 1977 at a cost of almost $4 billion, according to the House Subcommittee on Oversight and Investigations. (The American Medical Association has argued that unneeded surgery constitutes a "very, very tiny percentage" of all surgical procedures.) Second-opinion surgical programs, such as the American Federation of State, County and Municipal Employees (AFSCME) program in New York, have significantly reduced the incidence of unneeded surgery (in this case by over one-third).[67] Current incentives in hospital-reimbursement practice often encourage unnecessary treatment, delay patient discharges, or weaken admissions. Hospital pre-admission testing by Professional Standard Review Organizations can shorten lengths of stay; a recent nationwide survey of PSROs concluded that hundreds of millions of dollars could be saved through effective coordinated application of PSRO audit findings.[68]

Prescription drugs cost Americans $12 to $14 billion a year, or nearly 10 percent of the nation's health-care expenditures.[69] There is an extraordinary price differential between drugs prescribed under trade names and products marketed under generic names. The FDA could undermine deceptive claims about the safety and effectiveness of generic drugs by publicizing a list of interchangeable drugs. The FDA also has the authority to inform the medical profession and the public when there is no difference between two products.

The most fundamental long-range step in stabilizing the health-sector component of overall inflation is an increasing emphasis on prevention. There is no alternative here but government regulation to reduce pollution, achieve food safety, protect occupational health and safety, and promote education for individual responsibility for health.

D. Housing

If the housing component of sectoral inflation is to be checked, several new policy departures will be necessary over the coming decade. In the context of an overall program to reduce inflation, both speculative and interest rate components of housing costs can be addressed. At the outset, it is important to recognize that we face a significant supply/demand imbalance in certain types of housing, and in certain geographic markets. The baby boom is now a family boom, with high housing demand and shortages in key areas. The trend toward more single-family units is also important. New households increased from an average yearly rate of 925,000 in the 1950s to 1,060,000 in the 1960s;[70] from 1975 to 1978, new household formations averaged 1,636,000 annually. Unbalanced economic growth has also contributed additional problems by concentrating population in areas of short supply, and by shifting industry and population out of other areas, leaving excess units behind.

Over the long haul greater regional economic balance is an important factor. But the larger capital and supply problems are central: In the stop-start economy of the 1970s, high interest rates regularly choked off housing starts even as family-formation rates put growing pressures on restricted supply. If the food- and energy-initiating sources of overall inflation can be reduced, longer-term interest rates and housing production will improve automatically. Beyond this, the explicit allocation of capital, an approach common in other nations, is likely to be of growing importance during the coming decade. During the 1970s former Federal Reserve Board member Andrew Brimmer and former Secretary of the Treasury G. William Miller (before taking office) proposed different systems of allocation. Under the Credit Control Act of 1969 the president was given authority to request the Federal Reserve Board to require that a certain percentage of a bank's portfolio be in the form of mortgages or housing loans. Alternatively, selective-reserve-asset systems have been suggested which can achieve lower interest rates for various types of low- and moderate-income housing. Other credit-control or allocation strategies should also be explored.[71]

Additional government action to expand investment in moderate- and low-income houses is also important. In 1977 the median ratio of shelter costs (including utilities, property taxes, maintenance, and insurance) to income was 25 percent for renters and 19 percent for owners with mortgages. But for renters with annual incomes below $5,000 and mortgaged owners with incomes below $7,000 the median ratio was over 35 percent.[72] There are a variety of well-known measurement problems, but several factors add to the severity of the growing shortage: First, new residential construction has become increasingly luxury-oriented; units produced are not easily filtered down. Second, production of new rental housing is very limited. In 1978 the nation's rental-housing stock actually declined as rental-unit losses exceeded rental-unit production.

Government housing subsidies for new construction, moderate rehabilitation, and in some cases substantial rehabilitation are required if a serious attack on the problems is to be mounted over the decade. Though currently politically vulnerable, subsidies have become central to housing strategies in virtually all other advanced industrial nations; they are particularly important in connection with rental housing—in fact, roughly two-thirds of all new U.S. rental units currently involve subsidy programs. (Low- and moderate-income persons are obviously the most dependent on rental housing —roughly 45 percent of low- and moderate-income families are renters versus only 15 percent of upper-income families.) Over the coming decade public housing (particularly expansion of the successful low-rise unit program) is also likely to be of renewed significance.

The supply of low- and moderate-income multifamily units in urban areas may also be increased by turning over abandoned property to individuals, nonprofit community, and tenant groups. Such properties can often be renovated by potential tenants themselves (so called "sweat equity") at substantial savings, and incorporated as nonprofit housing cooperatives (in the case of multifamily buildings) or occupied as "urban homesteads" in the case of single-family homes. Urban homesteading has been promoted since 1973 by several cities—and recently by the federal government.[73]

Current tax laws permitting interest-rate deductions (and the skewed income distribution) assure the excessive production of luxury, single-family housing. Tax provisions also lead to wasteful speculation; as many have noted, full-scale tax reform, including some limit on deductibility, is long overdue. Housing density will also have to be increased gradually over the decade to prevent further energy and land-wasting suburban sprawl. Local job-stabilization programs could mitigate the present situation in which housing stands empty in Youngstown while families double up in San Diego. Strategies that permit the expansion of capacity in critical building-materials industries, and which orient public-employment and training programs to develop marketable skills in housing construction and solar-energy retrofitting, could help eliminate potential bottleneck areas.

The conversion of existing rental buildings to cooperatives can contribute to the control of housing inflation by taking apartments out of the for-profit market and putting them under the control of a nonprofit corporation, or, in some cases, a community organization. While rents have risen more slowly than homeownership costs, they have been accelerating in recent years, and the national vacancy rate continues to hit record lows as more and more middle-income people are priced out of the home-purchase market. Low- and moderate-income tenants are increasingly being displaced, directly through condominium conversion, or indirectly through exorbitant increases in rents. Though obviously a last resort, if combined with supply expansion and conversion strategies for the long haul, rent control in certain markets may on balance be the only short-run way to avoid the excessive costs and social displacements of temporary housing shortages.[74]

Finally, the land issue will have to be confronted directly if longer-term inflation in housing is to be curbed. Land has been a major recent source of housing inflation. From 1969 to 1977, the costs of labor and materials for the average single-family home rose 66 percent while land prices for those homes soared 127 percent. From 1949 to 1977 land as a percentage of average single-family home costs more than doubled from 11 to 25 percent (in contrast, labor and material costs in that period as a percentage of the average-price home dropped from 69 to 46.7 percent).[75] There are no generalized approaches to the stabilization of land prices; the nation is too huge and the forces that impinge on land values too varied. However, some obvious principles are important, the most significant of which is that rewards from private speculation in land should be reduced.

Taxing speculative profits from land development is an idea dating from the nineteenth-century economist Henry George. George held that land values—as opposed to the value of improvements—rose because of population and other outside forces not caused by a productive investment of the landowner. He proposed that the entire increment of land values be taxed at a rate of 100 percent. A modified modern tax on land speculation was established by the state of Vermont in 1973. Under the Vermont statute, anyone buying and selling land within a period of six years must pay a declining capital-gains tax on profits: If land is bought and sold at a higher price within six months, the state tax is 70 percent; it reaches zero at six years.

A second general approach is for the public to buy development rights. Property is a "bundle" of rights—to use land, to sell it, to keep other people off it, to develop it. To a large degree, returns from speculation depend on possibilities for development. The idea is to separate development rights from the rest of the bundle and permit the public to control them. Since 1978 the Massachusetts Agricultural Preservation and Restriction Program has been authorized to buy development rights to farmland on a limited basis.

A third alternative is public ownership. In recent years responsible policy analysts have focused increasing attention on this tool of urban development. One proposal, for instance, comes from former HUD Secretary Robert Wood:

> Fundamentally, we are at the point where public ownership and public planning are probably the essential components for a genuine land reform program. Certain levels of density no longer make tolerable private ownership and development even though zoning and planning requirements are available to affect them directly. Only a general plan with land ownership and control being the decisive forces in critical areas can do the job.[76]

The American Institute of Architects in 1972 offered a detailed proposal for the joint federal, state, and local acquisition and development of one million acres of land in selected urban-fringe areas of the country. The AIA estimated that one million acres could accommodate one-third of the nation's growth over the next thirty years at the relatively low average density of twenty-five persons per acre.[77] "The appreciating value of this land," the AIA argued, "...realized by lease and sale over the next thirty years—would be enough to cover its original cost plus a large proportion of the cost preparing the land for development."[78]

VI. THE ROLE OF CONTROLS
IN A COMPREHENSIVE PROGRAM

This list of strategies aimed at reducing important sources of longer-term sectoral inflation during the 1980s can obviously be expanded and refined. As we have seen, however, the significant point is that unless structural problems in the key areas are attacked directly, there is little likelihood of controlling major initiating sources of overall inflation, which are likely to resume.

It may well be that if inflation is not checked, political pressures will force the reimposition of wage-price controls at some point during the 1980s. In this regard, it is important to remember that the 1970s controls were instituted not by a Democratic Administration but by Richard Nixon. For most of the Carter period poll data showed that a majority (often a large majority) of the public has favored wage-price controls. Early in 1980 the conservative Salomon Brothers financial analyst Henry Kaufman urged wage-price controls because chaos in the financial markets had become intolerable. So, too, did Barry Bosworth and a number of traditional liberal proponents of controls. The Joint Economic Committee in early 1981 urged stand-by legislation.

Wage-price controls are not a solution to the problem of sectoral based inflation. In fact, only if appropriate measures to deal with the structural problems are developed could wage-price controls work with even moderate effectiveness. From the point of view of social justice, there are additional problems: unless a focus on the sectors is sharpened, if wage-price controls were put into effect family income would be severely burdened. One Nixon Administration official commented that the 1970s controls "zapped labor." Family real income was also put under severe pressure in the period of the voluntary Carter guidelines, as key items in the family budget —heating oil and food, for example—were allowed to skyrocket while wages were held down. A program of wage-price controls that did not deal with underlying pressures in the key sectors would put real income in a legal vise and systematically squeeze the household budget.

Beyond the fundamental equity issue lies a practical one. If the 1970s scenario were to be played out again in the 1980s, wages—and then prices—would almost certainly explode after controls were lifted as families attempted to make up the real income lost while they were in effect. Then, in all likelihood, we would see a replay of the last six years: A worsening inflationary spiral, then (once again) an attempt to engineer a recession, and probably (thereafter) reimposition of controls when everything else had failed.

This is not to say that controls should not be considered as part of an overall program, since experience shows they can affect expectations and slow inflation in the short run. But the basic point before, during, or after controls is that they cannot succeed unless the underlying sectoral problems that are fueling inflation are dealt with.

VII. TRADE, PRODUCTIVITY, GROWTH, INCOME POLICIES

We have suggested that in the political-economic context of the remaining decades of the twentieth century, the social-justice implications of new forms of inflation extend beyond their direct impact on the consumption needs of different income groups, and even beyond the indirect (but powerful) fact that uncontrolled inflation leads to attacks on spending for social programs, and, regularly, to engineered recessions which disproportionately throw members of low- and moderate-income groups out of work. The additional political-economic effects of the new inflation cannot be separated from the primary effects.

Nor, it may be added, can we significantly improve our export position without managing domestic price levels more effectively. Directly stabilizing the initiating sources of U.S. inflation would in fact be a powerful strategy for improving our overall export position—one likely to have a much greater effect than well-publicized but essentially limited "winner picking" or other specially targeted export-enhancing policies. Lowering domestic inflation would also permit reduction of the high interest rates that have artificially increased the value of the dollar and undercut our trading position. The U.S. is in a relatively favored resource position vis a vis most other nations (especially in food and domestic energy); if we so choose, price-stabilizing sectoral strategies could even be a significant component of an aggressive longer-term trade initiative. Beyond this, the economic performance and growth rates of productivity in Germany, Japan, and a number of other industrial competitors have been outpacing us for some time. In the period 1970-79, for instance, output per man-hour in manufacturing increased 23 percent in the U.S., but 58 percent in Germany and 57 percent in Japan. U.S. manufacturing productivity rates turned negative during 1979.[79] If the next decade repeats this performance, the compounding effects guarantee that the very heart of our industrial economy will be threatened as we stagger in productivity, while our major competitors race forward. But self-evidently the problem of overall stability can also not be understood without reference to the special sectors.

It is unlikely that we will significantly alter our present unfortunate general productivity pattern until we develop a serious fundamental strategy to challenge the stop/start, go/no-go management of our economy. No intelligent executive can plan for long-term investment in high-productivity equipment unless he has confidence in a growing market that can be counted on. In a continually uncertain economy, moreover, we build in supply bottlenecks that prevent future expansion. To the extent investment is limited by expectation of weak performance (or simply uncertainty), future inflation is guaranteed when an upward swing is throttled by limited capacity— itself the inevitable result of stop/go expectations.

Our only real alternative if we are to resume an upward, steady-growth path in the 1980s is to deal with the underlying causes of continued instability. But it is precisely at this point that traditional remedies for inflation are most at odds with the realities. Tightening the monetary screws another notch is a prescription for economic suicide, especially for the innovative small-business sector. Broad-brush demands for more fiscal restraint do more to weaken a strategy of careful expansion than to help control inflation. Finally, viewed in the larger perspective of the growing sector-specific problems, generalized tax reductions can create large budget deficits while contributing little to planned growth.

If the United States is to resume a steady forward trend, broad public support for policy is also necessary. But no consensus on economic issues is likely to be sustained (beyond the short term) unless it is equitable. Organized labor has demonstrated considerable moderation in its wage demands in light of the rate of nonwage-based inflation. A long-term consensus involving wage moderation is likely to hold, however, only if the special problems of the sectors most important to the average family budget are resolved. The AFL-CIO, in fact, has consistently declared its willingness to compromise on key points *if* food, housing, energy, and health-care issues are dealt with. A variety of different forms of incomes policies can be devised, but a strategy designed to cover the key areas could simultaneously reduce nonwage-based inflation and remove major barriers to resumption of stable growth. Though not often discussed in the context of incomes policies in the U.S., sector-specific policies are commonly included in such approaches abroad. A comprehensive effort including the sectors, as has been suggested, might more than compensate for small-order micro-inefficiencies with significant macro-gains. If carefully crafted, the addition for a brief period of a tax-based incomes policy (TIP) involving tax relief in exchange for price or wage restraint could possibly help solve some problems of transition caused by past failures.

VII. CONCLUSION

We may now summarize several political/economic points drawn from our analysis of social equity and the new inflation: Our main conclusion is that because of its primary impact (high prices of necessity-related items on low- and middle-income groups) and its secondary impact (the consequences of failure to solve inflation for overall policymaking, the budget, unemployment, and productivity growth), direct strategies to reduce inflation in the necessity-related sectors are an important element in any serious effort to achieve social justice in the coming decades.

It is likely (beyond price moderation caused by temporary gluts) that once economic growth resumes we will see a resumption of inflation in the 1980s. During the years of the Carter Administration a broad-based coalition proposed that the "necessities of life" be made the central thrust of an equitable anti-inflation program which could also help achieve sustained economic growth. More than 70 consumer, labor, environmental, senior-citizen, and minority organizations—Consumers Opposed to Inflation in the Necessities (COIN)—proposed policies to hold down price increases in the four key sectors. The poll data also shows strong support for direct measures, including not only wage-price controls, but energy- and food-price controls, and even rationing.[80] If traditional solutions to the problem of inflation once again falter during the 1980s, if massive recession is rejected, and if the resulting economic burdens and social inequities increase, there is likely to be need for a carefully refined list of new policy initiatives. We can expect at some point that the public will demand that the pain be stopped—and that the economy be put back to work. Economists who invest their intellectual capital in the necessary advance-research effort are likely to find that the returns, both for social equity and overall economic policy, are substantial.

NOTES

1. We are here referring to the equity implications of specific prices, not of general inflation. For two notable recent exceptions, see Ray Canterbery, *The Making of Economics,* (Belmont, Calif.: Wadsworth Publishing Co., 1980); and Paul Blumberg, *Inequity in an Age of Decline* (New

York: Oxford University Press, 1980). Historically, the work of the nine-teenth-century German statistician Ernest Engel is obviously significant.

2. The Necessities Related Index is calculated from data provided by the Bureau of Labor Statistics in its monthly Consumer Price Index releases. The Index is a weighted average of the price indexes for food, shelter, medical care, and energy. The weights used are fixed-quantity weights provided by the Bureau of Labor Statistics which are based on the average proportion of family income spent on those items in 1973 according to a survey conducted by the BLS. These weights are identical with those used by the BLS in calculating the CPI. The proportional weight of each item in the Index is the same relative to each of the other necessity-related items as it is in the CPI.

3. For a discussion of definitional and other problems related to the key sectors, see *Challenge,* January/February 1981.

4. Council of Economic Advisors, *Economic Report of the President,* (Washington, D.C.: U.S. Government Printing Office, 1978), p. 141.

5. "Volcker: Standard of Living Has to Decline." *Wall Street Journal,* October 29, 1979.

6. National Advisory Council on Economic Opportunity, *Critical Choice for the 80's* (Washington, D.C.: U.S. Government Printing Office, August 1980), p. 85; and Leslie Nulty, *Understanding the New Inflation: The Importance of the Basic Necessities* (Washington, D.C.: Exploratory Project for Economic Alternatives, 1977), p. 7. The Nulty study is one of the most important, and first, analyses of several sectoral issues reviewed in this paper.

7. Lester Brown with Erik P. Eckholm, *By Bread Alone* (New York: Praeger, 1974), pp. 5-6.

8. Energy Information Administration; cited in *Energy Policy,* Congressional Quarterly, Inc., 1981, p. 5.

9. National Advisory Council, p. 85.

10. Anthony Gallo, James A. Zellner, and David M. Smallwood, "The Rich, the Poor and the Money They Spend for Food" in *National Food Review,* Summer 1980, U.S. Department of Agriculture, pp. 16-18.

11. Fuel Oil Marketing Advisory Committee, *Low-Income Energy Assistance Programs: A Profile of Need and Policy Options,* U.S. Department of Energy (Washington, D.C., U.S. Government Printing Office, July 1980), pp. 9-10.

12. Joseph J. Minarik, "A Critique"; Gar Alperovitz and Jeff Faux, "Missing the Point: A Reply"; and Joseph Bowring, "Necessities Inflation and Distributional Impact," in *Challenge,* January/February 1981.

13. Lester Thurow, *The Zero-Sum Society* (New York: Basic Books, 1980), pp. 41-54. For a critique of Thurow's arguments on the impact of inflation on different income groups, see Joseph Bowring, "How Bad Were the Seventies?" *Challenge,* July/August 1981, pp. 42-50.

14. Beverly L. Johnson, "Changes in Marital and Family Characteristics of Workers, 1970-80," *Monthly Labor Review,* April 1979, p. 49.

15. Gar Alperovitz and Jeff Faux, "Controls and the Basic Necessities," *Challenge,* May/June 1980, p. 21.

16. National Advisory Council, p. 99.

17. Joseph Bowring, "How Bad Were the Seventies?" and Larry Olsen, *Inflation and the Elderly,* Data Resources, Inc., March 1980.

18. National Advisory Council, pp. 88-89.

19. Michael Mazerov and Robert Howard, *The Triple Threat: Inflation and Low-Income Families,* National Community Action Agency Executive Directors Association, May 1980, p. 6.

20. Blumberg, p. 79.

21. Federal Fuel Oil Marketing Advisory Committee, p. 12.

22. According to the Federal Fuel Oil Marketing Advisory Committee, the average poor household spent 21.8 percent of its family budget for household energy in 1980 (in contrast, middle-income households spent, on the average, only 5.1 percent of their budget on household energy). Ibid., p. 10.

23. Congressional Budget Office, *Entering the 1980s: Fiscal Policy Choices* (Washington, D.C.: U.S. Government Printing Office, January 1980), p. 90.

24. Council of Economic Advisors, *Economic Report of the President* (Washington, D.C.: U.S. Government Printing Office, January 1981), p. 42.

25. Data Resources, *The Macroeconomic Impact of Federal Pollution Control Programs: 1978 Assessment,* submitted to the Environmental Protection Agency, January 29, 1979.

26. Barry P. Bosworth, *Address Before the Associated Press Annual Meeting,* May 1, 1978, p. 10.

27. Ibid., p. 7.

28. Arthur M. Okun, "Efficient Disinflationary Policies," *American Economic Review,* May 1978, p. 348.

29. Thurow, p. 53.

30. "The Employment Situation: July 1981," Department of Labor, Bureau of Labor Statistics press release, August 2, 1981.

31. Gerald F. Seib, "Recessions Cause Death Rate to Rise, As Pressures of Coping Take Hold," *Wall Street Journal,* August 24, 1980. See also M. Harvey Brenner, "Mortality and the National Economy: A Review and the Experience of England and Wales 1936-1976, *Lancet,* September 15, 1979, pp. 568-73; and "Health and the National Economy: Commentary and General Principles," *Mental Health and the Economy* (Kalamazoo, Mich.: Upjohn Institute, 1979), pp. 63-87.

32. Dan Morgan, *Merchants of Grain* (New York: Viking Press, 1979).

33. Over time, as international demand increases, the income could be substantial, especially in years of acute shortage. Accumulated financial surpluses could appropriately be used to assist developing nations, as could expanded grain reserves in times of difficulty.

34. See John Schnittker, *"Stabilizing Domestic Food Prices by Changing the Export Marketing System,"* prepared for the National Center for Economic Alternatives, January 1979.

35. See "U.S. Drive for Grain Exports Stirs Doubts Both at Home and Abroad," *New York Times,* September 1, 1981; and "Food Exports: Worries in Land of Plenty," *Washington Post,* August 17, 1981. For further discussion of export increases and resource constraints, see U.S. Department of Agriculture: *Summary Report on the Structure of Agriculture,* Washington, D.C., January 1981, pp. 23-28.

36. A 1978 unpublished Department of Agriculture paper found that if the U.S. in 1978 had unilaterally set its wheat and coarse-grain export prices at the level at which they are supported internally in other countries —thereby eliminating subsidies to foreign governments—export volume would have fallen 13 percent while the value of exports would have risen 39 percent. This would have produced $3.3 billion in additional revenues. See U.S. Department of Agriculture, *Economic Effects of Differential Export Pricing of Agricultural Products—A Case Study,* unpublished paper, photocopy, 1978, p. 3.

37. A portion of the inflation in the marketing bill has been the result of higher energy costs in recent years. See below for a discussion of strategies to reduce this source of sectoral inflation.

38. Statement of Russell Parker and John M. Connor, *Impact of Market Concentration on Rising Food Prices,* Hearing before the Subcommittee on Antitrust, Monopoly and Business Rights of the Senate Judiciary Committee (Washington, D.C.: U.S. Government Printing Office, April 6, 1979).

39. Despite the sorry record of recent antitrust policy, there is probably no alternative to more vigorous enforcement in the food sector in the short run. Success will require new legislation to deal with conglomerate mergers that are rampant in the industry. Senator Edward Kennedy has introduced legislation to make mergers by companies with over $2 billion in assets or sales illegal. His proposal would also simplify a finding that monopolization is occurring. The late Senator Phillip Hart's Industrial Reorganization Act would have required divestiture if four or fewer companies accounted for 50 percent or more of sales in any line of commerce in any year out of the three preceding the filing of the complaint, if there was no price competition within an industry, or if the average rate of return of a company exceeded 15 percent for five of the seven preceding years. (Industrial Reorganization Act, S. 1167, *Congressional Record,* vol. 119, part 6, pp. 7319 et seq.)

40. See, for instance, Congressional Budget Office, "A Strategy for Oil Proliferation," Staff Working Paper by Craig Roach, February 23, 1979.

41. Ibid., p. 6.

42. Ibid., p. 5.

43. *The Energy Factbook,* Congressional Research Service Committee Print for the Subcommittee on Energy and Power, Committee on

Interstate and Foreign Commerce, November 1980, p. 374.

44. "A Strategy for Oil Proliferation."

45. "Ways to Foil the Oil Cartel," interview with M.A. Adelman, *U.S. News and World Report,* April 9, 1979.

46. H.R. 3604, Oil Imports Act of 1979, *Congressional Record,* April 10, 1979.

47. Robert Stobaugh and David Yergin, eds., *Energy Future: Report of the Energy Project at the Harvard Business School* (New York: Ballantine Books, 1979), p. 229.

48. Ibid., p. 184.

49. National Highway Traffic Safety Administration, *Analysis of Post-1985 Fuel Economy,* January 1981, pp. 1-9.

50. *Energy Future,* p. 193.

51. Dr. Robert H. Williams, "Industrial Cogeneration." *Annual Review of Energy* (Palo Alto, Calif.: Annual Reviews, 1978), p. 352.

52. *Energy Future,* p. 200.

53. Ibid., p. 214.

54. See ibid., p. 208.

55. Council on Environmental Quality, *Solar Energy: Progress and Promise,* Executive Office of the President, 1978.

56. Roger W. Sant, *The Least-Cost Strategy: Minimizing Consumer Costs Through Competiton* (Pittsburgh: Energy Productivity Center, Mellon Institute, 1979, p. 39.

57. Research by the Energy Action Educational Foundation shows that "controlled [natural gas] prices below oil-equivalent levels are not only sufficient to encourage exploration by most companies, but that despite controlled prices, producers preferred to search for and develop gas." See *The Decontrol of Natural Gas Prices: A Price Americans Can't Afford,* Energy Action Educational Foundation, February 19, 1981, pp. 12-18. In 1979 (with domestic crude-oil prices at $11 per barrel compared with $35 in 1981) the Congressional Budget Office estimated that oil decontrol would increase domestic oil supply by 405,000 barrels per day by 1985—an increase of 5.4 percent over production had controls been continued. See Congressional Budget Office, *The Decontrol of Domestic Oil Prices: An Overview,* May 1979, p. 25. For a discussion of arguments for oil price controls, see Paul Davidson, "What Is the Energy Crisis?" *Challenge,* July/August 1979, pp. 41-46.

58. See Congressional Budget Office, *Managing Oil Disruptions: Issues and Policy Options,* September 1981.

59. Office of Research, Demonstrations and Statistics; Health Care Administration; cited in *Health Policy: The Legislative Agenda, Congressional Quarterly,* 1980, p. 3.

60. Paul Starr and Gosta Espring-Anderson,"Passive Intervention," *Working Papers for a New Society,* July-August 1979, p. 22.

61. Karen Davis, *Rising Hospital Costs: Possible Causes and Cures,* Brookings Institution Reprint 262, 1972.

62. Health Care Financing Administration, *Case Study of Prospective Reimbursement in Maryland,* April 1980, p. 98.

63. Edmund Faltermayer, "Where Doctors Scramble for Patients' Dollars," *Fortune,* November 6, 1978, p. 115.

64. Harold S. Luft, "How Do Health-Maintenance Organizations Achieve Their 'Savings'?" *New England Journal of Medicine,* June 15, 1978.

65. *Health Policy: The Legislative Agenda,* p. 68.

66. H.R. 3884, National Health Service Act of 1981. For a critique of the major conservative alternative (the so-called competitive approach), see Dan Sigelman, "The Competitive Prescription for Health Care: Survival of the Fittest?" *Health Law Project Library Bulletin,* April 1981.

67. Consumers Opposed to Inflation in the Necessities, *There Are Alternatives,* p. 82.

68. Elliot Segal and Kenneth Gardner, "Preadmission Certification and Denied Hospital Stays: Two Surveys of PSROs," *Inquiry,* Summer 1981, p. 124.

69. *There Are Alternatives,* p. 83.

70. See Anthony Downs, "Public Policy and the Rising Cost of Housing," *Real Estate Review,* Spring 1978, p. 34, and *Current Population Reports,* Series P-20, No. 357, October 1980.

71. John Brown, Special Reserve Requirements of Mortgage Assets to Lower Mortgage Rates for Necessity Housing and Raise Mortgage Rates for Luxury Housing, Public Interest Research Group, Winter 1978-79. See also "Monetary Policy, Selective Credit Policy and Industrial Policy in France, Britain, West Germany and Sweden," Joint Economic Committee, U.S. Congress, Washington, D.C., June 26, 1981. Andrew Brimmer, *Monetary Policy and Sectoral Credit Flows: Assessment of Alternative Policy Strategies,* speech to the American Economic Association, December 28, 1973. See also G. William Miller, "A Businessman's Anti-Inflation Formula," *Business Week,* October 5, 1974, p. 16.

72. National Low Income Housing Coalition, *Briefing Paper on Low Income Housing Needs and Progress: 1981-82 Budget Proposals and Their Impact,* 1981, p. 1.

73. Urban Homesteading: *A Good Program Needs Improvement,* U.S. Government Accounting Office, November 13, 1979.

74. For a positive assessment of the effects of rent controls on neighborhood deterioration problems, see Peter Marcuse, "Abandonment: A Preventable Tragedy," *Ways and Means,* May/June 1981.

75. Office of Management and Budget, *Housing Affordability in an Inflationary Environment,* June 1979, p. 7.

76. Robert C. Wood, *The Necessity Majority: Middle America and the Urban Crisis* (New York: Columbia University Press, 1972), pp. 87-88.

77. *American Institute of Architects, A Plan for Urban Growth: Report of the National Policy Task Force,* January 1972.

78. Ibid.

79. U.S. Department of Commerce, Bureau of the Census, *Statistical Abstract, 1980* (Washington, D.C.: 1980), p. 913; and Council of Economic Advisors, *Economic Report of the President,* (Washington, D.C.: U.S. Government Printing Office, 1981), p. 276.

80. In July 1981 the Gallup Poll found that Americans favored wage-price controls 50 percent to 38 percent. See "Most Americans Still Favor Wage and Price Controls," *Washington Post,* July 2, 1981.

Justice and Mathematics: Two Simple Ideas

ROBERT D. COOTER

INTRODUCTION

Mathematics is the perfection of analytical skill just as poetry is the perfection of the imagination. In mathematics we pass from one proposition to another according to explicit rules, whereas in poetry we pass from one image to another without rules to guide us. Mathematical reasoning is constrained by well-defined concepts of consistency, whereas the play of imagination in poetry is constrained by sensibility or taste.

Is justice a sensibility or can it be analyzed mathematically? Political justice resides in the allocation of duties and rights to individuals by law and political practice. These allocations are complex, but the political theories advanced to explain them are simple. We shall show that two traditions of political theory are erected upon two simple mathematical ideas.

The idea of a contract was raised to the level of political theory by the contractarians or social-contract theorists, such as Hobbes, Locke, and Rousseau.[1] Contractarians conceive of the state as a bargained agreement analogous to an ordinary business contract. From this perspective the state is viewed as a cooperative venture for mutual gain.

The ideas in this essay first took shape when I was writing my thesis under the direction of Richard Musgrave, John Rawls, and Jerry Green. The ideas acquired their present shape as a consequence of the invitation to lecture at Notre Dame. The rough draft was revised in light of comments received at Notre Dame, and at the Stanford University law and economics seminar directed by Mitch Polinsky. I received helpful comments from Jules Coleman and others. Finally, I am grateful to Philippe Monet who saved me from numerous errors.

The idea of a maximum was raised to the level of political theory by the utilitarians, especially Bentham.[2] The utilitarians conceive of the state as maximizing social welfare, which is analogous to a private firm maximizing profits. The contractarian and utilitarian political philosophies are the two traditions which we shall try to explain with the help of simple mathematics.

These two traditions do not claim any true believers among contemporary lawmakers. However, contractarianism and utilitarianism are part of the intellectual culture pervading the law. The classical contractarian texts are a reference point for interpreting the American constitution, and utilitarianism motivated many reforms of British law.[3] Lawmakers reflect upon difficult decisions from the vantage point of these traditions. It is helpful to think of contractarianism and utilitarianism as deep metaphors for thinking about almost any legal issue.

Our aim is to clarify these two metaphors by describing their mathematical structure. It is characteristic of mathematics that it illuminates political disputes without resolving them. Although our analysis cannot resolve disputes about justice and the law, it can increase the quality of the debate by making the disputants lighter on their feet.

Before beginning, a comment is due on the relationship between describing the law and criticizing it. The positive-normative distinction is one line of demarcation between science and nonscience in positivist methodology. For example, some economists believe that economics can be separated from ethics by separating explanation from evaluation. This boundary receives little respect in the work of most utilitarians or contractarians. For example, Bentham passes from explanation to evaluation with ease because his aim is to rationalize the law, i.e., to criticize the parts that do not conform to the fundamental principles. In his view the law as a whole conforms to the principle of utility, although parts of it diverge. Thus the principle of utility can be used to explain the basic structure of law and to criticize the laws that are inconsistent with its fundamental design. This essay concerns the attempt by utilitarians and contractarians to rationalize the law.

The essay is divided into two parts. First, the simple mathematical ideas underlying utilitarianism and contractarianism are explained, and the historical antagonism between these philosophies is explained by the tension between the mathematical ideas (Part I). The second step is to relate these two philosophies to the fundamental structure of the law, which is accomplished by connecting the underlying mathematical ideas to the formal logic of rules (Part II). A formal connection is established between the economic logic of preferences and deontic logic.

I

A. Mathematics and Pictures

A useful artifice of economic theory is to imagine a timeless and certain world. We replace the complexity of real choices with "time slices" that have no past or future. These time slices are called "states of the world," which consist of detailed descriptions of nature and society.[4] There are many possible states of the world s_1, s_2, s_3, etc., where the s indicates a state of the world and the subscript indicates which one it is. The basic idea in economic theories of choice is that states of the world can be ranked according to their overall goodness or desirability. For example the set of states listed in Figure 1 might be ranked $s_1 < s_2 < s_3$, where the states get better as we move from left to right.

Figure 1
Associating States with Numbers

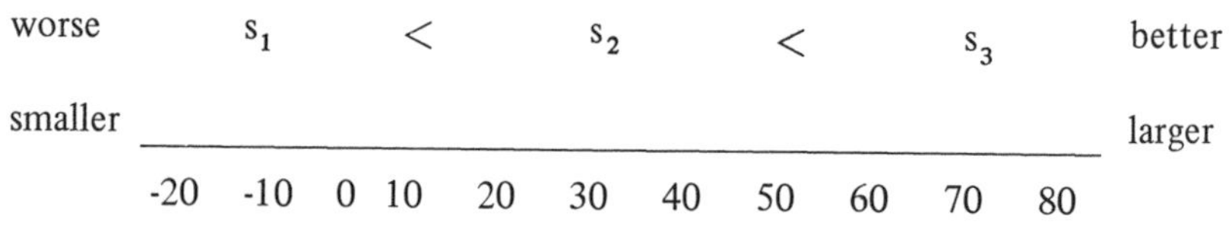

| worse | s_1 | $<$ | s_2 | $<$ | s_3 | better |

| smaller | | | | | | larger |

| | -20 | -10 | 0 | 10 | 20 | 30 | 40 | 50 | 60 | 70 | 80 | |

Many relations between objects are orders; for example, "heavier than" or "faster than." There are also many unordered relations; for example squash players find that player A can beat B, and B can beat C, but C can beat A. Each of the three players beats someone and loses to someone, so we cannot set them in order of skill and identify a best player. A relation that cannot be ordered is called "intransitive."[5] Microeconomic theory assumes that overall goodness is like weight and unlike skill at squash: A rational person can set states of the world in order of goodness.

An example from commercial life illustrates why economists think that transitivity is a requirement of rationality. Suppose that someone takes his desk lamp to swap at the flea market. He finds another lamp that he prefers, so he swaps lamp number 1 and a dollar for lamp number 2. Next he finds a lamp that he likes better than number 2, so he swaps number 2 and a dollar for lamp number 3. But now he finds that he likes lamp number 1 better than lamp number 3, so he swaps number 3 and a dollar for number 1. He spends three dollars and ends up with the lamp that he initially brought to the market. This example shows that an intransitive consumer, like the proverbial fool, will soon be parted from his wealth.

In economics states of the world can be set in order from bad to good; in mathematics real numbers can be set in order from small to large; so we could associate a real number with each state of the world. In Figure 1 we have associated three states with real numbers. It is this correspondence between "better" and "larger" which permits quantification of the economic theory of individual values.

Figure 2
Constrained Maximum

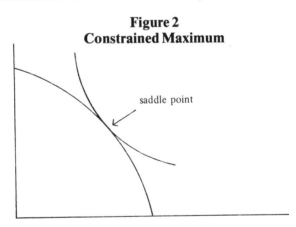

saddle point

As soon as we accept transitivity as an axiom of rationality, so that states can be ordered, there is a drift to accept maximization as the basis for choice. After all, why do worse when you can do better? It would be irrational to choose a state that is worse when a better one is available.

The first principle of decision theory in economics is to maximize goodness subject to the constraints inherent in the choice situation. For example, firms judge goodness by profits alone in the conventional formulation, so firms maximize profits subject to the constraints imposed by the technology of production. A constrained maximum can be represented by a saddle point in a two-dimensional diagram (Figure 2), which is familiar to any student of introductory economic theory. There is no habit of thought among microeconomists which is more compelling than the urge to characterize each human choice as a saddle point on an appropriately chosen pair of axes.

Transitivity connects a theory of value to the real number system, and maximization connects it to calculus and related optimization techniques. It is possible in principle to have a theory of a value which is ordered, in the sense of being transitive, but which does not postulate maximization. To my knowledge, philosophers have not advanced such theories. Economists and psychologists have made the attempt through so-called satisficing or learning-behavior models, but these beginnings do not compare in scope or power to the utilitarian tradition.[6] The utility theory of choice, as incorporated in economics, is the outstanding form of value theory based upon the real numbers.

We have explained the mathematical idea of maximization which is fundamental to utilitarianism. Now we turn to contractarianism. The theory of contract in jurisprudence has focused upon the questions, "When does a contract exist?" and "What are its terms?" For example, the proposal has been made that a contract comes into existence when each side offers the other a tangible benefit (called "consideration") or the promise of it.[7] The terms of a contract are taken to be those explicitly stated in writing or words, plus those that can be imputed by virtue of established conventions and practices.

The criteria for existence and identification of contracts, which are central to jurisprudence, are taken for granted in economics. Economists usually assume that a wide range of possible contracts are available, each with well-defined terms. The relevant problem of contract which economists have addressed could be called "contract selection," i.e., "What will be the terms on which individuals will strike a bargain?" Economists try to predict the terms of the contract which will prevail at the end of the bargaining process.

Economists have developed their own jargon for describing bargaining.[8] The level of welfare that a person can achieve on his own without entering into a contract with the parties in question is called his "threat value." Each person must receive at least his threat value, or there would be no advantage for him in entering the agreement. A bargaining situation is viable if both parties could benefit from cooperation. The problem of contract selection studied by economists is to predict the likelihood and terms of cooperation. There is a question of efficiency—namely, "Will the parties cooperate?"—and a question of distribution—namely, "How will the advantages of cooperation be divided among individuals?"

Some economic theories assume that bargaining can be described in money terms.[9] For example, consider a business contract between, say, a cotton grower and a textile manufacturer. The threat value is the profit level that each can achieve without exchange between them, e.g., the manufacturer's profit when buying cotton from the best alternative source. The sum of the grower's and manufacturer's threat values is the "noncooperative value" of the game. The "cooperative value" of the game is the sum of profits under a contract whose terms maximize the joint profits of the grower and the manufacturer. The surplus from cooperation is the difference between the cooperative and the noncooperative values of the game. The bargaining problem is to find terms for splitting the surplus which both parties will accept.

The solution to this bargaining problem is called a "bargaining equilibrium." The exact nature of this equilibrium is a subject of dispute, but we can explain the equilibrium concept in abstract terms.[10] A game situation is an equilibrium if no player wishes to revise his move. Let $(x_1, x_2, \ldots, x_n)$ describe the moves of players $1, 2 \ldots n,$ respectively. Let f describe how each player revises his move in light of what other players are doing. f is called a "reaction function" because it describes how players react to each other. For example, the moves $(\bar{x}_1, \bar{x}_2, \ldots, \bar{x}_n)$ may cause the reaction $(\bar{\bar{x}}_1, \bar{\bar{x}}_2, \ldots, \bar{\bar{x}}_n)$ as specified by f:

$$(\bar{\bar{x}}_1, \bar{\bar{x}}_2, \ldots, \bar{\bar{x}}_n) = f(\bar{x}_1, \bar{x}_2, \ldots, \bar{x}_n).$$

An equilibrium is a situation where no player wishes to revise his move given what the other players are doing, i.e., and $(x_1^*, x_2^*, \ldots, x_n^*)$ such that

$$(x_1^*, x_2^*, \ldots, x_n^*) = f(x_1^*, x_2^*, \ldots, x_n^*).$$

From a mathematical standpoint, an equilibrium is a fixed point in the reaction function f.

The most familiar example of a fixed point in economics is the equilibrium of a competitive market, which is represented by the intersection of supply and demand curves. This example is not useful for our purposes because there is no scope for bargaining in competitive markets. But we can use a less familiar economic model, the Cournot duopoly game, to illustrate a bargaining equilibrium.

Figure 3
Fixed Point or Equilibrium

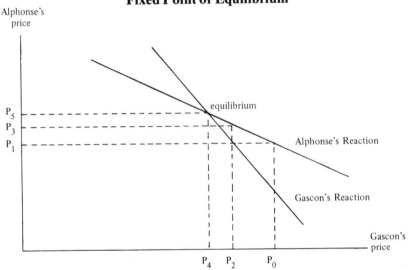

Consider Figure 3. Suppose Alphonse and Gascon operate gas stations across the street from each other. Imagine that they are bargaining with each other in an attempt to set prices cooperatively. One curve in Figure 3 depicts the price that Alphonse will favor in reaction to Gascon's suggested price, and the other curve represents the price that Gascon will favor in reaction to Alphonse's suggested price. Starting from any arbitrary prices, the reactions of the players cause the prices to converge to the intersection of the lines, as illustrated by the sequences of prices (P_0, P_1, P_2, P_3, P_4, P_5, . . .). The point of intersection is the equilibrium or fixed point in the reaction functions.

A fixed point and a saddle point are mathematically distinct ideas. A fixed point presupposes a measure of value which is maximized. For example, in economics the behavior of a firm is described as a saddle point, i.e., a point where profts are maximized. However, the interaction of firms in duopoly is described as a fixed point, i.e., an equilibrium in the reaction of firms to each other.

It matters whether we think of politics as concerned with a maximum equilibrium or a fixed-point equilibrium. Under the first description we think of government as if it were disciplined to pursue a common purpose, like a business firm pursuing profits. Under the second description, we do not think of political life as having a single, shared purpose. Rather, we think of politics as an agreement specifying the extent to which different individuals are entitled to pursue their private ends. The utilitarian conception emphasizes harmony and common values, whereas the contractarian conception emphasizes restraint and private goals. This contrast is implicit in the difference between maximizing value and an equilibrium in the reaction function of individuals. We shall use this distinction in mathematical ideas to compare the utilitarian and contractarian traditions in political theory.

B. The Structure of Utilitarianism

The first systematic utilitarian was Jeremy Bentham, who was twenty-five years younger than Adam Smith. We begin by reviewing some salient features of Bentham's cardinal utility theory.[11]   First, Bentham identified the utility of a situation with a definite quantity of pleasure or pain produced by it. His concept of pleasure was broad, encompassing such similar (but different) ideas as benefit, happiness, advantage, and goodness.[12] He discussed various qualities of pleasure which affect the quantity of it afforded by particular circumstances, such as intensity, duration, and certainty. The total pleasure afforded by a situation can be found by adding up the pleasure from its different aspects, after allowing for these qualities. No special problems arise if the pleasure belongs to more than one person. Bentham believed that the pleasure of different individuals can be added together just like their body weights can be summed. He gave no instructions for how to carry this out, which is an unfortunate tradition maintained by his intellectual heirs in philosophy.

A second feature of Bentham's theory is the equity rule, "Each to count for one and none to count for more than one." This rule requires everyone's pleasure to be given equal weight in social choice. Bentham did not pay much attention to this equity rule; in fact, the above statement of it is by Mill.[13] In Bentham's view the idea that one person's pleasure could count more than another's is a misunderstanding of the metric, rather like the confusion that an ounce of lead weighs more than an ounce of feathers. Once we understand the metric, there is no further problem of fairness among individuals. In utilitarianism, efficiency and equity get collapsed into the idea of a single metric that measures social welfare. The concept of justice in Benthamism is the concept of a correct measure.

The equity rule introduces a bias toward income redistribution in utilitarian thinking. Bentham noted that the pleasure from spending money depends upon the intensity of the wants satisfied by the expenditure, and poor people have more urgent unsatisfied wants than rich people. The implications of such an outlook for economics were fully developed by A.C. Pigou.[14] According to Pigou, there is no *precise* way to compare one person's pleasure with another's, but all the evidence of common sense directs economists to proceed on the assumption that a dollar is more valuable to a poor person than to a rich person. Pigou concluded that economists should recommend policies that distribute national income more equally without appreciably diminishing its sum total. Thus the requirement that each person's pleasure receive equal weight was egalitarian in its implications.

A third feature of this doctrine is that it is strictly forward-looking, by which I mean that there is rigorous application of the maxim "Bygones are bygones." Only the present and future can afford us pleasure; we have no access to retroactive enjoyment.[15] In order to act we need to know how much present and future pleasure alternative actions will afford. That is all we need to know. The past is fully represented in our decision by the causal propensity of the present to afford pleasure. Past actions cannot create obligations or duties that are distinct from causal propensities. Philosophers call such a theory "consequentialist," because decisions are guided by the action's consequences, but not by its antecedents. This feature of utilitarian doctrine represents a reforming and critical spirit toward the past, which prompted many proposals to reform the law.[16]

The final feature of Bentham's doctrine is that actions can be ranked according to the magnitude of the pleasure which they afford. Since all situations can be ranked according to pleasure, and pleasure is the ultimate standard of goodness, it follows immediately that rational behavior requires maximizing pleasure. The individual is deemed as maximizing his own pleasure, and the interaction of individuals is described as maximizing the sum of individual pleasures. This optimistic account of the ecology of interaction, according to which self-interested individuals accomplish social goals, is reminiscent of Adam Smith's account of how private greed serves public purposes in free markets.

One of the glaring faults in Bentham's philosophy is his failure to justify this optimism. Adam Smith had described an "Invisible Hand" that directs self-interested traders to benefit the public by exchanging in competitive markets. This argument anticipated contemporary proofs that individuals who maximize their own utility by exchanging in a competitive market will reach an equilibrium which is efficient. Bentham possessed one of the fundamental concepts in this proof—namely, maximization—but not the other—namely, equilibrium. Consequently, he did not perceive clearly the need to identify a mechanism comparable to the hidden hand that operates in government. There is no account of a mechanism that guides self-interested individuals in politics or the courts to act so that social welfare will be maximized.

By thinking of pleasure as a quantity to be maximized, Bentham established a link between rational choice and the calculus. The exploitation of this linkage by Bentham's successors established the pre-eminent place of utilitarian ethics in economic reasoning.

In summary, Bentham's utilitarianism has four attributes discussed in ethics: (1) hedonism (broadly conceived); (2) egalitarianism; (3) consequentialism; and (4) maximization. Attribute (4) permits government to be described as a saddle point, and attributes (1)-(3) characterize the metric. These four attributes have a natural affinity for each other, rather like the elements of an art style. For example, Greek columns go with mathematically symmetrical buildings, and income redistribution goes with maximizing social welfare. If we think of government as a saddle point, then we tend to think of the metric as possessing attributes (1)-(3), although it is possible to separate them.

C. The Structure of Contractarianism

The social-contract tradition is an aggregation of related theories without a dominating figure comparable to Bentham.[17] There is room for disagreement about the most salient features of the tradition. We shall describe features of contractarian thought which correspond perfectly to the economic model of bargaining and imperfectly to any particular contractarian doctrine. In effect we consider an abstract social-contract doctrine that is purified of its noneconomic elements, and we use this abstraction to classify the major contractarian philosophers. Our approach provides a unified perspective on a complex tradition, but we do not claim to uncover the hidden unity in diverse philosophies. In order to avoid false appearances, we shall refer to the doctrine which we explain as "economic contractarianism."

A familiar definition of the state is the institution that possesses a monopoly of coercive force.[18] Contract theories can be viewed as explaining why people would be willing to create such a monopoly.

There are three steps in developing this argument. The first step is to find out what people would do in the absence of civil government, which is aptly called the "state of nature." The second step is to characterize the advantages available to them by creating a state. The third step is to show the terms for distributing the advantages of government. The terms of the contract are described concretely in the fundamental laws or constitution of the state.[19]

The three steps in constructing this political contract correspond to elements in the economic theory of business contracts. The state of nature is the noncooperative solution that prevails if the parties cannot agree. Civil society is the cooperative solution. The social surplus is the difference between the level of welfare in civil society and the state of nature. The political contract specifies the terms for dividing the surplus from cooperation. Cooperation can improve the well-being of everyone in the sense that each person can be raised above the standard of life that he enjoys in the state of nature. We use the phrase "economic contractarianism" to refer to any contract theory containing these three steps.

According to game theory, a rational player will bargain with the aim of achieving agreement on terms favorable to himself. The level of well-being that a person can achieve on his own, without the cooperation of others, is his threat value. In social-contract theory the threat value of an individual or group is what they could secure without the protection of government. The stronger the threat, the more the person or group must be given to make cooperation worthwhile. Bargaining theory predicts that individuals and groups will enjoy legal rights and advantages in proportion to what they could secure for themselves without the help of government.

We identified four features of Bentham's utilitarianism: (1) Pleasure measures value (hedonism); (2) each person's pleasure receives equal weight (egalitarianism); (3) the past is represented by the causal propensities of the present (consequentialism); and (4) value should be maximized (maximization). Let us contrast these attributes to a social-contract theory modeled upon the economic theory of bargaining.

Utilitarianism asserts that social arrangements tend to maximize the sum of individual pleasures. If the pleasures of different individuals can be summed, then they must be commensurable, i.e., the progress of individuals toward different goals must be reducible to a single measure of value, namely, utility or pleasure. By contrast, economic contractarianism postulates a reaction function describing how people bargain. Each person bargains so as to maximize progress toward his own goals, but the reaction function does not require private goals to be commensurable. One person may seek wealth, another may seek political power, and a third may seek scientific truth. There is no commitment to the view that disparate goals can be reduced to the same thing, namely, pleasure. In this respect contractarianism is amenable to ethical relativism and utilitarianism is not.

In most economic theories, bargaining achieves an equilibrium when the scope for mutual gain is exhausted. Equilibrium is typically a situation where no one can be made better off without making someone else worse off. Economists call this Pareto efficiency. A bargained agreement is likely to be Pareto efficient.[20] Pareto efficiency is a concept of value that is intended to avoid the problem of incommensurability. A Pareto optimum is not necessarily a maximum on a shared standard of value. Though the political contract may be described as Pareto efficient, it does not necessarily maximize anything.[21]

Social cooperation produces income and wealth that must be distributed to individuals. The utilitarian equity rule requires each person's pleasure to receive equal weight when distributing income and wealth. By contrast the economic theories of contract distribute the surplus from cooperation according to threat values in the state of nature. If threats are equal in nature, then rights are equal in society. The extent and form of civil inequality depend upon the extent and form of natural inequality. The political contract is egalitarian to the extent that the state of nature is egalitarian, but not more so.

We called utilitarianism "consequentialist" because the decision maker is supposed to be guided by the consequences of his actions, not by their antecedents. The consequences are completely described in their relevant aspect for utilitarians by the amount of pleasure produced. By contrast the antecedents of an action have a direct and compelling influence upon decision makers who follow a contractarian philosophy. The task of such government officials is to carry out the terms of the political contract, not to increase social welfare. Government officials are asked by contractarians to guide their behavior by looking back to the political contract, not forward to the sum of pleasures. The political contract may be described as the logical antecedent to the state. Thus the distinction is between guiding choice by its effects or guiding choice by its logical antecedents.

Obviously, no government official should be blind to future consequences or past commitments. A well-articulated political philosophy must contain forward-looking and backward-looking considerations.[22] The claim that utilitarians guide action by its consequences, and contractarians guide action by its antecedents, concerns the most fundamental orientation of government officials. The dispute concerns whether the *fundamental* guide for state action is future social welfare or a past social contract.

We have discussed the attributes of a social-contract theory that is purified by omitting features that do not belong to the economic theory of games. There are four attributes of such a theory which are antithetical to the four attributes of utilitarianism:

1. Value is private and relative; there is not necessarily a shared value such as pleasure.
2. Civil equality exists only to the extent of natural equality.
3. Collective choice is ultimately guided by its logical antecedents, not by its causal consequences or effects upon welfare.
4. The political contract is Pareto efficient, but a Pareto optimum is not necessarily a maximum on a shared standard of value.

The difference in attributes can be explained by the difference in the simple mathematical ideas underlying the two philosophies. In utilitarianism the individual and society are described by the same concept: maximization. Maximization presupposes a measure of value. Consequently, utilitarianism assumes that state action can be measured against a shared standard of value. The state is regarded as a kind of superperson who resolves conflicts of interest among persons in the same way that an individual supposedly resolves conflicts among his own motives, i.e., by maximizing pleasure. In contractarianism the individual and society are described by a different concept: The individual may be a maximizer, but the state is not. The state is regarded by economic contractarians as a kind of political market in which rights are exchanged. Contractarianism allows for more tension among individuals by allowing their goals to be incommensurable, and the incommensurability of individual goals prompts skepticism about collective action.

D. A Parable in Arithmetic

We have shown that the distinction in mathematical ideas underlying utilitarianism and economic contractarianism explains the contrast in their attributes. It is useful to illustrate this claim in a concrete example. Imagine a two-person world in which there are three activities: farming, defending, and robbing. The amount of corn that is produced depends upon how much time each person spends farming, and upon whether the mode of farming is cooperative or noncooperative. More is produced by cooperation because there is no need to devote time to defending or robbing. The exact numbers are given in Figure 4.

We wish to determine the consumption of each person in the state of nature and in civil society. From the figure we see that total production under noncooperation is 150, whereas by cooperating together the joint product is 250. The gain or surplus from cooperating is 100. The economic problem of forming a social contract is to distribute this surplus.

Figure 4
The Production and Distribution of Corn

		1st person	2nd person	Total
	Solitary Output	100	50	150
Non-cooperative	Gain from Theft	+10	+20	+30
	Loss from Theft	-20	-10	-30
	Solitary Consumption	90	60	150
Cooperative	Joint Output	0	0	250
	Hobbesian Consumption	140	110	250
	Lockean Consumption	150	100	250
	Rawlsian Consumption	125	125	250

Economic theorists are not unanimous about how the surplus will be distributed, but the simplest solution concept is due to Nash.[23] According to Nash, each player will receive his threat value plus an equal share of the surplus. An equal share of the surplus allots 50 to each player. Suppose that the parties would steal from each other in the absence of government. From the figure we see that if both engage in theft, the first party consumes 90, and the second party consumes 60. The threat values when the parties resort to mutual plunder are 90 and 60. Thus we can compute the equilibrium consumption by adding 50 to the threat values, yielding the distribution 140 and 110, which is labeled "Hobbesian Consumption" in Figure 4. This distribution describes the economic allocation under a social contract derived under the assumption that the state of nature involves mutual plunder.

Another possibility is that individuals would not engage in unrestrained plunder if government were absent. Perhaps the players would recognize certain natural rights in property. Even animals fight more vigorously when they defend their own territory. We could imagine that theft would be censured in the state of nature on moral grounds, even though no legal apparatus existed to enforce morals. Suppose that the parties could threaten nonparticipation in joint production, but not theft, when negotiating the social contract. We see from Figure 4 that solitary output is 100 and 50, which represents the consumption levels the parties can achieve on their own in the absence of theft. Thus the threat values when the parties resort to nonparticipation, but not theft, are 100 and 50. We can compute consumption under a bargained equilibrium with nonparticipation as the threat by adding 50 to the threat values, yielding the distribution 150 and 100, which is labeled "Lockean Consumption" in Figure 4. This distribution describes the economic allocation under a social contract derived under the assumption that the state of nature involves nonparticipation (solitary production, no theft).

In anarchy individuals would benefit from natural strengths such as intelligence and a strong body. Unequal outcomes in anarchy imply unequal threats, and unequal threats result in inequality in the bargained equilibrium. The two kinds of social contract discussed so far result in unequal economic distribution. Suppose that someone wished to build a contractarian theory that did not allow individuals with superior natural strength to bias the laws of distribution in their favor. How would such a theory be constructed? By changing the conception of the state of nature. Rather than thinking of nature as anarchy, we think of nature as a condition of primitive equality. We ask ourselves, "What would be the principles of distribution if all unfair advantages that result from inequalities in natural strength were removed?" If threats of plunder or nonparticipation were not allowed, then the parties represented in Figure 4 would not have any basis for claiming an unequal share of the cooperative product. Consequently the total cooperative product would be split equally among them, yielding the distribution 125 and 125, which is labeled "Rawlsian Consumption" in Figure 4.[24] This distribution describes the economic allocation under a social contract derived under the assumption that the state of nature involves primitive equality.

The methods by which a utilitarian would solve the problem of choosing a principle of distribution are different from those of the economic contractarian. A utilitarian would begin by identifying the utility or pleasure that each person receives from consuming corn. Figure 5 illustrates the relationship that might exist between utility and corn. Corn should be distributed between the two people so that the sum of utilities or pleasures is maximized, according to

Figure 5
Utility and Corn

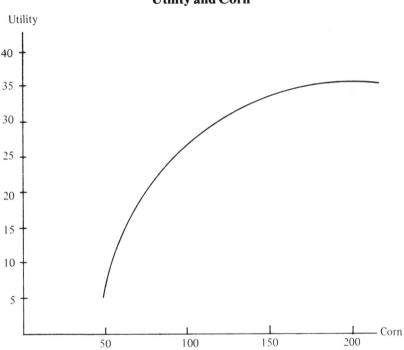

Bentham. The maximum occurs when the marginal utility from consuming a small additional amount of corn is the same for both individuals. If both people have similar needs (i.e., if they are "equally efficient pleasure machines"), then they will both have the same functional relationships between utility and corn. The sum of utilities would be maximized under this condition when each consumes an equal amount of corn, yielding the allocation 125 and 125.[25]

   The utilitarian solution to the parable in arithmetic (1) assumes that each person's consumption of corn can be reduced to the same measure of social value (utility or pleasure); (2) gives equal weight to each person's pleasure; and (3) maximizes total pleasure. The economic contractarian solutions assume that (1) each person has private reasons for wanting corn, which may be incommensurable; (2) inequalities in the distribution of corn result from unequal bargaining power; and (3) the social contract does not waste corn (Pareto efficient), nor does it maximize anything. Also, the principle of utility distributes corn on the basis of its effect upon the pleasure of individuals (consequentialism), whereas contractarians distribute corn on the basis of the threat values that are the logical antecedents to cooperation.

E. Three Contractarian Philosophies

The names used to describe the three distributions in the parable in arithmetic, Hobbesian, Lockean, and Rawlsian, are chosen because the structure of the argument is reminiscent of these philosophers. In Hobbes's philosophy natural behavior is not influenced by legal or moral norms, rapaciousness is unrestrained, it's every person for himself, there is a "war of all against all."[26] The definitive feature of this version is that dissolution of civil restraints results in dissolution of moral restraints.

In Locke's philosophy people in a state of nature perceive themselves as possessing natural rights and duties, independent of the legal system.[27] People fight each other in order to protect these rights or as retribution for their violation. Behavior is normative, not rapacious, because people recognize that others have rights similar to their own. The psychology is different from nature as normlessness, because the motive for harming others is to protect what is yours rather than to get as much for yourself as possible. Though some measure of peace and security is possible in Locke's state of nature because people practice moral restraint, the level of security is less than in civil society. The motive for erecting the state is to provide a more firm guarantee of each person's rights than anyone can assure by acting on his own or through private associations.

In our parable in arithmetic the Hobbesian distribution was reached by threatening mutual plunder, whereas the Lockean distribution was reached by threatening nonparticipation. The names were chosen because it is characteristic of Hobbes's philosophy that the state of nature involves normlessness, whereas the state of nature in Locke's conception involves moral norms but not statutes. The mathematical-bargaining theory used in our parable is contemporary, which is one reason why we have not claimed to offer a strict interpretation of these classical philosophies. Our use of bargaining theory elucidates these classical philosophies by clarifying one strand of thought found in them.

Hobbes and Locke described the state of nature as the historical condition of tribal people. These classical texts are cluttered with anthropological claptrap. However, the historical interpretation can be abandoned by giving the social contract a hypothetical interpretation. The dissolution of the civil state may be adopted as a goal at any time. Each generation reaffirms the social contract by rejecting anarchy and working to preserve or improve the state. The social contract is regarded as the logical antecedent to citizenship, not the historical antecedent to the state.

Plunder (Hobbes) and nonparticipation (Locke) do not exhaust the list of possible antecedents to citizenship. There is a long tradition in philosophy, reaching back to Plato's *Republic,* which holds that the first virtue of government is justice. Rather than thinking of the state of nature as a condition that would actually exist if government dissolved, we could think of the state of nature as a condition that would exist if all the unjust advantages that some people enjoy over others were removed. This is how Rawls approached the rehabilitation of contractarianism.[28] Rawls describes an original bargaining position in which a veil of ignorance disguises the natural inequalities that give some people advantages over others. Unfair advantages are removed by depriving the individual of the knowledge that would enable him to identify his self-interest.[29] No one can act upon threats in the original position because no one knows the identity of those who would be harmed or benefited by such acts. For Rawls the state of nature is a condition of primitive equality induced by ignorance about one's personal advantages.

In Hobbes's account *all* threats are allowed, in Rawls's account *no* threats are allowed, and in Locke's account most threats of nonparticipation are allowed. Nature as ignorance is the polar opposite of nature as normlessness, and nature as nonparticipation is in between.

F. Conclusion to Part I

We have shown that two leading traditions in political theory can be explicated by two simple mathematical ideas. Specifically, utilitarianism draws upon the idea of a maximum or saddle point, and contractarianism in its economic aspect draws upon the idea of a bargaining equilibrium or fixed point. The two mathematical ideas characterize the pattern of explanation that these political philosophies apply to law.

Political justice consists in the allocation of duties and rights to persons by law and political practice. The two traditions in philosophy which concern us are supposed to explain the allocation of duties and rights to individuals. Having shown how these two philosophies are connected to two mathematical ideas, we now try to connect the mathematical ideas to the structure of law.

II

A recent article on jurisprudence was subtitled "One View of the Cathedral."[30] This image suggests the massiveness of the structure of law and the reverence with which it is approached. Theories are required to make it comprehensible, although they are inevitably inadequate. In Part I we discussed two of the prominent traditions in jurisprudence, namely, utilitarianism and contractarianism. In Part II we shall try to connect these theories to the structure of law.

In order to make this connection it is necessary to reduce the law in all its complexity to a few simple ideas, just as we reduced the two traditions in political theory to simple ideas. We shall not think of the law as a body of living institutions, each with its own personalities and history. Rather, we shall think of the law as a body of rules with a definite logical structure. We conceive of the allocation of duties and rights as being articulated in rules. This reduction is illuminating because the structure of rules has been studied formally by logicians. Our strategy is to connect the logic of rules to the two political philosophies that we have discussed.

A. Preferences and Rules

Two topics in practical logic which have been developed axiomatically are the logic of preferences and the logic of rules. The logic of preferences has been developed by economists under such headings as "the calculus of utilities," "consumer demand theory," or "decision theory."[31] The logic of rules has been developed by philosophers under the heading "deontic logic."[32] We shall explain the connection between these axiomatic systems.

Economic theory defines "preference" as a behavioral relationship between a decision maker and a pair of alternatives. If a person could choose between state one s_1 or state two s_2, and he chooses s_2, then economists say that "s_2 is revealed to be preferred to s_1." In economics, ascribing a preference to someone amounts to predicting the choice that he would make when confronted with a pair of alternatives.

Choices must be made by institutions as well as by individuals. Economists often describe institutional choices as revealing institutional preferences. For example, economists speak of the revealed preferences of a corporation, legislature, or school board.

It is straightforward to extend this mode of speaking to legal systems. Many laws give directions about how to act. We can think of a law as revealing a preference for some actions rather than others. To elucidate, think of an action as changing the state of the world, and think of a law as an instruction to do an action or forbear from changing it. The instruction apparently reveals a preference on the part of the rule maker for the state favored by the action.

The argument can be clarified with the help of the notation used in the logic of rules. The elements of the logic of rules are somewhat different from those of the logic of preferences. We begin with actions, rather than with states of the world.[33] An action changes the world from one state into another. Let P_{ij} denote the action of changing the state of the world from s_i to s_j.[34] A rule in canonical form states that certain people ought to undertake a certain action under certain circumstances. Explicit statement of the class of persons and the circumstances is often omitted. For example, Op_{ij} is the notation for "Someone (unspecified) ought to do the action described by proposition p_{ij} under certain conditions (unspecified)." It seems reasonable to say that the duty to p_{ij} "reveals" a preference on the part of the rulemaker for s_j over s_i, which we write

$$Op_{ij} \ <=> \ s_i < s_j.$$

Logicians would say that s_j is a deontically ideal world relative to an actual world s_i.[35]

B. Contradiction

We connected preferences to rules by using the fact that rules guide actions and actions reveal preferences. Now we wish to connect *systems* of preferences to *systems* of rules. In a well-developed logical system, such as consumer-choice theory or deontic logic, there are axioms that characterize consistent reasoning. Violation of these axioms is said to be irrational or contradictory. We shall compare a simple concept of contradiction contained in the logic of preferences to a simple concept of contradiction in the logic of rules.

Let us review part of the argument developed previously. Utilitarianism is based upon the idea of maximization, which presupposes a measure of value. A measure of value exists when states of the world can be set in order according to their goodness. Preference relations between pairs of states can be set in order if the preference relations are transitive. For example, if s_2 is preferred to s_1, and s_3 is preferred to s_2, then transitivity requires that s_3 is preferred to s_1. Transitive preferences can be arranged along a line as in Figure 6.

Intransitive preferences cannot be set along a line; they run in a circle. For example, a person who chooses s_2 over s_1, s_3 over s_2, and s_1 over s_3 reveals the circular preferences depicted in Figure 6. Since intransitive choices cannot be represented by a measure of value, they cannot be described as maximizing anything. The failure to maximize is evidence of irrationality according to utilitarian philosophy. Consequently, the basic concept of contradiction in the logic of preferences, and in utilitarian philosophy, is intransitivity.

Figure 6

Transitive Preferences	$s_1 < s_2 < s_3$	Intransitive Preferences	$\begin{array}{cc} & s_1 \\ \swarrow & \nwarrow \\ s_3 & \rightarrow s_2 \end{array}$

If a decision maker is an individual with transitive preferences, then economists call his preferences a utility function. If the decision maker is an institution, then economists often call its transitive preferences a social ordering. The term "social" is used because it connotes a multiplicity of individuals. If a social ordering is consistent with an ethical or a normative ideal, then it is called a social-welfare function. Thus, the federal tax code is said to reveal a social ordering insofar as it is internally consistent. The tax code is said to reveal a social-welfare function insofar as it satisfies an ethical criterion such as basing marginal tax rates on ability to pay.

Now we leave the topic of contradictions among preferences and consider contradictions among rules. We develop the concept of contradictory rules informally at this stage and formally in a subsequent section. We shall distinguish two types of contradiction. The first kind of contradiction involves asserting and denying that a rule exists, i.e., asserting that a certain law is part of the legal order and also asserting that the law is not part of the legal order. For example, it is a contradiction to assert that there is a legal obligation to cross streets only at corners and also that there is *no* legal obligation to cross streets only at corners. Making both assertions provides no guidance to someone who is wondering whether to cross in the middle of the block. The second kind of contradiction involves asserting that there is an obligation to do an action and also an obligation not to do that action. For example, it is a contradiction to assert that drivers are legally obligated to drive at least 45 MPH on a certain road and also to drive under 45 MPH on that road. Rules which are contradictory in the second sense have the characteristic that obeying one rule violates the other. An ideal system of law would offer a guide to action. Contradictory rules offer no guide to action.

What is the connection between consistency in rules and preferences? One possibility is that a consistent set of rules necessarily reveals a consistent set of preferences. We are entertaining the possibility that consistent rules necessarily reveal transitive preferences. If this assumption were true, then rational laws would necessarily have the mathematical structure of utilitarianism, i.e., the law could be described as maximizing a conception of social value.

Utilitarian jurisprudence is not entitled to such an easy triumph. The fundamental concept of contradiction in rules is weaker than the utilitarian concept. A set of rules can offer an uncontradictory guide to action without revealing an ordered purpose. Rules that are consistent in the sense of offering a consistent guide to action need not be consistent in the sense of revealing a transitive ordering over states of the world.

This argument requires formal proof, which we provide in a subsequent section, but first we shall remove some of its obscurity by discussing a concrete application of it.

C. Distribution, Utility, and Justice

There is a tendency for people to judge whether an economic system is just by examining the distribution of income across classes. Utilitarians hold that that income distribution is best which maximizes the sum of utilities. In practice utilitarians have advocated income redistribution by such means as taxes, subsidies, free necessities (e.g., health care), minimum-wage laws, unionization (monopoly in labor markets), antitrust (no monopoly in product markets), etc. The underlying principle is that more equality is better if it does not cause less production.[36]

For example, in Figure 7 we have drawn a curve showing the levels of utility that can be obtained by tax transfers between persons A and B. The diagram assumes that both people choose how many hours to work and that A's hourly wage is greater than B's. The tax is levied on the earnings of high-income people such as A and transferred to low-income people such as B. At very high tax rates, neither A nor B works many hours, and both suffer low utility levels, as represented by the points on the utility possibility curve near the origin. By lowering the tax rate we move out to the right on the utility possibility curve, and both people are better off, up to a point. Eventually a point is reached where further decreases in the tax rate cause a decline in subsidy to B. Beyond this point decreases in tax rates benefit A and harm B. Economists call this part of the curve the "Pareto frontier." The sum of the utilities is maximized at the point of tangency between the Pareto frontier and a straight line sloping down at 45° as shown. This optimal point corresponds to a tax rate that is best according to a utilitarian philosophy. Any other point on the utility possibility curve represents a lower level of utilitarian social welfare than at the optimum.

One way to differentiate utilitarianism from contractarianism is to claim that contractarianism directs society to a different point

Figure 7
Optimal Tax—Transfer

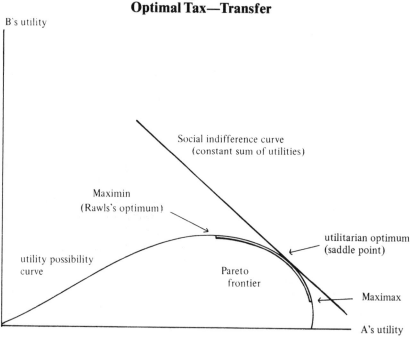

on the Pareto frontier from the utilitarian optimum. For example, the version of contractarianism developed by Rawls concludes that the just point on the Pareto frontier is where the worst-off individual is as well off as possible (maximin in Figure 7).

This way of thinking about income distribution was attacked by Robert Nozick. His interpretation of Locke rejects the whole approach of disputing about the just point on the Pareto frontier. Nozick argued that justice cannot be decided by a "time slice" or "end state" approach.[37] Nozick applies the predicate "just" to a process, not to a still photograph of income classes. He follows the contractarian logic of judging by the history of the world, not by the state of the world.

The object of distributive justice in Nozick's theory is the history of the relationship between people and things, not the pattern of that relationship. Static or time-slice theories apply the judgment about whether something is just to the wrong object. We cannot say that some points on the Pareto frontier are more just than others by looking at the distribution of property across persons; we must know the history of the connection between property and persons. To think otherwise confuses the relationship of people to things. We are not faced with a collection of things to be distributed and enjoyed; rather, we are faced with a collection of things to be transformed by our labor. The process of transformation and transfer is the correct object of our judgment about justice, not the final allocation, according to Nozick.

According to Nozick, any voluntary redistribution from an initially just situation is just, and any involuntary redistribution is unjust. For example, free exchange is voluntary and taxation is involuntary. Thus Nozick's philosophy condemns income taxation, social-security taxation, and minimum-wage laws or other interferences with free contracts.

Nozick's government prefers that contracts be kept, but has no preference over which contracts are made, i.e., no preference over the distribution of property. From the formal viewpoint, the preferences of Nozick's government are created and extinguished as individuals make contracts and carry them out. Nozick's government does not reveal stable preferences over states of the world, because it has no ordered purpose, i.e., no ranking of still photographs of the distribution of property.

A concise illustration of this point is provided by three fundamental laws of an imaginary civil code inspired by Nozick's libertarianism:

1. There is a set of actions called "free actions" which everyone is permitted to do. (Unfree actions are covered by the
   criminal code.)
2. Everyone is permitted to contract to do any free action.
3. Performing a free action extinguishes the contractual duty
   to do it.

Notice that this code does not impose civil duties upon anyone except as a consequence of his own voluntary action. If no one creates
a contract, then government is indifferent about what free actions
are performed. If someone makes a contract, then government prefers that the contract be kept. This preference is extinguished by
performance according to the contract's terms. Rules 1-3 reveal no
preference by the rule makers for one state of the world over another.
This civil code is an example of a consistent set of laws that does not
reveal an ordered purpose. The rule maker cannot be described as
maximizing social value. Rather, the rule maker allows maximum
freedom to individuals.

We have contrasted a utilitarian tax code with Nozick's conception of distributive justice. Utilitarians favor intervention in the
free exchange of contracts in order to achieve the optimal distribution of property, whereas Nozick holds that such intervention is unjust to individuals. The fundamental point is that utilitarianism
imposes a stronger purpose upon the law than some philosophers in
the contractarian tradition.[38] We develop this point formally in the
next section.

D. Formalization

Some formal notation will clarify our argument, although readers who are allergic to it may wish to skip this section. As before, we
let Op denote the rule that imposes a duty to do the action described
by proposition p. There are two forms of negation in the logic of
rules.[39] Internal negation states that there is an obligation *not* to do
an act p, which is written $O \sim p$. For example, there is an obligation
for drivers not to pass a school bus that is discharging children. External negation, written $\sim Op$, states that no obligation exists to do
the act p.[40]

There are two simple concepts of contradiction in the logic of
rules corresponding to the two forms of negation.[41] An internal contradiction is the assertion that there is an obligation to do some act
and an obligation not to do that act, which is written Op and $O \sim p$.

For example, it is an internal contradiction to assert that there is an obligation to stop for a school bus discharging children and an obligation *not* to stop for a school bus discharging children. By contrast, it is an external contradiction to assert that there is an obligation to do some action and also no obligation to do that action, which is written Op and $\sim Op$. Contradictory rules offer no guide for action, just as contradictory statements of fact offer no basis for belief.[42]

As before, we let P_{ij} denote the action that changes the world from state s_i to s_j. A rule that imposes the duty to do the action P_{ij} is said to reveal a strong preference for s_j over s_i:

$$Op_{ij} \; <=> \; s_i < s_j.$$

Similarly, the duty not to do P_{ij} reveals the opposite preference:

$$O \sim p_{ij} \; <=> \; s_j < s_i.$$

It is a feature of most systems of deontic logic that no obligation to p is identical to permission not to p. Consequently, the absence of a duty to P_{ij}, or the permission not to P_{ij}, seems to reveal that s_j is no better than s_i:

$$\sim Op_{ij} \; <=> \; s_i \leq s_j.$$

This notation enables us to impute preferences to lawmakers. Consider a pair of laws and what they reveal:

$$Op_{12} \; <=> \; s_1 < s_2$$
$$Op_{23} \; <=> \; s_2 < s_3.$$

This pair of duties suggests that lawmakers prefer s_3 over s_2, and s_2 over s_1. If the preferences of the lawmakers are transitive, then they also prefer s_3 over s_1. In this case we would also expect a rule to exist such as $O \sim p_{31} \; <=> \; s_1 \; < s_3$. The set of laws Op_{12}, Op_{23} and $O \sim p_{31}$ reveals the transitive preferences $s_1 < s_2 < s_3$.

The rules in the preceding paragraph are consistent and transitive. However, it is easy to write consistent rules that are intransitive, e.g.,

$$Op_{12} \; <=> \; s_1 < s_2$$
$$Op_{23} \; <=> \; s_2 < s_3$$
$$\sim O \sim p_{31} \; <=> \; s_3 \leq s_1$$

or

$$Op_{12} \; <=> \; s_1 < s_2$$
$$Op_{23} \; <=> \; s_2 < s_3$$
$$Op_{31} \; <=> \; s_3 < s_1$$

These two sets of rules do not contain an internal or external contradiction, but they do not reveal a transitive preference ordering. The conclusion can be generalized:

> *Theorem:* Consider a set of laws consisting of duties (e.g., Op_{ij}) and permissions (e.g. $\sim O \sim p_{ij}$). Assume the set of laws are consistent and transitive. Internal or external negation of any duty in a triple of duties will make the laws consistent and intransitive.[43]

The meaning of this theorem can be expressed in ordinary language. An ideal of legality is that laws should offer intelligible instructions. If one statute imposes a duty to p and another imposes the duty not to p, then at least one of them is illegal. However, a set of intelligible instructions may not have an ordered purpose, e.g., the instructions may not be transitive. In brief, the set of possible rules that are transitive is a subset of the possible rules that are consistent.

This theorem is potentially significant for the dispute between utilitarians and contractarians. Utilitarians hold that rational laws necessarily have an ordered purpose—namely, maximizing utility—and contractarians deny this claim. If parts of the law can be modeled by systems of deontic logic without the transitivity axiom, then the actual allocation of legal duties and rights must not be utilitarian.

As an illustration consider the Nozickian civil code discussed in the preceding section. We can represent rules 1-3 in our formal notation. Let Pp denote permission to do the action p (or equivalently, no obligation not to p, written $\sim O \sim p$). Let S represent the set of free actions or actions not covered by the criminal code. An appealing formalization is the following:

1. Pp_{ij} all p_{ij} in S. (Permission to P_{ij} for all P_{ij} in S.)
2. POp_{ij} all p_{ij} in S. (Permission to create the duty to P_{ij} for all p_{ij} in S.)
3. $\sim (p_{ij}$ and Op_{ij}) all p_{ij} in S. (There is not both the performance of p_{ij} and the duty to p_{ij} for all p_{ij} in S.)

Rule 1 reveals a weak preference of the form $s_i \leq s_j$. Rule 2 reveals a weak preference over the action of creating duties, i.e., making contracts. Rule 3 states that any strong preference created by making a contract according to rule 2 can be extinguished. Thus the fundamental rules of the Nozickian civil code do not reveal strong preferences over states of the world. We cannot set states in order of goodness by using the preferences revealed by these laws. Our conclusion is that Nozick's government has no ordered purpose, i.e., there is not a transitivity axiom.

The iteration of operators in rule 2 and the mixed form of rule 3 raise some controversial issues in deontic logic, but exploring them in this essay is inappropriate.[44]

F. Implications

Utilitarian jurisprudence is committed to the view that rational laws serve an ordered purpose, namely, maximizing utility. A set of laws is irrational by utilitarian standards if it does not reveal an ordered purpose. A minimal condition for utilitarian rationality is that obeying the law increases social welfare as measured by a shared standard of value.

Contractarian jurisprudence is not committed to viewing the law as maximizing welfare. Some contractarian philosophies postulate ordered purposes and others do not. Economic contract theory views law as a bargaining equilibrium, which presupposes a function describing how the bargainers react to each other. However, a reaction function does not presuppose a shared concept of value. Economic contractarianism is consistent with the view that the goals of individuals are incommensurable in the sense that they cannot be reduced to a single standard of value.

We have worked out the formal implications of the argument that contractarianism tolerates a weaker purpose in law than utilitarianism. We connected preferences to rules in order to show how the logic of law is different in utilitarian and contractarian models. Utilitarian laws satisfy the transitivity axiom, but contractarian laws are not necessarily transitive. The fundamental laws would not reveal stable preferences over pairs of states, or triples of states, in some versions of contractarianism.[45]

A set of laws without an ordered purpose may be described as a heterogeneous collection of rights and duties. The basic constitutional liberties are depicted this way by many contractarians. For example, Rawls describes "liberty" as a collection of conventional rights, e.g., freedom of speech, press, religion, association, etc. The value of these liberties is not derived by Rawls from their ability to advance some other purpose, such as maximizing pleasure. The absence of an underlying measure of value makes the comparison of liberty with other values impossible. For example, in Rawls's theory liberty cannot be balanced against economic advantage.[46] It is possible to find the set of liberties that afford maximum equal liberty for everyone, but it is not possible in Rawls's system to balance liberties against nonliberties. For Rawls liberty is a heterogeneous collection of rights that are valuable for their own sake.

The idea that a legal system might not be transitive is familiar to economists. Kenneth Arrow's Impossibility Theorem proved that a democratic political constitution cannot combine the preferences of different individuals into a transitive ordering.[47]   This conclusion is sometimes expressed by the proposition, "The social-welfare function does not exist." This result has been interpreted as a refutation of utilitarianism and a proof that politics is unavoidably irrational. Our argument shows that some contractarians would not *want* a constitution with an ordered purpose, even if it were possible to construct one.

SUMMARY

In our opening remarks we asked, "Is justice a sensibility or can it be analyzed mathematically?" Political justice resides in the allocation of rights and duties to individuals by law and political practice. Utilitarianism and contractarianism are two important theories of law. We showed that two simple mathematical ideas can be used to elucidate these political philosophies. The concept of a maximum was used to explicate utilitarianism, and the concept of a bargaining equilibrium was used to explicate contractarianism.

The concept of a maximum presupposes an ordered conception of value which guides social choice. Utilitarians view the individuals in society as combining their efforts toward advancing a single end, rather like the individuals in a firm who combine their efforts to maximize profits. A utilitarian allocation of rights and duties maximizes social welfare, which implies that the preferences revealed by such laws satisfy the transitivity axiom.

The concept of a bargaining equilibrium presupposes a reaction function for different individuals, but not a shared conception of value. Economic contractarians view the individuals in society as entering into an agreement to further their private ends, rather like the parties to a business contract. Contractarians do not necessarily view the law as having a unifying purpose such as maximizing social welfare. Contractarians do not believe that law is irrational just because it does not reveal an ordered purpose.

Judgments about justice turn upon subtle distinctions in thought which are buried in the mind. Ethical theories aim at unearthing these distinctions, a kind of archeology of the mind. We have shown that two simple mathematical ideas can explicate two traditions of political theory. The purpose of this demonstration is to unload the dross accumulated around our intuitions, so that we can think more clearly and build more confidently upon our moral instincts. The danger is that we will use mathematics as a substitute for thinking. If mathematics is used mechanically, then the crucial distinctions are compacted into a worthless conglomerate; such an operation is rather like excavating a Greek temple with a bulldozer. If mathematics is used with discernment and sensitivity, then we can uncover patterns of thought in philosophical traditions which are a precious inheritance.

NOTES

1. The classical texts are from the seventeenth and eighteenth centuries, but the origin of the social-contract tradition is much older. See Peter Laslett, "Social Contract," *Encyclopedia of Philosophy* (New York: Macmillan, 1967), for discussion and bibliography.

2. Bentham was the first *systematic* utilitarian. See J.J.C. Smark, "Utilitarianism," *Encyclopedia of Philosophy,* for discussion and bibliography.

3. George Keeton and George Schwarzenberger, *Jeremy Bentham and the Law* (London: Stevens, 1948).

4. A description of a state of the world is usually defined to include a complete account of causal propensities. As a result, a description of the present state of the world contains a complete prediction of what the future will be if no one acts to change the natural order of events. Arrow writes: "A state of the world is a description of the world so complete that, if true and known, the consequences of every action would be known." Kenneth Arrow, *Essays in The Theory of Risk Bearing* (Amsterdam: North-Holland, 1971), p. 45.

5. Formally, intransitive preferences are not transitive, and transitive preferences have the property that, for any triple $[s_1, s_2, s_3]$, s_2 preferred to s_1, and s_3 preferred to s_2, implies s_3 preferred to s_1.

6. Herbert Simon pioneered the satisficing approach. For a review, see his Nobel Prize lecture, "Rational Decision Making In Business Organizations," *American Economic Review,* September 1979, p. 493.

7. "The root of the whole matter [of contracts] is the reciprocal conventional inducement, each for the other, between consideration and promise." Oliver Wendell Holmes, Jr., *The Common Law* (Boston: Little, Brown, 1881), pp. 293-94.

8. An amusing introduction to the economic theory of games is J.D. Williams, *The Compleat Strategyst* (New York: McGraw-Hill, 1966).

9. More generally, these theories assume transferable cardinal utility.

10. The classical text on game theory, which is still the best, is R.

Duncan Luce and Howard Raiffa, *Games and Decisions* (New York: Wiley, 1957). Some of the solution concepts discussed are the core, the von Neumann-Morgenstern solution, the Nash-Zeuthen solution, and the Shapely value. The fixed-point solution discussed in this article is called the Nash equilibrium. The Nash equilibrium describes abstractly the conditions under which bargaining ceases, but not the final distribution of the surplus from cooperation. The other solution concepts attempt to describe the final distribution of the surplus that will be achieved when bargaining ceases. One of the solution concepts describing an exact distribution is the so-called Nash bargaining solution, which we discuss later in this essay. The Nash equilibrium and the Nash bargaining solution should not be confused.

11. Bentham was a prolix classifier. The attributes of utilitarianism listed by Bentham in such classics as *The Principles of Morals and Legislation* (New York: Hofner, 1973) are numerous and complicated. The list of four attributes used in this essay seems salient in retrospect.

12. "By utility is meant that property in any object, whereby it tends to produce benefit, advantage, pleasure, good, or happiness (all in the present case comes to the same thing) or (what comes again to the same thing) to prevent the happening to mischief, pain, evil, or unhappiness to the party whose interest is considered." Bentham, *The Principles of Morals and Legislation,* chap. I, section IV, p. 2.

13. John Stuart Mill, *Utilitarianism* (New York: Liberal Arts Press, 1953), chap. 5.

14. A.C. Pigou, *Economics of Welfare,* 4th ed. (London: Macmillan, 1932), and *A Study in Public Finance*, 3d (rev) ed. (London: Macmillan, 1947).

15. This is not to deny that future pleasures will be had from memories of past events.

16. Keeton and Schwarzenberger, *Jeremy Bentham and the Law.*

17. "*Social Contract* is the name given to a group of related and overlapping concepts and traditions in political theory. Like other aggregations in philosophy and intellectual history, it has at its center an extremely simple conceptual model, in this case that the collectivity is an agreement between the individuals who make it up." Peter Laslett, "Social Contract," *Encyclopedia of Philosophy,* p. 465.

18. "Political control involves not only authority but *ultimate* authority, backed at some point by the use of force." Kingsley Davis, *Human Society* (New York: Macmillan, 1949), p. 481.

19. This is the traditional view. More recently, Rawls has described the terms of the social contract as the conception of justice in light of which a political constitution is chosen. John Rawls, *Theory of Justice* (Cambridge, Mass.: Harvard University Press, 1971), pp. 195-201.

20. The economic theory is complicated. In games there may be multiple (Nash) equilibria, only some of which are Pareto efficient. There is no precise statement of the conditions under which bargaining has efficient outcomes. It is sometimes said that bargaining will be efficient if there are

no transaction costs. However, the concept of transaction costs has no satisfactory mathematical formulation. This problem is discussed and resolved in Robert Cooter and Stephen Marks, "Bargaining in the Shadow of the Law: Model of Strategic Behavior," Mimeograph, February 1981.

21. John Rawls argues that the ideal social contract is Pareto efficient but not maximal in the utilitarian sense. See *Theory of Justice,* p. 70.

22. Contractarians may argue that the social contract directs officials to maximize social welfare under certain circumstances, but the conditions under which this behavior is acceptable are carefully circumscribed in the social contract. Utilitarians may argue that government officials are obligated to keep past commitments, but this obligation is derived from the principle of utility, not from a social contract.

23. Nash's bargaining solution is described in Luce and Raiffa, pp. 128-34 and 140-43.

24. The principle of distribution advocated by Rawls is to maximize the minimum income. If redistribution does not influence the amount which is produced—i.e., if there is a "lump-sum tax" so that redistribution is costless—then the *maximum* results in equal shares for everyone, as in our parable in arithmetic.

25. Note that this line of reasoning makes the simplifying and unrealistic assumption that the cooperative product is unaffected by its distribution, i.e., the individuals work just as hard at producing corn in the cooperative venture regardless of how much each consumes. Our parable is too simple to address the problem of incentives.

26. "Out of civil state, there is always war of everyone against everyone." Thomas Hobbes, *Leviathan,* ed. Michael Oakeshott, (New York: Collier Books, 1962), p. 100. A contemporary example of a theory with this structure is James Buchanan's *Limits of Liberty* (Chicago: University of Chicago Press, 1975). He explains the creation and revision of property rights as an exercise of natural power. Property rights are created or revised whenever the balance of natural power shifts; in Buchanan's words, the "constitution is re-negotiated."

27. A contemporary theory that draws upon Locke to defend libertarianism is Robert Nozick's *Anarchy, State and Utopia* (New York: Basic Books, 1974).

28. Rawls begins his opus with the sentence, "Justice is the first virtue of social institutions, as truth is of systems of thought." *Theory of Justice,* p. 3.

29. It is a feature of our actual legal system that some contracts extracted by threatening nonparticipation are unenforceable. For example, the law will not enforce a contract which "sells" the cargo of a sinking ship for a trivial sum to the only ship's captain in a position to save it. (This case is discussed in M. Eisenberg, "Bargain Promise," mimeo, Berkeley Law School, 1980.) Such examples support Rawls's position that some free contracts are not fair contracts.

30. Guideo Calabresi and A. Douglas Malamed, "Property Rules, Liability Rules and Inalienability: One View of the Cathedral," *Harvard Law Review,* 85 (1972), 1089.

31. This topic is developed in any standard microeconomics textbook, such as J.M. Henderson and R.E. Quandt, *Microeconomic Theory: A Mathematical Approach* (New York: McGraw-Hill, 1971).

32. A good overview of deontic is found in Risto Hilpinen, ed., *Deontic Logic: Introductory and Systematic Readings* (Dordrecht: D. Reidel, 1971). The connection to modal logic is exhibited in A.N. Prior, *Formal Logic* (Oxford: Clarendon Press, 1962). A systematic book is Georg Henrik von Wright, *Norm and Action* (New York: Humanities Press, 1963).

33. In formal deontic logic the operator for obligation prefixes letters whose exact interpretation is disputed. These letters may stand for act predicates, sentences about acts, or states of affairs. This dispute has little bearing upon our discussion.

34. It may be helpful to relate our notation to von Wright's. For von Wright the state of the world is described by the truth values of a set of propositions. An "atomic event" is a change in the truth value of one of these propositions. An "atomic action" is an atomic event caused by an agent. So a change in the state of the world, which we called an action, is a conjunction of one of von Wright's atomic changes, or a "molecular action." In von Wright's notation, $pij = d(s^i T_{sj})$. Drr von Wright, chaps. 2 and 3.

35. In deontic logic each set of norms applicable to a real world is said to presuppose an ideal world in which those norms are not violated.

36. Pigou, p. 89.

37. This utility possibility curve appears in the literature on optimal income taxation. For example, see R. Cooter and E. Helpman, "Optimal Income Taxation for Transfer Payments Under Different Social Welfare Criteria," *Quarterly Journal of Economics,* 88 (1974), p. 660.

38. Nozick, *Anarchy, State and Utopia.*

39. Nozick is a libertarian who draws heavily upon Locke's contractarianism. Some contractarians advocate an ordered purpose in the laws governing economic life. For example, Rawls advocates the maximum, whose tax consequences are shown in Figure 6.

40. von Wright distinguishes between doing an action and forbearing from doing it. We use the term "internal negation" to refer to forbearing from doing an action. However, the phrase "not doing an action" sometimes means something stronger than forbearance. This phrase can also mean "doing something different." In von Wright's notation, $d(\sim pTp) = d(pTp) v \, d(\sim pT \sim p) \, v f(\sim pTp) \, v f(\sim pTp \sim p) \, v f(pT \sim p) \, v f(pTp)$. von Wright, pp. 64-65.

41. Our concept of external negation is defined by von Wright as "permission." Specifically, the negation of an obligation to do an action is equivalent to permission to forbear from doing it: $\sim Odp = Pfp$. Permis-

sion to do an action is no obligation not to do it: $Pd = \sim O \sim d$. See von Wright, p. 140.

42. A set of obligations is consistent only if all obligations in this set can be simultaneously fulfilled and each permission can be realized without violating any obligation. Hilpinen, p. 16. Obviously, the obligations Op and $O \sim p$ cannot be fulfilled simultaneously. A permission is no obligation not to do the act in question: $Pp = \sim O \sim p$. Consequently, we have
$$(Op \& \sim Op) = (Op \& P \sim p).$$
The permission cannot be acted upon without violating the obligation. We have shown that our concept of internal contradiction corresponds to two duties that cannot be simultaneously performed, and our concept of external contradiction corresponds to a permission that cannot be realized without violating an obligation. In a more formal approach, there is no simple concept of contradiction; rather there is a set of axioms whose violation is a contradiction of the system.

43. It is possible to construct a system of deontic logic without an axiom prohibiting what I call "internal contradiction." See John Lemmon, "Moral Dilemmas," *Philosophy Review,* April 1962, p. 139. The connection to morality is discussed in Ruth Marcus, "Moral Dilemmas and Consistency," *Journal of Philosophy,* March 1980, p. 121, and the application to law is discussed in Stephen Munzer, "Validity and Legal Conflict," *Yale Law Journal,* May 1973, p. 1140. I attempt to avoid this dispute by claiming that consistency, or the absence of dilemmas, is an ideal of legality, although not necessarily a characteristic of law.

44. Sketch of a proof by construction: Consider any duty Op_{ij}. It reveals a strict preference $s_j > s_i$. Internal negation reverses the strict preference, yielding $s_j < s_i$, and external negation weakly reverses the strict preference, yielding $s_j \leq s_i$. Either change results in intransitivity when Op_{ij} is embedded in a triple of strict duties, but neither change results in a deontic inconsistency.

45. For example, it is easy to prove that rules 1 and 3 imply (Pp and $P \sim p$ is possible). This result is unproblematic if we read the conclusion as "It is possible that doing p is permitted and undoing p is permitted," or "It is possible to p in such a way that no duty is violated and to not-p in such a way that no duty is violated." However, the conclusion is problematic if it is read "Everything is permitted."

46. Liberty is "lexically prior" to economic advantage in *Theory of Justice,* p. 61.

47. K. Arrow, *Social Choice and Individual Values,* 2d ed. (New York: Wiley, 1963).